American Indian Prose and Poetry

WE WAIT IN THE DARKNESS

American Indian Prose and Poetry

WE WAIT IN THE DARKNESS

EDITED AND INTRODUCED BY

Gloria Levitas

Frank Robert Vivelo

Jacqueline J. Vivelo

G. P. PUTNAM'S SONS, NEW YORK

CAPRICORN BOOKS, NEW YORK

*SBN: 399-11115-8
Library of Congress Catalog
Card Number: 72-97301*

PRINTED IN THE UNITED STATES OF AMERICA

DARKNESS SONG*

We wait in the darkness!
Come, all ye who listen,
Help in our night journey:
Now no sun is shining;
Now no star is glowing;
Come show us the pathway:
The night is not friendly;
The moon has forgot us,
We wait in the darkness!

           1823

the moon will rise
in painted fever
for all we have
known is darkness
& in darkness
the message will come

the sun will rise
dripping blood
for all we have
known is darkness
but our deaths were
dealt in blazing heat
of day   bones bleached
aged   we paint them
red & black

it is a time
of visions
it is a time
of painting
no more do we
hide our dreams
we wear them
on our shirts
round our necks
they make music
in our hair

           Karoniaktatie†
           1973

*From Harriet M. Converse, *Myths and Legends of the New York State Iroquois*, New York State Bulletin 125, December 15, 1908.
†From *Akwesasne Notes*, vol. 5, no. 5. Early Autumn 1973, p. 48.

Contents

NORTHEAST

EAST SUB-ARCTIC

PRAIRIES

PLATEAU

NORTHWEST COAST

SECTION II: AFTER THE WHITE MAN CAME

SOUTHEAST

NORTHEAST

SOUTHWEST

APACHE

HOPI

KERES (Acoma)

NAVAJO

TEWA

Introduction

WE decided at the outset of this project that our collection of American Indian prose and poetry should differ from others in its organization of and approach to selections. First and foremost, it was to be a sampling of the artistic expression of American Indians, a collection of literature in and of itself. Second, we wanted to arrange the selections in a historically meaningful way; that is, we wanted the organization to reflect major periods in what we know of American Indian history. Third, we also wanted the selections to be culturally meaningful; we wanted to supply some information on the sociocultural systems from which each selection is drawn. Consonant with this strategy, the following Introduction is divided into two parts. Part I deals with the literature *qua* literature and attempts to place it in some historical perspective. Part II offers some basic notes on the cultures that produced the literature.

I

Some time last year we visited the home of a missionary to the Indians, a home preserved by an antiquarian society that attempts to educate the general public about the meaning of the American past. The house was charming: a constructed symbol of colonial ingenuity, of stoicism in the face of danger and and appreciation of beauty in order. Not so charming was the guide, whose ability to identify herself with the long dead missionary and his wife seemed to transcend all historical reality. Her lecture was touched with sly insinuation and mockery of the Indians for whose worthless souls, she was certain, the colonists had risked life and limb. She seemed ambivalent about those Indians, regarding them as both childish innocents and fiendish devils. Her private fantasies had been nourished by the white man's version of history, and she seemed to have fattened upon the myths of film and video. We left abruptly, wandering through the ordered colonial garden, aware suddenly of the tyranny of history and the power of the myth which had condensed the varied lives and multiple truths of hundreds and thousands of native Americans into a bloody expletive—Indians!

It is difficult to know today what those Indians were really like. We were rarely concerned with them as people: Some whites, indeed, regarded them as little more than animals; others as "souls" to be saved; still others as historical curiosities. They were "noble" savages to those who viewed them romantically and "filthy" savages to those who saw them only as an obstruction to white colonization. In the end they became symbols: dual representations of the best and worst in man; a dream people of generosity and stoicism who saved and restored the past; a nightmare people of lust and death who killed—not for property (for that we could have understood) but for custom (which we could not).

We know them as Indians. The name itself is the first crime committed by white men against them. It represents a conceptual and perceptual error made by Columbus perpetuated into the present—now by the Indians themselves, as their only weapon in the battle against extinction. The word conceals the truth: The Indians comprise some six hundred different cultures and dozens of language groups.

Some lived in stone cities, on the products of irrigated fields, with a complex and unified town life rich in ritual and ceremony. Others made temporary camps in bark huts or skin tepees, hunting and gathering, moving to follow the restless migrations of birds and beasts or to answer the call of restless spirits that demanded vision quests. Still others lived in long houses, their lives encompassed within a framework of family loyalties and dissensions. In the far West were a simpler people who subsisted principally on a diet of pine nuts. North of them were numerous fishermen who built large canoes, intricately carved wooden houses, and who became famous because they achieved status through potlatching—the sponsoring of feasts in which the objective was to give away, rather than accumulate, wealth.

There were others, too—the Natchez—with their complex, kaleidoscopic status system of Suns, Nobles, and Stinkards. And before the white man came were the mound builders of the Middle West who may have teetered on the edge of civilization before their world disintegrated for reasons we can only surmise.

What did these people have in common with each other? Physical anthropologists classify Indians as a subgroup of the Mongoloid peoples of the world. But the classification reveals nothing except their prehistoric connections with the Asian continent. The Indians of the Americas are as physically varied as they are culturally and linguistically differentiated. Genetic drift and the mysterious processes of adaptation and selection have raised and flattened noses, lengthened and shortened limbs, darkened and lightened skins here as elsewhere. Ecology—the varied landscape of the Americas—and history took care of the rest. When Columbus landed, Indian cultures and languages were far more varied than those of their European discoverers. Today Indians are linked together by their recent past: Their common destruction at the hands of the white man provides a desperate bond among them.

Indians they were called, and Indians they remain. The beauty and configurations of their unique and varied cultures have remained concealed behind the tinsel myths of Western movies and pulp magazines.

Many aspects of Indian life that white men regard as typically Indian were often in reality a product of Indian-white contact. The tomahawk and the scalp, the colorful long dresses of the Seminole, the patterns of decoration of surviving skin clothing, all show white influence. The metal tomahawk entered early as a valued trade object for which the Indian readily exchanged furs or labor. The practice of scalp-taking itself seems to have been copied by the Indians from the whites, who offered a bounty for Indian scalps much as they did for the skins of bothersome animals. The brave astride his pony, who has supported the dream factories of Hollywood and the insomnia of late-night TV, developed his unique way of life only after the white man reintroduced the horse to the Americas. With the horse available to the Indian, he became an efficient hunter of buffalo—and gave up a previous existence as semisedentary farmer or woodland hunter for the freedom of the great American plains.

In the end, the only generalization that seems to be true of North American Indians is that they lacked complex civilizational states and the attributes of those states. No monumental architecture, kingdoms, accounting systems, storage depots, or bureaucracy is to be found here. Nor did the Indians possess that most useful, and dangerous, of tools: written language. Their literature is a folk literature, a collective enterprise handed down by word of mouth, dependent upon the memories of listeners and storytellers, translated by missionaries, explorers, folklorists, and the Indians themselves. Their rituals are often highly personal: Men and women created their own songs or made up their own prayers, which perished with them. Other rituals, like those of the Southwestern Pueblos and the sheepherding Navajo, are social affairs: Highly complex and difficult to remember, they constituted a test by which the novice

became a priest. More important, the rituals accompanied public ceremonies, communal affirmations of the moral legitimacy of human enterprise.

Until recently, however, the popular concept of Indian literature was
shaped not by the Indian and not even by his translator but by the white
American writer or moviemaker. The dime novels, the Saturday afternoon westerns, and, on a different level, the poems of a Longfellow and
the novels of a Cooper have done their work, have themselves become a
part of American tradition. There is no better way to correct the misrep-
resentations that have ingrained themselves in our folklore than to listen
to the genuine voices of the Indian peoples. Since their poems are really
songs meant to be chanted or sung as part of various rituals, it is indeed
the voices of the Indians, ancient and authentic, despite the drawbacks of
translation, that we hear when we read them.

Despite the variation in language stocks and the differences in technology and social organizations that marked even proximal Indian groups,
the literature of North America is often linked by common themes and
events. The similarities are, of course, at least in part an artifact of translation: Important formal differences in linguistic structures cannot be
translated into English. Thus differences in rhythms, phrasings, and, ultimately, impact are often glossed over in translation. Other similarities
derive from what anthropologists call "psychic unity," or the basic similarity of all human mental structures. Still others depend upon similarities
in life-ways: Societies engaged in hunting or fishing are likely to produce
social organizations appropriate to their activities; and the poetry and
stories that deal with the imperatives of social and economic life may
show many points of contact. Some similarities in themes may be due to
common sources; others to contact—acculturation was occurring among
Indians before the white man arrived, though its pace was necessarily
slow because of the lack of any form of political organization more extensive than the tribe. Diffusion of peoples and ideas accompanied migra-
tion, the trade, and warfare that were all operant in the Americas before
Columbus.

With few exceptions, most of these tales were transcribed during the
nineteenth century; hence it is impossible to say, categorically, that they
are precisely the same tales that were told before the coming of the white
man. Anthropologists have expended a good deal of energy searching for
systems that would adequately reconstruct culture history; that would
identify an original story and allow us to discover which versions of a
particular tale were derivative. Criteria depending upon complexity, upon

statistical differences in distribution, upon statistical distribution of various themes in an area, can often help us differentiate between earlier and later forms. For the purposes of this anthology, however, it seemed reasonable simply to present a representative sample of these early forms without concerning ourselves with relative degrees of historical precedence.

An anthology that covers such a broad spectrum of cultural and linguistic traditions can do little more than suggest the variety and subtleties of folk literature. Moreover, the problems of translation—often from languages in which the structure is totally different from our own —guarantee that what is presented here is but a feeble shadow of the original. Even when a translator can imitate the original rhythms, or subtle nuances or ambiguity of the original, the reader who has no knowledge of the culture will inevitably fail to perceive the mythic connections, the rich reverberation of memory that links present form to past experience and accounts for the emotional impact of a work of art upon its audience.

Another factor to note in the literature is the very one most often overlooked, and that is its diversity of tone. The selections here have been chosen to reflect the religious, the heroic, the belligerent, the whimsical, and the humorous moods of the Indian. While the Indians did express reverent awe for the natural world, they also saw and were amused by their own failings. With the advent of the white man, the Indian's candid gaze led him to laugh at the smugness of the overconfident intruder.

The images of the poetry and the subject matter of the prose are drawn from nature, from the simple, familiar objects of the everyday world. Father sky and mother earth are pervasive images. The animals the Indian saw daily became embodiments of human virtues and failings. Though as one Osage said, finding he had to explain to the white man, "We do not believe that our ancestors were really animals, birds, etc., as told in the traditions. These things are only [symbols] of something higher" (Dorsey 1888:396).

Like any literature, that of the American Indians should not be regarded as an object to be studied, as a tradition that has been frozen forever in its aboriginal form. Rather, it is the result of complex dynamic processes that lead to social change. To give some idea of the nature of that process, this anthology has been organized in three sections to reveal the changes, over time, in the literature of the North American Indians.

The first section represents, as closely as we can approximate it, the indigenous literary traditions of the various bands and tribes that occupied

North America. Among these we find origin stories, nature stories, myths about supernatural powers, and more mundane narratives that outline daily life or assert specific moral lessons. Most such stories seem designed to answer the ubiquitous "whys" of human beings. Of course, there are other levels of understanding also touched by such literature. Some, like the Old Man Coyote stories, resemble the nonsense tales of Edward Lear or foolish chronicles, like Simple Simon. The absurdity of such tales is designed as a cautionary lesson: Proper human beings do not behave—*must* not behave—like the outrageous coyote or his counterparts. But the tales serve other purposes as well: They allow for the harmless expression of scatological or unpermissible fantasies; and they can also be used as political weapons to symbolize the folly and nonhuman attributes of outsiders. Principally, such stories seem to provide reassurance that the boundaries between order and chaos, culture and nature, will not be violated.

Like the literature of all peoples, that of American Indians was an integral part of each culture. Language makes culture possible by allowing people to store the collective wisdom of past and present as a weapon against the future. Codified as myth, poetry, and ritual, this group knowledge is passed down over the centuries—more vital to survival than his stone tools, as man has come to depend more and more upon learning and less upon the instincts that once guided his ancestors safely through an arboreal existence. Without ignoring the expressive or psychological functions of language, or the cathartic role it may play, a major emphasis in the material presented in this anthology is to provide insight into the essentially social importance of literature. Literature—myth, poetry, song, fable—accompanied religious ritual, crisis rites, and curing ceremonies. It often accompanied work, and its moral teachings helped define all manner of political and social relationships. Embodied in the stories and poetry, the narratives and songs of the Indians, are a series of rules about human behavior, lessons defining relationships among men, between man and nature, between man and the supernatural.

Often such stories were used to justify things as they are. For example, many of the nature stories purport to tell why animals behave the way they do, or why they have fur or lack it. More serious tales provide reasons for the origins of death or explain why people look and behave as they do. Such stories are quite obviously embedded in particular cultures and usually reiterate specific cultural values.

While the stories are often similar, the animal heroes change with the environment. Thus, quite obviously, the fishing cultures of the Northwest tend to emphasize stories about fish and sea mammals, while those of the Eastern Woodlands concern themselves with deer, fox, and rabbit. Coyotes and buffalo belong largely to the Plains, Plateau, and Prairie peoples.

More important, perhaps, than a simple association of certain kinds of animals with certain kinds of habitat is the difference in the nature of the concerns expressed by different Indian groups. By and large, these concerns derive from the tribe's economy and reflect the need for specific types of social organization in order to exploit specific types of environment. Obviously sedentary farmers who depend upon irrigation for their survival will have interests different from those of mounted buffalo hunters. These differences can be seen in many aspects of literary form and content.

Among many of the sedentary peoples of the Southwest, the emphasis in ritual is upon the need for group solidarity. The ritual itself is often spoken by a priest, but it demands the presence of the community. Need for cooperation in farming and irrigation activities is mirrored in ritual behavior; and the emphasis upon sun and rain, upon celestial events, seems to reflect a need for calendrical information by which they might regulate their planting and harvesting activities. The importance of work, of social tranquility and cooperation, are common themes. The ritual poetry itself is generally long and complex. Because such rituals must be recited exactly, with no deviation from the text, the similarity of the lines makes memorization extremely difficult. While the untutored might imagine that repetition facilitates memory, when such repetition is not exact but demands a slight change from line to line, the speaker gets no help from the context. Obviously, special gifts of perseverance, willingness to adhere to past forms, and concentration were required for priests. Such virtues are, indeed, the highest virtues of the Pueblos themselves and are thus celebrated both in the substance and form of the ritual poetry.

By contrast, the literature of Plains, Plateau, and Prairie—although there is some overlap in content and form—provides an entirely different picture. Concerns are often more personal and individualistic, as befits the needs of hunting societies. There are love songs, laments by women for lost lovers, reports of quarrels, hunting songs. Brevity is pronounced. Songs are made up by individuals and sung by them; they are the prop-

erty of the individual rather than the group and extol his virtues. Group
rituals are also found; but these, too, tend to be brief and tend to center
around major events in the lives of most of the people: hunting and warfare. Origin stories often concern clans rather than villages, for the
nomadic life of these people rested upon enduring social relationships
rather than spatial contiguity. Humor and scatology are more in evidence
here as well. Possibly the Plains Indians, who often practiced sexual ab-
stention to assure themselves success in battle or in the hunt, used both
humor and scatological references as a form of catharsis for severely re-
pressed sexual needs. It is also not surprising that thunder plays a great
role in their literature. The spectacular nature of electrical storms on the
Plains is still awesome, the dangers of lightning still evident.

The literature of the Northwest is, again, quite different both in substance and form. Town life, fishing, trade, and gambling are all common
themes. Justification of the status system that existed in the Northwest is
provided by origin myths. There is more concern with witchcraft and the
danger that it might backfire. A nonromantic viewpoint would suggest a
change in consciousness that derives from achievement of a settled life,
need for trade, and the development of marked status systems that accompanied the accumulation of wealth made possible by the predictability
of salmon and other foods from river and sea.

Both Northern Woodlands and the Southeast again reflect the concerns
of what appears to have been a mixed economy. In both areas farming
was supplemented by hunting. In both, we can find themes quite similar
to those of the Western areas. There are intimations here of a cultural
decline of some sort; memories of mound builders and a sedentary life
contrast with the simpler farming found there by the colonists. Also
worth noting are the extensive thanksgiving rituals of the Seneca which
resemble, in their length and complexity, the rituals of the Pueblos,
though they are not linked with them.

In many cases, the Indian's way of life is reflected in the imagery he
calls forth in song and story. The Pueblo Indians, for instance, often
make use of weaving terms. The sparse desert rain falling like uneven
threads becomes the "skyloom." Perhaps more surprising to non-Indians
is the fact that much of what we consider poetry was created by the
Indian to be chanted or sung. The brief, highly repetitive verses were
made up for many reasons, upon many occasions, and could remain the
property of the creator or become part of a traditional body of songs.
Indians created these songs as parts of rites or initiations, to praise their

gods or entreat them, in hunting, planting, or warfare. Some were simple expressions of their maker's private experiences; others were written as boasts. Still others derived from tribal games and were an integral part of such games.

We had some difficulty in deciding which selections should go into the first section and which into the second. The categories, like all such human devices, are somewhat arbitrary. Should we, for example, place the literature of the Plains culture (which was, after all, in part a product of contact with the whites) wholly in section two? Or should we, on the grounds that the Plains culture had developed more or less indigenously (once the presence of the horse is discounted), regard its rituals, literature, and poetry as representing a precontact situation? We chose to do the latter. Hence, the war songs, vision quest poetry, and the like, are to be found largely in section one.

Section two deals principally with the overt effects upon Indian literature of white contact. While in the beginning contact created a renaissance for some Indian groups, the destructive impact of the white world upon the Indian is the most prominent theme of the Indian literature of the nineteenth century. Here, again, we had to make some hard decisions. For example, pressure exerted by the white men as they moved westward created friction among many Indian groups as well as between white and Indian. White cultivation of former Indian hunting territory forced groups into more and more constricted areas, and warfare, once relatively nonlethal and sporadic, became more malignant, more pervasive, and more prevalent. Though a statistical study of forms of literature might well indicate an increase in the numbers of war poems, revenge songs, mortuary laments, there is no way to indicate this situation in this kind of book. Hence, we generally placed war songs in section one and confined section two to works commemorating specific historical events.

What the white man did not achieve through direct conquest or indirectly by setting tribe against tribe, he achieved through disease, through provision of guns and alcohol to the Indians, through destruction of indigenous religion and myth by Christianity. Measles and smallpox decimated the Indians. These epidemics are mentioned in numerous accounts of the day. Later, alcohol and the incursions of missionary activity further undermined the delicate network of thought, social organization, and religious belief that constitutes the cohesion of culture.

The process of moral dissolution, religious decay, and economic destruction is discernible in the literature of the time. Native forms and styles give way to inferior European varieties. A concern with alcoholism and its effects, self-mockery, and bitterness replace traditional concerns. Nevertheless, the literature suggests that Indians did not succumb but fought back constantly with verbal as well as military weapons. White men are incorporated into myth and legend. They often appear as fools in the narratives: What Indians could not say directly to them, they could express indirectly in their literature. Much of the literature is made up of oratory—eloquent political statements of Indian leaders whose attempts to deal with the American government were doomed to failure. The oratory provides a tragic picture of beleaguered men whose pleas, threats, and entreaties testify to continual betrayal.

Other European influences can be seen in the assimilation of Christian forms, like the hymn, and Biblical themes, such as the story of the Flood or of the Tower of Babel, to Indian folk forms. Even European fairy tales make an appearance—their non-Indian origins apparent, but their transformations at the hands of the Indians a creative blending of two different worlds.

Social disorganization, brought about by the conflict engendered between the white man's national, expansionist goals and Indian ways, emerges in autobiographical accounts of villages wracked by disease, dissension, and warfare. Attempts to resolve the continuing crises included warfare and endless debates between Indian chiefs and government officials. Less well known to American audiences are what anthropologists call "revitalization movements." Generally such movements preach salvation in return for the surrender of technology. The earliest movement derived from the Delaware prophet who promised that the white man would leave if the Indians abandoned the customs and material goods they had borrowed from the whites. Wave after wave of similar protests washed over the Indians, moving westward with migrating tribes. The names of the leaders—Handsome Lake, Smoholloh, Isatai, Pautapety, Poinkia, Taivo—are a litany of hope and despair. Best known of the movements and the prophets was the famous Ghost Dance of 1890 led by the Paiute Wovoka, who stirred up the now pitiful remnant of the once great Plains tribes. Each tribe interpreted Wovoka's message in its own way. Some prophesied an earthquake; the Arapaho foresaw a flood; the Shoshone predicted a four-day sleep; the Walapai awaited a hurricane. All believed the whites would be annihilated. A number of Sioux turned the ghost dance into an active resistance movement. Both they and the movement perished in the massacre at Wounded Knee.

The Peyote cult proved more enduring. Associated with the Native

American Church, the Peyote cult linked Christian and Indian rituals: Members ate the buttons of peyote and accompanied their visions with hymn singing and testimonials.

A few Indian groups managed to escape annihilation through disease, warfare, alcohol, and neglect. The Navajo, who have increased in number, represent an interesting mixture of Indian, Spanish, and American cultural traits. The Pueblo groups, who acculturated first to the Spaniards, have succeeded in keeping much of their way of life intact —through secrecy and the use of powerful sanctions against assimilation. Whether they can continue to resist the encroaching industries and cities of the white man is a question to which, at the moment, there is no answer.

Presently, Indian life and literature are in a state of transition. In section three we have put together some samples of Indian writing that is, quite obviously, still uniquely Indian in its view of the world. But changes are apparent—in the use of individual names to sign the pieces, in a decreasing emphasis on tribal affiliation (evident everywhere except among the tightly bound Pueblos) and an increasing focus on Indians in general.

It would be a disservice, we therefore decided, to classify present-day Indian literature according to tribal breakdown. The keynote of modern native American voices is unity. We do not wish to imply that the aim of the current pan-Indian movement is to deny or obscure tribal differences. The various tribal group traditions and identities are reflected within the larger, all-encompassing Indian identity. Consequently, in order to mirror this historical period, as we have tried to do in ordering our selections for past periods, our selections for section three are offered without divisions according to "tribe."

The renaissance in Indian art has affected painting and handicrafts; in literature it is most obvious in the Indian experimentation with English poetic forms. Prose narratives are, oddly, little in evidence. Novels by Indians are virtually nonexistent. Indian newspapers have proliferated and with them the first Indian journalists. As a whole, and in separate groups, Indians have come to realize their need for political organization. Like their great chiefs of the nineteenth century, they are developing a new political eloquence.

The necessity of preserving the voice of the Indian was explained by a Navajo elder as follows: "You look at me," he said, "and you see only an ugly old man, but within I am filled with great beauty. I sit on a mountaintop and I look into the future. I see my people and your people living together. In time my people will have forgotten their early way of life unless they learn it from white men's books. So you must write down all that I will tell you and you must have it made into a book that coming generations may know this truth" (O'Bryan 1956: vii).

II

The American Indian does not exist. The one characteristic that is immediately apparent to the student of American Indian cultures is their great diversity—diversity in language and in sociocultural systems in general. (American Indians have been called [Spencer, Jennings, *et al.* 1965:1] "the most interesting and diverse human population on earth.") Devising a meaningful arrangement of selections of prose and poetry from these cultures for a volume such as this can pose a problem.

One of our aims was to organize selections so that they were related for the reader to the societies that produced them and were not just free-floating entities divorced from context and hence from social significance. We considered various arrangements in our efforts to lend to this collection at least a hint of the flavor of the sociocultural systems that produced the literature. We wanted, however, to keep the organization simple for the general reader with little knowledge of American Indians. Yet we also wanted to avoid oversimplifying to the point of serious distortion.

We finally settled on that old anthropological standby, the culture area concept.

A culture area is a geographic area in which similar cultures are found at a given point in time. One authority on American Indians (Driver 1961:12) has described a culture area as "a geographical area occupied by a number of peoples whose cultures show a significant degree of similarity with each other and at the same time a significant degree of dissimilarity with the cultures of the peoples of other such areas."

The culture area concept has proved a poor analytic device, yet it is still a useful tool for organizing a mass of data. It helps one to catalog and depict a range of variation and similarity over a large area (in this case, the forty-eight states of the continental United States).

(The concept of culture area, however, has a number of drawbacks. One is that a culture area map is a static representation of its subject matter; it belies the dynamism of ongoing cultures. It can be used only to depict a distribution of cultures at one point in time. Since Indian cultures are anything but static, we would have to choose one time period for our map if we wanted to pinpoint geographical locations of the various Indian groups. We thought at first of indicating the distribution of cultures at about the time of white contact. But we rejected this, for it introduces distortions. For one, many Indian groups roamed over wide areas, whereas the map would indicate they remained in one relatively small area. For another, different groups of Indians came into contact with whites at different times. We therefore decided simply to indicate general culture areas on the map and to provide an accompanying list of specific tribal groups found in the areas. Though this manner of presentation has its obvious faults, the map we provide nevertheless offers a general orientation for those readers without any other guides. We refer those interested in detailed accuracy to the more comprehensive and scholarly literature on the subject [references cited below]. Another drawback concerns the boundaries between culture areas. Let the reader be cautioned that culture areas shade into one another. The lines on the map separating the various culture areas are only general guides.*)

The three classic culture area descriptions for American Indians are Wissler's (1938, orig. 1917), Kroeber's (1939), and Driver's (orig. 1961; second revised edition 1969). Probably the most sophisticated classification of American Indian diversity is that by Driver et al. (1972). We have used Driver's earlier work as the basis of our culture area breakdown.

According to this scheme (Driver 1969:17-24), there are a total of thirteen culture areas for North America. Though the selections for this anthology were drawn primarily from the geographical area of the forty-eight United States, we occasionally strayed outside this boundary and crossed the Canadian border. We have thus drawn selections from nine culture areas. These are:

Northwest Coast
Plateau
California
Great Basin
Southwest

*"How many 'culture areas' there are in North America depends in part simply on how far back you stand, what degree of detail you use to lump or split. It also depends on whether some attempt is made to take differences in language or social organization into account, rather than simply patterns of adaptation to the physical environment" (Keesing and Keesing 1971:113).

Plains
Prairies
East Sub-Arctic
Eastern
    (a) Northeast
    (b) Southeast

Each area is characterized by a specific environment, linguistic constellations, and types of food-getting technology. (See Driver 1969: 19-23 for a brief summary description for each area.)

Following this Introduction there is a culture area map, and with it are shown the various "tribes" from which we have drawn our selections of prose and poetry. (The term "tribe" is in some cases—perhaps most cases—a misnomer but is used here for convenience. See, for example, Swanton 1952: 1-3 and Spencer, Jennings, *et al*. 1965:1-6 on some problems with "tribe.") There is also a table listing the tribes in alphabetical order and indicating for each its culture area, techno-economic level, and linguistic affiliation.*

Thus it will be seen that, in addition to arranging the selections in a historically meaningful order, we achieved our objective of having all major language phyla and culture areas represented.

The major language phyla (according to Driver 1969:43-45) roughly coincident with the forty-eight states of the continental United States are all represented in this volume.

The ideal arrangement would have been to organize our selections first on the basis of historical period and then to have represented each language phylum and each culture area within every historical period. Though we endeavored to, and did, follow this schema as closely as possible, we did not succeed completely. In general, however, this is the plan of the book. If other factors—especially time limitations—had not intervened, the ideal would have been the actual. The product which

---

*The diversity of American Indian cultures is well illustrated by language differences. The number of Indian languages (for both North and South America) ranges from 1,000 to 2,000, all mutually unintelligible (see Driver 1969:25-52). "The Navaho sheepherder of the Southwest can no more communicate with a Blackfoot warrior than a monolingual English speaker with a monolingual Chinese. And just as languages differ, so also do cultures" (Spencer, Jennings, *et al*. 1965:2). Even some peoples in the same area, for example the Pueblos of the Southwest, speak languages as different from each other as is Chinese from English (see Spencer, Jennings, *et al*. 1965:110-118). In California alone there were over 135 different languages.

Phylum	Number of Tribes Representing
Na-Dene	5
Macro-Algonkian	15
Macro-Siouan	13
Hokan	3
Penutian	6
Aztec-Tanoan	9
Other language isolates and families	5

Similarly, all culture areas are represented as well:

Culture Area	Number of Tribes Representing
Northwest Coast	9
Plateau	3
California	2
Great Basin	1
Southwest	13
Plains	9
Prairies	8
East Sub-Arctic	1
Eastern	
(a) Northeast	8
(b) Southeast	6

is this volume nevertheless represents as close an approximation of the ideal as was possible under the circumstances.

Finally, we would advise those readers desiring a broader perspective and deeper understanding of the richness and diversity of American Indian cultures to consult as a first step the following helpful sources (full references are given in the bibliography under author and date): Driver 1969; Driver and Massey 1957; Driver, Massey, *et al.* 1953; Kroeber 1939; Mooney 1928; Murdock 1949; Powell 1891; Spencer, Jennings, *et al.* 1965; Swanton 1952; Voegelin and Voegelin 1966; Wissler 1938, 1966.

Yet despite the drawbacks or advantages of any particular framework of presentation, the literature as art remains the primary focus in a volume such as this. It is helpful to offer historical and cultural background, but in the final analysis all art must stand on its own merits. It must speak for itself. We therefore restrict our further comments to a minimum number of notes beyond this Introduction. Extensive footnotes throughout

MAP OF CULTURE AREAS

I. EAST SUB-ARCTIC
Ojibwa

II. EAST
  NORTHEAST
    Cayuga
    Delaware
    Mohegan
    Onondaga
    Pokonokets
    Scaticook
    Seneca
    Wawenock
    Wyandot

  SOUTHEAST

    Caddo (also Prairies
    Cherokee
    Chitimacha
    Creek
    Seminole
    Shawnee

III. PRAIRIES

Caddo (also Southeast)
Dakota (also Plains
Fox
Menomini
Omaha
Osage
Pawnee
Winnebago

IV. PLAINS

Arapaho
Assinibone
Blackfoot
Cheyenne
Comanche
Crow
Dakota (also Prairies)
Kiowa
Shoshoni (also Great Basin)

V. PLATEAU
Kutenai
Modoc
Nez Percé

VI. GREAT BASIN

Shoshoni (also Plains)

VII. SOUTHWEST
Apache
    Eastern: Jicarilla
    Western: Mescalero
                San Carlos

Havasupai
Hopi
Keres: Acoma
        Sia
Mojave
Navajo
Papago
Picuris
Pima
Tewa
Zuñi

VIII. NORTHWEST COAST

Alsea
Chinook
Duwamish
Haida
Kwakiutl
Coast Salish
Tlingit
Tsimshian
Yurok

IX. CALIFORNIA

Luiseño
Yokuts

the text would be distracting and might tend to obscure the aesthetic impact of the selections. There are a great number of works devoted to ethnographic descriptions and historical accounts of Indians, but this volume is not one of them. This is, rather, a collection of literature and is thereby a tribute to the aesthetic sense (similar in many respects to that manifest in Japanese haiku) of the American Indian.

TRIBAL DESIGNATION	TECHNO-ECONOMIC LEVEL	CULTURE AREA	LANGUAGE (Phylum & Family, where possible)
Alsea	Hunting-gathering (fishing)	Northwest Coast	Penutian (Yakonan)
Apache			
Eastern Apache	Hunting-gathering and farming	Southwest	Na-Dene (Athapascan)
Western Apache	Hunting-gathering and farming	Southwest	Na-Dene (Athapascan)
Arapaho	Hunting-gathering	Plains	Macro-Algonkian (Algonkian)
Assinibone	Hunting-gathering	Plains	Macro-Siouan (Siouan)
Blackfoot	Hunting-gathering	Plains	Macro-Algonkian (Algonkian)
Caddo	Farming	Prairies and Southeast	Macro-Siouan (Caddoan)
Cayuga	Farming	Northeast	Macro-Siouan (Iroquoian)
Cherokee	Farming	Southeast	Macro-Siouan (Iroquoian)
Cheyenne	Farming (later hunting)	Plains	Macro-Algonkian (Algonkian)
Chinook	Hunting-gathering (fishing)	Northwest Coast	Penutian (Chinookan)
Chippewa (see Ojibwa)			
Chitimacha	Farming	Southeast	Macro-Algonkian (Language Isolate)
Comanche	Hunting-gathering	Plains	Aztec-Tanoan (Uto-Aztecan)
Creek	Farming	Southeast	Macro-Algonkian (Muskogean)
Crow	Hunting-gathering	Plains and Prairies	Macro-Siouan (Siouan)
		Northeast	Macro-Siouan (Siouan)
Dakota	Hunting-gathering	Northwest Coast	Macro-Algonkian (Algonkian)
			Salish Family Isolate

TRIBAL DESIGNATION	TECHNO-ECONOMIC LEVEL	CULTURE AREA	LANGUAGE (Phylum & Family where possible)
Delaware	Farming	Prairies	Macro-Algonkian (Algonkian)
Duwamish	Hunting-gathering (fishing)	Northwest Coast	Na-Dene (Language Isolate)
Fox	Farming	Southwest	Hokan (Yuman)
Haida	Hunting-gathering (fishing)	Southwest	Aztec-Tanoan (Uto-Aztecan)
Havasupai	Farming		
Hopi	Farming		
Huron			
(see Wyandot)			

Iroquois: not a tribe but a confederation of tribes, including originally Mohawk, Oneida, Onondaga, Cayuga, and Seneca, and later the Tuscarora.

Jicarilla Apache (see Eastern Apache)

Keres (Acoma)	Farming	Southwest	Keres Language Isolate
Keres (Sia)	Farming	Southwest	Keres Language Isolate
Kiowa	Hunting-gathering	Plains	Aztec-Tanoan (Kiowa-Tanoan)
Kutenai	Hunting-gathering	Plateau	Kutenai Language Isolate
Kwakiutl	Hunting-gathering (fishing)	Northwest Coast	Wakashan Family Isolate
Luiseño	Hunting-gathering	California	Aztec-Tanoan (Uto-Aztecan)
Menomini	Farming	Prairies	Macro-Algonkian (Algonkian)

TRIBAL DESIGNATION	TECHNO-ECONOMIC LEVEL	CULTURE AREA	LANGUAGE (Phylum & Family where possible)
Mescalero Apache (see Western Apache)			
Modoc	Hunting-gathering	Plateau	Penutian (Klamath-Modoc Language Isolate)
Mohegan	Farming	Northeast	Macro-Algonkian (Algonkian)
Mohawk			
Mojave	Farming	Southwest	Hokan (Yuman)
Navajo	farming (later sheep-herders)	Southwest	Na-Dene (Athapascan)
Nez Percé	Hunting-gathering (including fishing)	Plateau	Hokan (Sahaptin-Nez Percé)
Ojibwa	Hunting-gathering (incl. some fishing)	East Sub-Arctic	Macro-Algonkian (Algonkian)
Omaha	Farming	Prairies	Macro-Siouan (Siouan)
Oneida	Farming	Northeast	Macro-Siouan (Iroquoian)
Onondaga			
Osage	Farming	Prairies	Macro-Siouan (Siouan)
Papago	Farming	Southwest	Aztec-Tanoan (Uto-Aztecan)
Pawnee	Farming	Prairies	Macro-Siouan (Caddoan)
Picuris	Farming	Southwest	Aztec-Tanoan (Kiowa-Tanoan)
Pima	Farming	Southwest	Aztec-Tanoan (Uto-Aztecan)
Pokonets	Hunting-gathering (fishing)	Northeast	Macro-Algonkian (Algonkian)
Coast Salish	Hunting-gathering (fishing)	Northwest Coast	Salish Family Isolate

TRIBAL DESIGNATION	TECHNO-ECONOMIC LEVEL	CULTURE AREA	LANGUAGE (Phylum & Family, where possible)
San Carlos Apache (see Western Apache)			
Scaticook	Farming	Northeast	Macro-Algonkian (Algonkian)
Seminole	Farming	Southeast	Macro-Algonkian (Muskogean)
Seneca	Farming	Northeast	Macro-Siouan (Iroquoian)
Shawnee	Hunting-gathering	Southeast	Macro-Algonkian (Muskogean)
Shoshoni	Hunting-gathering	Great Basin and Plains	Aztec-Tanoan (Uto-Aztecan)
Sioux: a linguistic term used to designate a category of related peoples primarily from the Plains Culture Area. It is used herein when the particular tribe is unspecified.			
Tewa	Farming	Southwest	Aztec-Tanoan (Uto-Aztecan)
Tlingit	Hunting-gathering (fishing)	Northwest Coast	Na-Dene (Language Isolate)
Tsimshian	Hunting-gathering (fishing)	Northwest Coast	Penutian (Language Isolate)
Wawenock (Abnaki)	Hunting-gathering (fishing)	Northeast	Macro-Algonkian (Algonkian)
Winnebago	Farming	Prairies	Macro-Siouan (Siouan)
Wyandot	Farming (and hunting-gathering)	Northeast	Macro-Siouan (Iroquoian)
Yokuts	Hunting-gathering	California	Penutian (Yokuts)
Yurok	Hunting-gathering (fishing)	Northwest Coast	Macro-Algonkian (Yurok Language Isolate)
Zuñi	Farming	Southwest	Penutian (Language Isolate)

SECTION I

Before the Coming
of the White Man

Southeast

HOW THE WORLD WAS MADE*

THE earth is a great island floating in a sea of water, and suspended at each of the four cardinal points by a cord hanging down from the sky vault, which is of solid rock. When the world grows old and worn out, the people will die and the cords will break and let the earth sink down into the ocean, and all will be water again. The Indians are afraid of this.

When all was water, the animals were above in Galûñ'lati, beyond the arch; but it was very much crowded, and they were wanting more room. They wondered what was below the water, and at last Dâyuni'si, "Beaver's Grandchild," the little Water-beetle, offered to go and see if it could learn. It darted in every direction over the surface of the water, but could find no firm place to rest. Then it dived to the bottom and came up with some soft mud, which began to grow and spread on every side until it became the island which we call the earth. It was afterward fastened to the sky with four cords, but no one remembers who did this.

At first the earth was flat and very soft and wet. The animals were anxious to get down, and sent out different birds to see if it was yet dry, but they found no place to alight and came back again to Galûñ'lati. At last it seemed to be time, and they sent out the Buzzard and told him to go and make ready for them. This was the Great Buzzard, the father of all the buzzards we see now. He flew all over the earth, low down near the ground, and it was still soft. When he reached the Cherokee country, he was very tired, and his wings began to flap and strike the

*From James Mooney, *Myths of the Cherokees*, 1900 p. 239-240.

ground, and wherever they struck the earth there was a valley, and where they turned up again there was a mountain. When the animals above saw this, they were afraid that the whole world would be mountains, so they called him back, but the Cherokee country remains full of mountains to this day.

When the earth was dry and the animals came down, it was still dark, so they got the sun and set it in a track to go every day across the island from east to west, just overhead. It was too hot this way, and Tsiska′gili, the Red Crawfish, had his shell scorched a bright red, so that his meat was spoiled; and the Cherokee do not eat it. The conjurers put the sun another hand-breadth higher in the air, but it was still too hot. They raised it another time, and another, until it was seven hand-breadths high and just under the sky arch. Then it was right, and they left it so. This is why the conjurers call the highest place Gûlkwâ′gine Di′galûñ-′latiyûñ′, "the seventh height," because it is seven hand-breadths above the earth. Every day the sun goes along under this arch, and returns at night on the upper side to the starting place.

There is another world under this, and it is like ours in everything —animals, plants, and people—save that the seasons are different. The streams that come down from the mountains are the trails by which we reach this underworld, and the springs at their heads are the doorways by which we enter it, but to do this one must fast and go to water and have one of the underground people for a guide. We know that the seasons in the underworld are different from ours, because the water in the springs is always warmer in winter and cooler in summer than the outer air.

When the animals and plants were first made—we do not know by whom—they were told to watch and keep awake for seven nights, just as young men now fast and keep awake when they pray to their medicine. They tried to do this, and nearly all were awake through the first night, but the next night several dropped off to sleep, and the third night others were asleep, and then others, until, on the seventh night, of all the animals only the owl, the panther, and one or two more were still awake. To these were given the power to see and to go about in the dark, and to make prey of the birds and animals which must sleep at night. Of the trees only the cedar, the pine, the spruce, the holly, and the laurel were awake to the end, and to them it was given to be always green and to be greatest for medicine, but to the others it was said: "Because you have not endured to the end you shall lose your hair every winter."

Men came after the animals and plants. At first there were only a brother and sister until he struck her with a fish and told her to multiply, and so it was. In seven days a child was born to her, and thereafter every seven days another, and they increased very fast until there was danger that the world could not keep them. Then it was made that a woman should have only one child in a year, and it has been so ever since.

WHAT THE STARS ARE LIKE*

There are different opinions about the stars. Some say they are balls of light, others say they are human, but most people say they are living creatures covered with luminous fur or feathers.

One night a hunting party camping in the mountains noticed two lights like large stars moving along the top of a distant ridge. They wondered and watched until the light disappeared on the other side. The next night, and the next, they saw the lights again moving along the ridge, and after talking over the matter decided to go on the morrow and try to learn the cause. In the morning they started out and went until they came to the ridge, where, after searching some time, they found two strange creatures about *so* large (making a circle with outstretched arms), with round bodies covered with fine fur or downy feathers, from which small heads stuck out like the heads of terrapins. As the breeze played upon these feathers showers of sparks flew out.

The hunters carried the strange creatures back to the camp, intending to take them home to the settlements on their return. They kept them several days and noticed that every night they would grow bright and shine like great stars, although by day were only balls of gray fur, except when the wind stirred and made the sparks fly out. They kept very quiet, and no one thought of their trying to escape, when, on the seventh night, they suddenly rose from the ground like balls of fire and were soon above the tops of the trees. Higher and higher they went, while the wondering hunters watched, until at last they were only two bright points of light in the dark sky, and then the hunters knew that they were stars.

*From James Mooney, *Myths of the Cherokees*, p. 257-258.

THE MOUNDS AND THE CONSTANT FIRE: THE OLD SACRED THINGS*

When they were ready to build the mound they began by laying a circle of stones on the surface of the ground. Next they made a fire in the center of the circle and put near it the body of some prominent chief or priest who had lately died—some say seven chief men from the different clans—together with an Ulûñsû'ti stone, an uktena scale or horn, a feather from the right wing of an eagle or great tla'nuwa, which lived in those days, and beads of seven colors, red, white, black, blue, purple, yellow, and gray-blue. The priest then conjured all these with disease, so that, if ever an enemy invaded the country, even though he should burn and destroy the town and the townhouse, he would never live to return home.

The mound was then built up with earth, which the women brought in baskets, and as they piled it above the stones, the bodies of their great men, and the sacred things, they left an open place at the fire in the center and let down a hollow cedar trunk, with the bark on, which fitted around the fire and protected it from the earth. This cedar log was cut long enough to reach nearly to the surface inside the townhouse when everything was done. The earth was piled up around it, and the whole mound was finished off smoothly, and then the townhouse was built upon it. One man, called the fire keeper, stayed always in the townhouse to feed and tend the fire. When there was to be a dance or a council he pushed long stalks of the *ihyâ'ga* weed, which some call *atsil'-sûñ'ti*, "the fire-maker" (*Erigeron canadense* or fleabane), down through the opening in the cedar log to the fire at the bottom. He left the ends of the stalks sticking out and piled lichens and punk around, after which he prayed, and as he prayed the fire climbed up along the stalks until it caught the punk. Then he put on wood, and by the time the dancers were ready there was a large fire blazing in the townhouse. After the dance he covered the hole over again with ashes, but the fire was always smolder-ing below. Just before the Green-corn dance, in the old times, every fire in the settlement was extinguished and all the people came and got new fire from the townhouse. This was called *atsi'la galûñkw'ti'yu*, "the honored or sacred fire." Sometimes when the fire in a house went out, the woman came to the fire keeper, who made a new fire by rubbing an

*From James Mooney, *Myths of the Cherokees*, p. 395-397.

ihyâ'ga stalk against the under side of a hard dry fungus that grows upon locust trees.

Some say this everlasting fire was only in the larger mounds at Nikwasi', Kitu'hwa, and a few other towns, and that when the new fire was thus drawn up for the Green-corn dance it was distributed from them to the other settlements. The fire burns yet at the bottom of these great mounds, and when the Cherokee soldiers were camped near Kitu'hwa during the civil war they saw smoke still rising from the mound.

The Cherokee once had a wooden box, nearly square and wrapped up in buckskin, in which they kept the most sacred things of their old religion. Upon every important expedition two priests carried it in turn and watched over it in camp so that nothing could come near to disturb it. The Delawares captured it more than a hundred years ago, and after that the old religion was neglected and trouble came to the Nation. They had also a great peace pipe, carved from white stone, with seven stem-holes, so that seven men could sit around and smoke from it at once at their peace councils. In the old town of Keowee they had a drum of stone, cut in the shape of a turtle, which was hung up inside the townhouse and used at all the town dances. The other towns of the Lower Cherokee used to borrow it, too, for their own dances.

All the old things are gone now and the Indians are different.

THE IGNORANT HOUSEKEEPER*

An old man whose wife had died lived alone with his son. One day he said to the young man, "We need a cook here, so you would better get married." So the young man got a wife and brought her home. Then his father said, "Now we must work together and do all we can to help her. You go hunting and bring in the meat and I'll look after the corn and beans, and then she can cook." The young man went into the woods to look for a deer and his father went out into the field to attend to the corn. When they came home at night they were hungry, and the young woman set out a bowl of walnut hominy (*kanâ'talu'ki*) before them. It looked queer, somehow, and when the old man examined it he found that the walnuts had been put in whole. "Why didn't you shell the walnuts and then beat up the kernels," said he to the young woman. "I didn't

*From James Mooney, *Myths of the Cherokees,* p. 401.

know they had to be shelled," she replied. Then the old man said, "You think about marrying and don't know how to cook," and he sent her away.

WHEN BABIES ARE BORN: THE WREN AND THE CRICKET*

The little Wren is the messenger of the birds, and pries into everything. She gets up early in the morning and goes round to every house in the settlement to get news for the bird council. When a new baby is born she finds out whether it is a boy or girl and reports to the council. If it is a boy the birds sing in mournful chorus: "Alas! the whistle of the arrow! my shins will burn," because the birds know that when the boy grows older he will hunt them with his blowgun and arrows and roast them on a stick.

But if the baby is a girl, they are glad and sing: "Thanks! the sound of the pestle! At her home I shall surely be able to scratch where she sweeps," because they know that after a while they will be able to pick up stray grains where she beats the corn into meal.

When the Cricket hears that a girl is born, it also is glad, and says, "Thanks, I shall sing in the house where she lives." But if it is a boy, the Cricket laments: "*Gwe-he!* He will shoot me! He will shoot me! He will shoot me!" because boys make little bows to shoot crickets and grasshoppers.

When inquiring as to the sex of the new arrival the Cherokee asks, "Is it a bow or a (meal) sifter?" or, "Is it ballsticks or bread?"

BATTLE CHARM**

Now! Blue Thunder, very quickly. You have just come to
    make a home.
Now! Tiy ga. You have just come to join the body.
Now! Red Thunder!
Ha! You splattered blood.

Among the Cherokee, red was the color of the war club and symbolized success, while blue indicated failure or depression. This brief verse, abrupt and quite to the point, was intended to affect the enemy magically by wishing failure (blue) upon him and success (red) upon the speakers. Black indicated evil and white signified peace.

*From James Mooney, *Myths of the Cherokees*, p. 401.
**From Jack F. and Anna G. Kilpatrick, *The Shadow of Sequoyah*, p. 46.

CHITIMACHA

THE OLD COUPLE THAT TURNED INTO BEARS*

LONG ago an old couple raised two nephews. When the boys could talk they called the old people their grandparents. One day the old woman said that she was going into the woods to get some firewood, and she went away. The children were about half grown at that time.

Late that evening the boys went to look for their grandmother and instead they saw a bear. The younger boy said, "That is not a bear. That is grandmother." He wanted to go to her but the older boy said, "No, let her alone." The children went home and said to the old man, "We saw grandmother but she was hairy. The face and ears were grandmother's but her body was hairy."

Soon afterward the old man went for wood. Next morning the children went for wood and saw a bear that ran from them.

Later the old woman came back, and again she went for wood. The children sought her a second time and saw only a bear. Both children cried, and the older boy began to sing a song so they would forget the change in their grandmother. It was said that each song occurring in the stories had a different melody, though none was remembered.

Three times the grandparents went away, returned and found that the children had been all right without them. Then they went away a fourth time and never came back. They did this so the children would become self-reliant and able to make their own living.

Among many primitive peoples, clan or family names are taken from animals. Members of such clans or families are usually forbidden to eat the flesh of the animal for which they are named except under unusual—and usually communal —circumstances. Human attitudes toward bears are particularly intriguing since there is evidence of some kind of mystic tie between men and bears in fossil deposits that extend back more than 50,000 years. While this story contains elements that recall that of Little Red Riding Hood, it was not derived from that European folktale but represents a wholly indigenous and original creation.

*From Frances Densmore, *A Search for Songs Among the Chitimacha Indians in Louisiana*, pp. 13-14.

SEMINOLE

THE RABBIT WHO STOLE THE FIRE*

THE people were having a Stomp Dance. Rabbit was a great singer and leader so they let him lead. Twice he ran up to the fire and made signs. The people thought he was wonderful. The third time he picked up a brand from the fire and ran toward the woods. He ran so fast that the people could not catch him, so they made medicine for rain to put out the fire.

When Rabbit came back, some people said, "Do not let him lead again as he steals the fire." Others said, "Don't let us be stingy." So they let him lead and he picked up a firebrand as before. They made medicine for rain again and it put out the fire.

Rabbit came back. Some said, "Don't let him lead again," but he had some friends who got him to lead. The same thing happened right over. But Rabbit found a hollow rock out in the woods. He could get in this hollow and keep the rain from putting out the fire. He rubbed some sort of oil on his hair, for he was afraid it might catch fire.

They let him lead again, and this time he went up toward the fire and stuck out his head. His hair caught fire and he ran out. The people ran after him but could not catch him, so they made another rain, but he had gone into the hollow rock that he had prepared. It rained and rained but he was safe.

He came out once in a while and set fire to grass but the people made rain and put it out. He did this four times and then they never saw any more fire. They thought Rabbit was finished up but he still had some fire, so he got out of the rock and got into the ocean, carrying the fire and intending to swim across.

The people saw the smoke across the ocean and knew that Rabbit had carried the fire across and spread it out. They were angry at him but couldn't reach him.

That is the way that everybody got fire.

*From Frances Densmore, *Seminole Music*, p. 194.

THE ORIGIN OF WHITE CORN*

The Seminole always refer to themselves as "A jia tki," which means *white corn*, and in the beginning they were white people.

An old woman was living with her grandchild. She made good *sofki* for the boy and it tasted good to him. He would go out and hunt, kill game and bring it to this grandmother. They all ate together, drank *sofki* and ate deer meat.

The boy did not know how his grandmother got the corn to make the *sofki*. He wanted to know where she got the corn, and he told his grandmother that he was going hunting again. Instead of going, he sneaked back to watch her make the *sofki*. He saw her go into a shack and sit down. She had very sore ankles that were so very dry that she could scrape off the flakes of skin. The boy watched her scrape off the flakes and bring them into the house. She got the pot and some water and put the flakes in the water. The boy found out that the *sofki* came from his grandmother's sore ankles.

After that he would not drink the *sofki*. His grandmother said, "Why don't you drink *sofki*?" He did not explain because he knew where it came from. The grandmother suspected that the boy had watched her, so she asked him, "Did you watch me doing something?" The boy did not reply, but said he would not drink *sofki* any more.

His grandmother told him that he must burn their house and everything. The reason was that the boy had found out her secret and she did not want to live any more. She told the boy to tell the people to burn the house over her, while she was in it.

A few days after the house was burned they came to see the ruins and found the old house restored and full of corn. From there the corn spread over all the earth.

That is the end of the story.

*From Frances Densmore, *Seminole Music*, p. 195.

THE OPOSSUM CALLS HER LOST BABY*

She came to a house. Somebody was there and she asked if they had seen anybody going by, carrying a baby. The person in the house said "Yes." The opossum went in the direction they indicated and on the road she met two people and asked them the same question. Then she had been to two places and met two people, and sang her "lonesome song" twice.

After a while she came to another place. In that place the baby had been hidden. There were four or five houses, some occupied and some empty. The opossum asked her question and somebody pointed to a house saying, "They got the baby in there." She went over, opened the door and found the baby inside. Somebody had killed a rattlesnake, cooked it, and given it to the baby to eat. The mother was angry and told them to take it away. She took the baby and started home. She killed a little fawn, ate some of the meat, and gave some to the baby. They stayed there a while. That made three times she sang the song.

A wolf came to that place and smelled the meat. The opossum lied and said she had no meat, but the wolf smelled the meat. The wolf got a bow and arrow. Then the opossum was afraid she would be killed. She went up a big tree, took the baby with her and stayed up in the top of the tree. The baby died up there in the tree. That was the fourth time she sang the song.

The old opossum came down and walked away. She found a skunk who was her friend and went home with the skunk. They lay down together and sang. They sang another "lonesome song" and then they both died.

WHY THE RABBIT IS WILD**

At first the Indians were under the ground, in a big hole, then they all came out. When they came out they bathed in a little creek. When they got through bathing they had nothing to eat and no fire.

One man told them what to do and how to make a fire. He told them to take dry, soft bark, twirl a stick between their hands, and then a spark lighted the bark. He got some dry punk. One man made the spark,

*From Frances Densmore, *Seminole Music*, p. 195.
**From Frances Densmore, *Seminole Music*, p. 177.

another caught it on the punk, then they made a fire, but they had no pots or kettles.

The man heard a noise a half a mile or so toward the north. He thought some animals were there. He sent two men to get little trees and out of these he made bows and arrows. He got ready, then sent the boys and men to find something to eat.

They found deer, turkey, and bear and brought them back to camp. Then they had plenty of meat but nothing else. The man tried to find something else and found swamp cabbage. He cut it down and told the people to eat it raw, as they had no kettles. Then he taught them to roast it in the ashes of a fire.

The two men talked it over. One man had made the bows and arrows and the other had taught them to roast the swamp cabbage and to cook meat in the same way, putting some in the fire. One man said to the other, "What shall we live in?" They had been sleeping in the grass. So they made themselves a house, like those the Seminole live in now. Then a horse and dog talked to the man, talking like people. At that time the rabbit stayed with the people and he told lies all the time, but the dog and horse told the truth.

Somebody found out that the rabbit lied. Then the rabbit tried to do something all the time. He would go away, and when he came back he would say he had seen things that he had not seen. He would say he had seen snakes, alligators, and turtles.

The man said to the rabbit, "If you find a snake, kill him and bring him back to camp." The rabbit killed a snake and brought it to the camp, and he sang a song with words that meant "On his back."

IT MOVES ABOUT AS IT FEEDS*

Yellow nose, small eyes, round ears, dark body, big hind quarters, short tall. It moves about as it feeds.

*From Frances Densmore, *Seminole Music,* p. 177.

Northeast

THE BEAR AND THE FOX*

A FOX was traveling along when suddenly he came upon a sleeping horse. He sucked milk from the horse until, when he had had his fill, he took another mouthful along back with him for his lunch.

He hadn't gone very far when he met a bear. The bear said, "What is that mouthful of stuff that you're going along with bulging in your cheek?" The fox said, "There's a horse sleeping over here; I sucked milk from her." "Gosh!" said the bear, "How about showing me where she is sleeping, so I can suck too!"

They they went back and arrived again at the place where the horse was sleeping. The bear started in at once, and drank the milk until he had gotten his fill.

The fox said, "I think it would be a very good idea for us to take her with us; then we can always have her." The bear said, "How will we manage to take her with us, she is so heavy?" The fox said, "That's easy, you are very strong, you will do the pulling." Then the bear said, "How will I manage to pull her?" The fox answered, "There's nothing hard about that; I will splice your tails together and tie them up; I'll make them good and tight. And I'll get behind and push." And so the bear consented.

Soon the fox said, "Okay, I'm finished; are you ready?" And he went around and bit the horse on her snout. Immediately the horse jumped up and away she ran, with the bear hanging on behind. It was quite

*From Floyd G. Lounsbury, *Oneida Verb Morphology*, pp. 95-109.

a distance, they say, that the bear was hanging, before finally his tail broke and he got himself loose.

Then the bear got mad, and he just made up his mind he would kill the fox the next time he met him. Now, they say, he traveled around looking for the fox. And it was some time later that he caught up with him again. The bear said, "It's been a long time that I've been looking for you. Now then, we'll straighten out the matter of that trick you played on me. Right here and now I'm going to beat the daylights out of you."

Said the fox, "It doesn't make any difference with me, except that there is so much difference in size between us, it's plain to see that you will get the best of me." Fox continued, "It's all right with me, only let's each of us get up a gang." Then he asked the bear, "When would you like to fight?" The bear said, "There's a great big tree on top of the hill; there's where we will meet, at two o'clock tomorrow." Then they parted once more.

The bear at once began collecting fighters. After a while he met a pig. Said the bear, "Darned if you don't look like a pretty tough one; that's just what I'm looking for, a good fighter." The pig answered, "That's exactly what I'm looking for, myself. I've never been licked by anybody yet." Immediately the bear invited the pig along to go back there where they were going to fight.

The fox in the meantime was also looking for help. It was quite some distance he had gone, when he met up with a dog that had broad shoulders and was walking lame. Then the fox said, "Well, it sure is a good thing we met; I am going to have a fight tomorrow." The dog answered, "That's exactly what my business is. I've never been beaten by anyone yet." So immediately he invited him along.

Just a little farther on they met up with a cat. And so he asked him if he could fight. It was okay by him. And so the fox said, "Now I guess we might as well head straight for the place where we're going to do the fighting."

Now the bear and the pig had already arrived in the vicinity of the big tree. And the bear said, "I guess I will climb this tree here, so I can see whether they are coming anywhere in sight yet." Then the pig said, "I think I will rest here in the shade; I'll cover myself up with leaves while we are waiting."

And, so they say, the bear was sitting way up on top of the tree, looking around. "Ow, here comes that gang," said the bear. "Now I realize we made a mistake. It's a sure thing we're going to get cleaned up, he has such a tough crowd coming." "What's the reason?" asked the pig. The bear answered, "One of them is carrying a sack on his shoulders and going along picking up stones" (that was the limping dog with the broad shoulders), "and one of them is carrying a club on his shoulders" (that was the cat with his tail in the air). Then the pig said, "Maybe it would be best if you would make up with the fox when they get here."

And so, it is said, the one perched up high called down when they arrived, and said, "I think we would prefer to make up with you; let's be friends and go our separate ways in peace." Then the fox said, "Shucks! That's funny! But, it's perfectly okay by me."

Now it is said, that the cat spoke up too, saying, "That's queer! I am very sorry that it looks as though we're not going to have a fight." Then the cat said further, "As for me, this is the way I would have done if we had fought." And he immediately jumped onto where there was a movement in the leaves. And he put his claws into the pig's snout. And the pig let out a squeal.

Immediately the cat let him go again, he got so scared. He just climbed right up the tree that the bear was sitting in. Then the bear got so scared that he let out a yell, saying, "This is the end of me!" Well, so the story goes, the only thing he could think of was to jump. And the bear landed flat as a pancake on the ground.

SENECA

THANKSGIVING RITUALS*

The People

AND now, we are gathered in a group. And this is what the Sky Dwellers did: they told us that we should always have love, we who move about on the earth. And this will always be first when people come to gather, the people who move about on the earth. It is the way it begins when two people meet: they first have the obligation to be grateful that they are happy. They greet each other, and after that they take up the matter

*From Wallace L. Chafe, *Seneca Thanksgiving Rituals*, pp. 17-33.

with which just they two are concerned. And this is what Our Creator did: he decided, "The people moving about on the earth will simply come to express their gratitude." And that is the obligation of those of us who are gathered: that we continue to be grateful. This, too, is the way things are: we have not heard of any unfortunate occurrence that there might be in the community. And the way things are, there are people lying here and there, held down by illness; and even that, certainly, is the responsibility of the Creator. And therefore let there be gratitude; we are always going to be grateful, we who remain, we who can claim to be happy. And give it your thought: the first thing for us to do is to be thankful for each other. And our minds will continue to be so.

The Earth

And now this is what Our Creator did: he decided, "I shall establish the earth, on which the people will move about. The new people, too, will be taking their places on the earth. And there will be a relationship when they want to refer to the earth: they will always say 'our mother, who supports our feet.' " And it is true: we are using it every day and every night; we are moving about on the earth. And we are also obtaining from the earth the things that bring us happiness. And therefore let there be gratitude, for we believe that she has indeed done all that she was obligated to do, the responsibility that he assigned her, our mother, who supports our feet. And give it your thought, that we may do it properly: we now give thanks for that which supports our feet. And our minds will continue to be so.

The Animals

And now this is what Our Creator did: he decided, "I shall now establish various animals to run about on the earth. Indeed, they will always be a source of amusement for those who are called warriors, whose bodies are strong." He decided to provide the warriors, whose bodies are strong, with the animals running about, to be a source of amusement for them. "And they will be available as food to the people moving about on the earth." And up to the present time we have indeed seen the small animals running about along the edges of the forests, and within the forests as well. And at the present time we even catch glimpses of the large animals again. There were in fact a number of years during which we no longer saw the large animals. But now at the present time we again see the large animals running about, and at the present time they are actually available to us again as food. And we are using them as Our Creator intended. And therefore let there be gratitude that it all does still continue as he intended. And give it your thought, that we may do it properly: we now give thanks for the animals running about. And our minds will continue to be so.

The Wind

And now this is what Our Creator did: he decided, "Now it can't always be just this way." And this, in fact, is what he decided. "There must be wind, and it will strengthen the people moving about whom I left on the earth. And in the west he made the thing that is covered by a veil; slowly it moves and revolves. There the wind is formed, and we are happy. It indeed strengthens our breath, for us who move about on the earth. And the wind is just the strength for us to be content with it and be happy. But the Sky Dwellers told us: they said, "We believe that your kinsmen will see that in future days it may happen that it will be beyond our control. It is the most important thing for us to watch. It may become strong in its revolving, and we believe that it will scrape off everything on the earth. The wind may become strong, we believe, and bring harm to the people moving about." That is what they said.

The Thunderers

And now this is what Our Creator did: he decided, "I shall have helpers who will live in the west. They will come from that direction and will move about among the clouds, carrying fresh water." They will sprinkle all the gardens which he provided, which grow of their own accord on the earth. And he decided, "There will be a relationship when people want to refer to them: they will say 'our grandparents, *hiʔnɔʔ,* the Thunderers'. That is what they will do." And he left them in the west; they will always come from that direction. And truly they will always be of such a strength that the people, their grandchildren, who move about will be content with them. And they are performing their obligation, moving about all through the summer among the clouds, making fresh water, rivers, ponds, and lakes. And give it your thought, that we may do it properly: we now give thanks for them, our grandparents, *hiʔnɔʔ,* the Thunderers. And our minds will continue to be so.

THE GHOST WOMAN AND THE HUNTER*

Once there was a young man in a village who was an orphan; he had neither relatives nor home. He lived in first one lodge and then in another.

Once in the fall of the year when warriors were preparing to go to hunt deer the orphan wanted to go but could not get a chance to do so; no one wanted him as a companion. So he was left alone in the village. When all the men had gone he determined to go, too, and he went off by himself. Toward night he came to a sort of clearing and saw a lodge on one side of it near the bushes; he looked into it but he could see no one. In the dooryard was a pile of wood and everything inside was comfortable; so the orphan decided to pass the night there. He made a fire, arranged a place to sleep, and lay down. About midnight he heard some one coming in and, looking up, he saw that it was a woman. She came in and stood gazing at him, but she said nothing. Finally she moved toward his couch but stopped; at last she said: "I have come to help you. You must not be afraid. I shall stay all night in the lodge. I know you are going out hunting." The orphan said, "If you help me, you may stay." "I have passed out of this world," said she; "I know that you are poor; you have no relatives; you were left alone. None of the hunters would let you go with them. This is why I have come to help you. Tomorrow start on your journey and keep on until you think it is time to camp, and then I will be there." Toward daybreak she went out, starting off in the direction from which she said she had come.

In the morning after preparing and eating some food he started on. In the afternoon when he thought it was about time to stop he looked for a stream. He soon found one and had just finished his camp as it became dark. In the forepart of the night the woman came, saying, "We must now live together as man and wife, for I have been sent to live with you and help you." The next day the man began to kill all kinds of game. The woman stayed with him all the time and did all the necessary work at the camp.

When the hunting season was over, she said, "There is no hunter in the woods who has killed so much game as you have." They started for home. "We shall stop," said she, "at the first lodge, where we met";

*From Jeremiah Curtin and J.N.B. Hewitt, *Seneca Fiction, Legends, and Myths,* pp. 90-92.

and they slept at the lodge that night. The next morning she said: "I shall remain here, but you go on to the village, and when you get there everybody will find out that you have brought all kinds of meat and skins. One will come to you and say, 'You must marry my daughter.' An old woman will say, 'You must marry my granddaughter,' but do not listen to them. Remain true to me. Come back next year and you shall have the same good luck. [This was at a time when the best hunter was the best man, the most desirable husband.] The next year when getting ready to hunt, a man will try to come with you, do not take him. No one would take you. Come alone. We will meet here." Before daylight they parted and he went on his journey with a great load of meat on his back.

In the village he found that some of the hunters had got home, while others came soon after. All told how much they had killed. This lone man said, "I will give each man all he wants if he will go to my camp and get it." Accepting his offer, many went and brought back all they could carry. Still there was much meat left. Everyone who had a daughter or a granddaughter now asked him to come and live with the family. At last the chief came and asked him to marry his daughter. The orphan was afraid if he refused harm would come to him, for the chief was a powerful man. At last he consented and married the chief's daughter.

The next fall the chief thought he had the best hunter for a son-in-law and a great many wanted to go with him, but the son-in-law said, "I do not think I shall go this year." All started off, one after another. When all had gone he went alone to the lodge where he was to meet the woman. Arriving there he prepared the bed, and early in the night the woman came in; stopping halfway between the door and the couch, she said, "I am sorry you have not done as I told you to do. I cannot stay with you, but I decided to come once more and tell you that I know everything you did at home and I cannot stay." She disappeared as suddenly as she came.

Day after day the orphan went hunting, but he saw no game. He ate all his provisions, and had to shoot small game—squirrels and birds—to eat, for he was hungry. Returning home, he told the people that he had seen no game. This woman who had befriended the orphan, it was said, was a ghost woman.

HINON AND THE SENECA WARRIORS*

Once a war party of Seneca while on the warpath against the Cherokee became very hungry. Seeing a bear, they chased it into its den, one of the party following it. When he had gone some distance into the den he could no longer see the bear, but he saw instead a fire burning briskly and three men sitting around it. The eldest asked the Seneca warrior why he had tried to shoot one of his men whom he had sent to entice him into the den. He continued, "I want to send word to the eldest man at your camp to tell him that his friend is here and wants some tobacco, and that tomorrow as many of his warriors as wish may come to see me here." So the warrior went back to the camp of his comrades and reported what he had heard.

The next day, accompanied by five of his companions, each bearing a pouch of native tobacco, he returned to the den of the bears. When they gave the tobacco to the old man, he was very glad, and said to them: "I am thankful to you for this present of tobacco. I shall enjoy it a long time, for it will last me many days." While in the den one of the warriors remarked, "Oh! I am very tired and sleepy." Overhearing this remark, the old man said to him, "Lie down, then."

When the others also had laid themselves down the old man arose, and going over to the spot where the first warrior lay, rubbed his body from his feet to his head. Then setting down a vessel which he held in one hand he proceeded to dismember this warrior's body joint by joint until he had taken him to pieces. Placing each piece in a mortar, with a pestle he pounded the bones to a jelly, which he poured into a bowl. Then he took the bowl and the other vessel into another part of the den, where he left them. Returning and sitting down, he began to smoke.

After a while he called out: "My nephew, come out now. You have been there long enough." When the young warrior came out, he appeared as light, fresh, and lithe as a boy. Then another of the Seneca warriors said, "Can you do this for me, too?" The old man answered, "Yes, if you wish me to do so."

Then the warrior laid himself down, and the old man went through the same process as he had with the other warrior. After he had carried the two vessels into the remote part of the den, the old man, returning, began to smoke. Shortly he called out, "Oh, my nephew, you have now

*From Jeremiah Curtin and J.N.B. Hewitt, *Seneca Fiction, Legends, and Myths*, pp. 197-199.

slept long enough!" At once the warrior arose and came forth so fresh and lithe that he felt no weight in his body. Thereupon another Seneca warrior asked the old man to treat him in the same manner. The latter man consented and, after going through the same process as that which renewed the others, this warrior, too, was made young and as light as a feather, and consequently was very happy.

Then a fourth warrior asked the old man to transform him likewise, but the old man refused, saying: "I have now done enough. I will tell you why I have taken the trouble to do this to four of your people. There is a large opening extending from one end of the world to the other. In this opening is a great rock, and in this rock is a man possessed of enormous horns. We have tried to kill him, but cannot do so. Now, I want two of you to try to crush this rock and so kill him; but first you must go out and try your strength in orenda" [magic power]. So, going out, they shot at a rock, which crumbled to pieces when they hit it. Then they shot at an enormous tree; this, too, they brought down when they hit it, leaving nothing but a stump. "Now," said the old man, "you may go to the opening and see what you can do with that enchanted rock. Your companions may remain here; they will not die, for we never die here. I always help my grandchildren. I cover your trail whenever you need to conceal it. It is I who cause it to rain."

The two transfigured warriors went to the opening, as directed, and seeing the great enchanted rock, they shot at it; then, returning to the old man, they told him what they had done. He quickly asked them, "Did you use all your orenda?" They replied, "No. We could have struck the rock a harder blow"; whereupon the old man said, "Go back there and employ all your magical strength." Returning to the opening where the great rock stood, the two warriors shot it with all their orenda. After waiting for some time, they heard a person coming toward them. Soon they saw that it was a man carrying the head of an enormous horned snake securely strapped to his back. This man was the old man who had transformed them. Returning to the den, the two warriors said, "Now our work is done; the great horned snake is dead." Then they went back to their homes.

THE CRAWFISH AND THE RACCOON*

The chief of the Crawfish settlement one day told his people that he

*From Jeremiah Curtin and J.N.B. Hewitt, *Seneca Fiction, Legends, and Myths*, p. 229.

was going about to inspect things and to see if the Ongwe Ias was around.

Starting out, he went to every lodge; he found that everyone was in and well. On his way home, as he was walking along the edge of the water he found what he judged to be the body of Ongwe Ias. "Oh! This is good luck," said he; "I will go and tell all the people to come to see Ongwe Ias lying here dead." So he invited all to turn out and see their enemy, whom he supposed was dead.

The whole multitude came and saw the Ongwe Ias lying on the ground with his face black and covered with flies. One of them went up and pinched his lips hard, but he did not move. Then saying, "We will sing a song of rejoicing," they formed in a circle around the Ongwe Ias to dance. While they were dancing and singing, all at once their enemy, the Ongwe Ias, springing up, ate the whole tribe except two or three who escaped. The Ongwe Ias knew the fondness of the Crawfish for dead meat of any kind, so his ruse was successful in providing him with a meal.

THE STORY OF BLOODY HAND*

According to tradition several tribes of the Iroquois claim the honor of having produced a great man, whose name was Bloody Hand, and whose fame as a hunter was not less than his reputation as a bold and resolute war captain.

Now, Bloody Hand had great love for the birds of the air and the animals on the earth that eat flesh. He greatly respected them and paid them marked attention. When he had killed a deer while out hunting he would skin it and cut the meat into small pieces; then he would call Gaqga to come to eat the flesh. When he killed another animal, he would dress it in like manner and call Nonhgwatgwa and his people to come to eat the flesh which he had given them. Sometimes he would carry home a portion of the game he had killed, but generally he gave it all to the various birds and animals whose chief food is flesh.

According to a Seneca legend a number of Seneca warriors went on a warlike expedition against a tribe which was hostile to them, and it so happened that Bloody Hand was one of this warlike band. In an

*From Jeremiah Curtin and J.N.B. Hewitt, *Seneca Fiction, Legends, and Myths*, pp. 224-226.

encounter with the enemy he and a number of others were killed and their remains were left on the ground. The body of Bloody Hand lay in the forest stark naked; the enemy, having scalped him, had borne away the scalp as a great trophy.

The birds of the air, having seen Bloody Hand killed and mutilated, held a council at which they bemoaned the death of their human friend. Finally one of the assembly said: "Let us try to bring him back to life. But before we can begin to resuscitate his body we must recover his scalp, which hangs before the door of the chief of the enemy who killed him. Let us send for it." The assembly, after agreeing to what had been proposed with regard to the preparations necessary to bring their friend back to life, first sent the Black Hawk to secure the scalp. Having arrived at the place where hung the scalp, Black Hawk was able by means of his sharp and powerful bill to break easily the cords that held the scalp; thus securing it, he bore it in triumph to the council of the birds. Then one among them said, "Let us first try our medicine to see whether it has retained its virtue or not. We must try first to bring to life that dead tree which lies there on the ground." Thereupon they proceeded to prepare their medicine. To make it, each representative placed in the pot a piece of his own flesh. (These representatives were, of course, birds of the elder time, not such as live now.) In experimenting with their medicine they caused a stalk of corn to grow out of the ground without sowing seed. In this stalk there was blood. After noting the efficacy of the medicine they broke the stalk, and after obtaining blood from it, caused it to disappear. With this medicine is compounded the seed of the squash.

When the medicine was made they held a sanctifying council, in which part of the assembly sat on one side of the tree, and the other part on the opposite side. The wolves and the snakes attended, also other animals and birds of great orenda (magic power). The birds sang and the rattlesnakes rattled; all present made music, every one in his own way.

Above the clouds and mists of the sky dwells a bird who is the chief of all the birds. His name is S'hadahgeah. This assembly of bird and animal sorcerers chose the chief of the crows to notify him of all that was taking place. This is the reason, according to the tradition, the crow today sings the note "caw, caw." The eagle is another chief who is under this great bird that dwells above the clouds and mists of the firmament.

When the leaders of this assembly saw that the trees and plants were coming to life and putting forth green leaves and waxen buds, the presiding chief said to his associates: "This is enough. We have sung enough. Our medicine will now act, and we must select someone to put it into the man's body." For this purpose they chose the chickadee. This canny bird first drank the medicine; then going by way of the man's mouth into his stomach, it emitted the medicine. While this was taking place the others were engaged in rubbing the body of the dead man with the medicine. When his body was well anointed they all sat down and began to sing. For two days and two nights they did not cease from singing, until they perceived that the body was becoming warm again. After his resuscitation the man reported that he felt suddenly as though he had just been aroused from a sound sleep; he heard the singing of the birds and the various sounds made by the beasts around him, and finally came to life again. Remaining silent, he merely listened to the singing of the songs of orenda that arose on all sides. He listened because he could understand the words that were used in these chants of the sorcerers. As soon as his body began to show signs of motion the birds and the beasts drew back a little, but continued to sing and chant.

When the chief of the assembly saw that the man had fully recovered his life, he said to him: "We bestow this medicine on you and your people. Your people shall have it for their healing. If it so happens that one of them is injured by a fall, by a blow, or by an arrow shot, he must have recourse to this medicine. You must make use of it at once. You must also from time to time strengthen and renew this medicine by giving a feast in its honor. When you make use of it you must burn tobacco in our behalf and turn your thoughts toward us. As long as you shall have this medicine, you shall assemble at intervals at appointed feasts to strengthen it, and for this purpose you shall burn tobacco of the old kind. While doing this you shall say, among the other things: 'Let all the birds and the beasts on the earth and above the earth share this fragrant smell of the tobacco. As long as people live and are born this ceremony must be maintained to fix the use of this medicine.' " Thus, after the birds and beasts had brought the man to life, they taught him how to make use of the medicine and how to sing the songs that put it in action. Then they dismissed him, telling him to go to his home, where he must inform his people, through their appointed authorities, what he had learned for their benefit and welfare. Thereupon the man went to his home.

The men who had seen him scalped and killed had related the story to their people, who believed him dead. So, when they saw him return alive, they quickly gathered around him, asking, "How has it come to pass that you have returned alive?'' Then the man gave them, in detail, an account of how he had been killed, and how the birds and the animals, in return for the kindness which he had shown them at all times, had concocted the medicine which had brought him back to life. Then, selecting a small number of wise men of great experience, he taught them how to use this medicine and confided its preservation to their custody. He strictly enjoined them not to make light of the songs which belonged to it; should they so far forget themselves as to do so, they would suffer great misfortune, for the songs possessed great orenda, which would become active against them. He told them, further, that no one should sing the songs unless he had some of this powerful medicine (which is called *nigahnegahah,* "small dose"). This medicine is still held in great repute among the Iroquois.

THE VAMPIRE SKELETON*

A man with his wife, starting from a Seneca village, went from it two days' journey to hunt. Having built a lodge, the man began hunting. When he had obtained a sufficient store of meat, they started for home. They packed all the meat they could carry and left the rest at the lodge. Setting out in the morning, after traveling all day they came to a cabin in which they found all the people dead. The last person to die was the owner of the lodge. The people of the village had put the body on a shelf in a bark box which they had made. When the man and his wife came it was already dark. The husband thought it better to spend the night there than to continue the journey. He gathered a quantity of wood with which he made a fire. The woman began to cook, broiling meat and making a cake of pounded corn, which she placed under the hot ashes to bake. The man lay down to rest a while and fell asleep. While cooking, the woman heard a noise behind her, near the place where the husband lay; it sounded like the noise made in the chewing of flesh. She began to think about the corpse on the shelf and remembered that the dead man was a wizard. Putting on more wood and making the fire blaze up, she looked toward the bunk, where she saw a stream of blood trickling out. From this she knew at once that her husband had been killed by the dead man.

*From Jeremiah Curtin and J.N.B. Hewitt, *Seneca Fiction, Legends, and Myths,* pp. 458-460.

The bread under the ashes was baked. She then spoke, saying, "I must make a torch and bring some water." Thereupon she prepared a torch of hickory bark taken from the lodge, making it long enough to last until she could run home. Taking the pail, she stole out, but once outside of the door she quickly dropped the pail, and ran through the woods with all her might. She had gotten more than halfway home when the dead man, the vampire, found that she was gone. At once he rushed out, whooping, and ran after her. She heard him, and knew that he was following her. The sound of the whooping came nearer and nearer, and for a while, unnerved completely by fear, she could scarcely move, but at last, having regained her strength, she ran on. Again the vampire whooped, and the woman fell down from fear and exhaustion; but she arose again and ran on, until finally she came within sight of a place near her own village where there was a dance. The pursuing man-eating skeleton was gaining on her, and her torch was almost gone; but, running ahead, she fell into the lodge in which the dancing was in progress, and then fainted. When she came to her senses, she told what had occurred to her and her husband.

In the morning a body of men went over to the cabin, in which they found the bones of her husband, from which all the flesh had been eaten. Taking down the bark box, they looked at the skeleton of the dead man and found his face and hands bloody. The chief said it was not right to leave dead people in that way; therefore they dug a hole, in which they buried the man-eating skeleton, and took the bones of the other man home. The chief had him buried and ordered that thereafter all dead people should be buried in the ground. At first the dead were put on scaffolds, but the people used to see sights which frightened them, for the dead would rise and run after the living. Then it was resolved to build bark lodges for the dead and to put them on shelves therein. This plan did not work well, as the foregoing story shows. About one hundred years ago, says the relator, the present system of earth burial was begun. Before the burial system was adopted they used to put the corpse on the ground, into a chamber like a room dug into a hillside. If the deceased was married, the husband or wife had to watch with the corpse in this place, and every ten days for a year friends brought food to the watcher. If the watcher lived through the year, he or she was then brought out and became free to marry again. The watcher often died in the excavation, however, for it was dark and foul.

Once a man left with the body of his wife heard, after a time, an occasional noise of craunching and eating. The next time his friends came with food he told them of this. Thereupon they held a council, and the chief sent several men into the excavation to ascertain the cause of the noise. They found that the bodies had been eaten, and that a deep hole led down into the ground, which must have been made by a great serpent. After that the Seneca ceased to bury in this way and put their dead into the ground as they do at present.

When it was the custom to place bodies in the bark lodges the husband or wife had to remain in the lodge and look after the dead for a year. At the end of this period the bones were taken out and fastened to a post in an erect position, and a great dance was held around them.

HI-NU DESTROYING THE GIANT ANIMALS*

A hunter in the woods was once caught in a thunder-shower, when he heard a voice calling upon him to follow. This he did until he found himself in the clouds, the height of many trees from the ground. Beings which seemed to be men surrounded him, with one among them who seemed to be their chief. He was told to look below and tell whether he could see a huge water-serpent. Replying that he could not, the old man anointed his eyes, after which he could see the monster in the depths below him. They then ordered one of their number to try and kill this enemy to the human race. Upon his failing, the hunter was told to accomplish the feat. He accordingly drew his bow and killed the foe. He was then conducted back to the place where he had sought shelter from the storm, which had now ceased.

This was man's first acquaintance with the Thunder God and his assistants, and by it he learned that they were friendly toward the human race, and protected it from dragons, serpents, and other enemies.

WAWENOCK

THE ORIGIN AND THE USE OF WAMPUM**

ACCORDINGLY, then, whenever they held a council there were sha-

---

*From Erminnie A. Smith, *Myths of the Iroquois,* p. 54.
**From Frank G. Speck, *Wawenock Texts from Maine,* p. 196.

mans there. And according to their strength among these shamans it was known who was the most powerful. After they held their council they lighted their pipes and smoked. In the case of an exceedingly great shaman every time he drew upon his pipe, wampum fell from his mouth. If the wampum was white, then it denoted that the shaman was of medium power. If the wampum was half white and half reddish it denoted the least powerful shaman. But if, in the case of a shaman, his wampum was almost black, then he would win over these shamans, the others who had the most wampum, after the shamans had smoked their pipes. And so whenever these two nations wanted to make a treaty they gave wampum to each other as a payment, the beads woven into a belt designed with two hands, meaning that they had agreed to the treaty and would fight no more and forever would not hunt one another down again. And that is all.

East Sub-Arctic

TO THE BUFFALO*

Strike ye now our land with your great curvéd
    horns;
In your mighty rage toss the turf in the air.
Strike ye now our land with your great curvéd
    horns;
We will hear the sound and our hearts will be
    strong.
When we go to war,
Give us of your strength in the time of our need,
King of all the plain—buffalo, buffalo.
Strike ye now our land with your great curvéd
    horns;
Lead us forth to the fight.

I SIT HERE THINKING OF HER**

I sit here thinking of her;
I am sad as I think of her.
Come, I beseech you, let us sing;
Why are you offended?

*From Frances Densmore, *Poems from Sioux and Chippewa Songs*.
**From Frances Densmore, *Poems from Sioux and Chippewa Songs*.

I do not care for you any more;
Someone else is in my thoughts.

You desire vainly that I seek you;
The reason is, I come to see your younger sister.

Come, let us drink.

Love songs were not very prevalent among Eastern Woodlands Indians before the coming of the whites. According to Frances Densmore, perhaps the foremost collector of Indian songs, love songs are to be found primarily among those Indians who have been living in close contact with white civilization. Most of the songs, like this one, express disappointment rather than affection.

I AM ARRAYED LIKE THE ROSES*

What are you saying to me?
I am arrayed like the roses
And beautiful as they.

I can charm the man.
He is completely fascinated by me

In the center of the earth
Wherever he may be
Or under the earth.

Magical love charms, like the one above, were used occasionally—although many Indians regarded them with a good deal of uneasiness, possibly because they suggested the possibility that one person might control another.

SONG OF THE THUNDER**

Sometimes
I go about pitying
Myself
While I am carried by the wind
Across the sky

*From Frances Densmore, *Chippewa Music*, p. 89.
**From Frances Densmore, *Chippewa Music*, p. 127.

Prairies

Menomini

KAKU'ENE, THE JUMPER, AND THE ORIGIN OF TOBACCO*

ONE day Mä'näbush was passing by a high mountain, when he detected a delightful odor which seemed to come from a crevice in the cliffs. On going closer he found the mountain inhabited by a giant who was known to be the keeper of the tobacco. Mä'näbush then went to the mouth of a cavern, which he entered, and following the passage which led down into the very center of the mountain he found a large chamber occupied by the giant, who asked him in a very stern manner what he wanted. Mä'näbush replied that he had come for some tobacco, but the giant replied that he would have to come again in one year from that time, as the ma'nuidos had just been there for their smoke, and that the ceremony occurred but once a year. Mä'näbush, on looking around the chamber, observed a great number of bags filled with tobacco. One of these he snatched and with it darted out of the mountain, closely pursued by the giant. Mä'näbush ascended to the mountain tops and leaped from peak to peak, but the giant followed so rapidly that when Mä'näbush reached a certain prominent peak, the opposite side of which was a high vertical cliff, he suddenly laid flat on the rocks while the giant leaped over him and down into the chasm beyond. The giant was much bruised, but he managed to climp up the face of the cliff until he almost reached the summit, where he

A recurrent figure in the mythology of some of the Prairies and Plains Indians was Mä'näbush or Ma'naboz'ho. Sometimes depicted as absurd—and very much like Old Man Coyote—he also appeared, as he does here, in the guise of a very traditional folk hero.

*From Walter James Hoffman, *The Menomini Indians*, pp. 205-206.

hung, as all his fingernails had been worn off. Then Mä′näbush grasped the giant by the back, and drawing him upward, threw him violently to the ground and said, "For your meanness you shall become Kaku′ene [the jumper—grasshopper], and you shall be known by your stained mouth. You shall become the pest of those who raise tobacco."

Then Mä′näbush took the tobacco and divided it amongst his brothers and younger brothers, giving to each some of the seed, that they might never be without this plant for their use and enjoyment.

THE PORCUPINE*

There was once a village in which dwelt two sisters who were considered the swiftest runners in the Menomini tribe. Toward the setting sun was another village, though so far away that an ordinary walker would have to travel two days to reach it. Once these two sisters decided to visit the distant village; so, starting out, they ran at great speed until nearly noon, when they came to a hollow tree lying across the trail.

Snow was on the ground, and the sisters saw the track of a Porcupine leading to the hollow of the trunk. One of them broke off a stick and began to poke it into the cavity to make the porcupine come out, saying, "Let us have some fun with him." "No, my sister," said the other, "he is a ma′nido, and we had better let him alone." The former, however, continued to drive the Porcupine farther and farther through the trunk until at last he came out, when she caught him and pulled all the long quills out of his body, throwing them in the snow. The other remonstrated against such cruelty, for she thought it was too cold to deprive the Porcupine of his robe. Then the girls, who had wasted some time and still had a great distance to travel, continued their running toward the village for which they were bound.

When they left the hollow log, the Porcupine crawled up a tall pine tree until he reached the very top, where he faced the north and began to shake before his breast his small tshi′saqka rattle, singing in time to its sound. Soon the sky began to darken and the snow to fall, while the progress of the girls, who were still running along, became more and more impeded by the constantly increasing depth of snow.

One of the sisters looked back and saw the Porcupine on the treetop,

*From Walter James Hoffman, *The Menomini Indians*, pp. 210-211.

using his rattle. Then she said to her sister who had plucked out his quills, "My sister, let us go back to our own village, for I fear some harm will befall us."

"No; let us go on," replied her companion, "we need not fear the Porcupine." As the depth of the snow impeded their progress, they rolled up their blankets and continued the journey.

The day was drawing to a close and the sisters had not yet reached a point from which they could see the village they were striving to reach. Traveling on, they came to a stream which they recognized as being near the village, but night had come on, and the snow was now so deep that they were compelled by exhaustion to stop. They could hear the voices of the people in the village, but could not call loud enough to be heard; so they perished in the snow which the Porcupine had caused to fall. One should never harm the Porcupine, because he is a tshi'saqka and a ma'nido.

THE CATFISH*

Once when the Catfish were assembled in the water an old chief said to them, "I have often seen a Moose come to the edge of the water to eat grass; let us watch for him, and kill and eat him. He always comes when the sun is a little way up in the sky."

The Catfish who heard this agreed to go and attack the Moose; so they went to watch. They were scattered everywhere among the grass and rushes, when the Moose came slowly along picking grass. He waded down into the water, where he began to feast. The catfish all watched to see what the old chief would do, and presently one of them worked his way slowly through the grass to where the Moose's leg was, when he thrust his spear into it. Then the Moose said, "What is it that has thrust a spear into my leg?" and looking down he saw the Catfish, when he immediately began to trample upon them with his hoofs, killing a great number of them, while those that escaped swam down the river as fast as they could. The Catfish still carry spears, but their heads have never recovered from the flattening they received when they were trampled by the Moose into the mud.

*From Walter James Hoffman, *The Menomini Indians,* p. 214.

OMAHA

THUNDER SONG*

Grandfather! far above on high,
The hair like a shadow passes before you.
Grandfather! far above on high,
Dark like a shadow the hair sweeps before you into the midst of your
    realm.
Grandfather! there above, on high,
Dark like a shadow the hair passes before you.
Grandfather! dwelling afar on high,
Like a dark shadow the hair sweeps before you into the midst of your
    realm.
Grandfather! far above on high,
The hair like a shadow passes before you.

The term Grandfather was an address of the highest respect in the language and used for the thunder god. In this ceremonial poem a lock of hair, symbol of life, is given to the thunder god to insure the protection of the child. Later, a lock on the crown of the boy's head was separated from the rest of his hair and kept distinct. Upon this lock of hair the war honors were worn. It was this lock that was cut from the head of a slain enemy because it represented the life of the slain man.

OSAGE

THE TRIBE THAT GREW OUT OF A SHELL**

THERE was a snail living on the banks of the river Missouri, where he found plenty of food, and wanted nothing. But at length the waters began to rise and overflow its banks, and although the little animal clung to a log, the flood carried them both away; they floated along for many days. When the water fell, the poor snail was left in the mud and slime,

*From Alice C. Fletcher and Francis La Flesche, *The Omaha Tribe,* p. 124.
**From Henry Rowe Schoolcraft, *Algic Researches,* pp. 263-264.

on shore. The heat of the sun came out so strong, that he was soon fixed in the slime and could not stir. He could no longer get any nourishment. He became oppressed with heat and drought. He resigned himself to his fate and prepared to die. But all at once, he felt a renewed vigor. His shell burst open, and he began to rise. His head gradually rose above the ground; he felt his lower extremities assuming the character of feet and legs. Arms extended from his sides. He felt their extremities divide into fingers. In fine he rose, under the influence of one day's sun, into a tall and noble man. For a while he remained in a dull and stupid state. He had but little activity, and no clear thoughts. These all came by degrees, and when his recollections returned, he resolved to travel back to his native land.

But he was naked and ignorant. The first want he felt was hunger. He saw beast and birds, as he walked along, but he knew not how to kill them. He wished himself again a snail, for he knew how, in *that* form, to get his food. At length he became so weak, by walking and fasting, that he laid himself down, on a grassy bank, to die. He had not laid long, when he heard a voice calling him by name. "Was-bas-has," exclaimed the voice. He looked up, and beheld the Great Spirit sitting on a white horse. His eyes glistened like stars. The hair of his head shone like the sun. He could not bear to look upon him. He trembled from head to foot. Again the voice spoke to him in a mild tone, "Was-bas-has! Why do you look terrified?" "I tremble," he replied, "because I stand before Him who raised me from the ground. I am faint and hungry—I have eaten nothing since the floods left me upon the shore—a little shell."

The Great Spirit here lifted up his hands and displaying a bow and arrows, told him to look at him. At a distance sat a bird on a tree. He put an arrow to the string, and pulling it with force, brought down the beautiful object. At this moment a deer came in sight. He placed another arrow to the string, and pierced it through and through. "These," said he, "are your food; and these are your arms," handing him the bow and arrows. He then instructed him how to remove the skin of the deer, and prepare it for a garment. "You are naked," said he, "and must be clothed; it is now warm, but the skies will change, and bring rains, and snow, and cold winds." Having said this, he also imparted the gift of fire, and instructed him how to roast the flesh. He then placed a collar of wampum around his neck. "This," said he, "is your authority over all beasts." Having done this, both horse and rider rose up, and vanished from his sight.

Was-bas-has refreshed himself, and now pursued his way to his native land. He had seated himself on the banks of the river, and was meditating on what had passed, when a large beaver rose up from the channel and addressed him. "Who art thou?" said the Beaver, "that comest here to disturb my ancient reign?" "I am a *man*," he replied, "I was once a *shell*, a creeping shell; but who art thou?" "I am king of the nation of beavers," he answered: "I lead my people up and down this stream; we are a busy people, and the river is my dominion." "I must divide it with you," retorted Was-bas-has. "The Great Spirit has placed me at the head of beasts and birds, fishes and fowl; and has provided me with the power of maintaining my rights." Here he held up the bow and arrows, and displayed the collar of shells around his neck. "Come, come," said the Beaver, modifying his tone, "I perceive we are brothers. Walk with me to my lodge, and refresh yourself after your journey," and so saying he led the way. The Snail-Man willingly obeyed his invitation, and had no reason to repent of his confidence. They soon entered a fine large village, and his host led him to the chief's lodge. It was a well-built room, of a cone-shape, and the floor nicely covered with mats. As soon as they were seated, the Beaver directed his wife and daughter to prepare food for their guest. While this was getting ready, the Beaver chief thought he would improve his opportunity by making a fast friend of so superior a being; whom he saw, at the same time, to be but a novice. He informed him of the method they had of cutting down trees with their teeth, and of felling them across streams so as to dam up the water, and described the method of finishing their dams with leaves and clay. He also instructed him in the way of erecting lodges, and with other wise and seasonable conversation beguiled the time. His wife and daughter now entered, bringing in vessels of fresh peeled poplar, and willow, and sassafras, and alder bark, which is the most choice food known to them. Of this, Was-bas-has made a merit of tasting, while his entertainer devoured it with pleasure. He was pleased with the modest looks and deportment of the chief's daughter, and her cleanly and neat attire, and her assiduous attention to the commands of her father. This was ripened into esteem by the visit he made her. A mutual attachment ensued. A union was proposed to the father, who was rejoiced to find so advantageous a match for his daughter. A great feast was prepared, to which all the beavers, and other animals on good terms with them, were invited. The Snail-Man and the Beaver-Maid were thus united, and this union is the origin of the Osages. So it is said by the old people.

HUNTING SONG*

1

It is stricken, it still lives and flees,
It is stricken, it still lives and flees,
I shall pursue and find it, wherever it goes,
I shall pursue and find it, wherever it goes.

2

It is stricken, it still lives and flees,
It is stricken, it still lives and flees,
Though it has gone afar I have found it,
Though it has gone afar I have found it.

WAR SONG**

Grandfather, O grandfather,
When I find the enemy,
I fall upon him unawares.

Grandfather, O grandfather,
When I find the enemy,
I make him fall to the earth in death.

Grandfather, O grandfather,
When I find the enemy,
I reduce his house to white smoke.

Grandfather, O grandfather,
When I find the enemy,
I reduce his house to gray ashes.

Grandfather, O grandfather,
When I find the enemy,
His bones lie whitened and scattered.

---

*From Francis La Flesche, *The Osage Tribe,* p. 189.
*From Francis La Flesche, *The Osage Tribe,* pp. 191-192.

PAWNEE

THE LESSON OF THE BIRDS*

ONE day a man whose mind was open to the teaching of the powers wandered on the prairie. As he walked, his eyes upon the ground, he spied a bird's nest hidden in the grass, and arrested his feet just in time to prevent stepping on it. He paused to look at the little nest tucked away so snug and warm, and noted that it held six eggs and that a peeping sound came from some of them. While he watched, one moved and soon a tiny bill pushed through the shell, uttering a shrill cry. At once the parent birds answered and he looked up to see where they were. They were not far off; they were flying about in search of food, chirping the while to each other and now and then calling to the little one in the nest.

The homely scene stirred the heart and the thoughts of the man as he stood there under the clear sky, glancing upward toward the old birds and then down to the helpless young in the nest at his feet. As he looked he thought of his people, who were so often careless and thoughtless of their children's needs, and his mind brooded over the matter. After many days he desired to see the nest again. So he went to the place where he had found it, and there it was as safe as when he left it. But a change had taken place. It was now full to overflowing with little birds, who were stretching their wings, balancing on their little legs and making ready to fly, while the parents with encouraging calls were coaxing the fledglings to venture forth.

"Ah!" said the man, "if my people would only learn of the birds, and, like them, care for their young and provide for their future, homes would be full and happy, and our tribe be strong and prosperous."

When this man became a priest, he told the story of the bird's nest and sang its song; and so it has come down to us from the days of our fathers.

THE LESSON OF THE WREN**

The wren is always spoken of as the laughing bird. It is a very happy

---

*From Alice C. Fletcher, *The Hako: A Pawnee Ceremony*, p. 170.
**From Alice C. Fletcher, *The Hako: A Pawnee Ceremony*, pp. 171-172.

little bird, and we have stories about it. Everyone likes to hear the wren sing. This song is very old; I do not know how old, how many generations old. There are very few words in the song, but there is a story which has come down with it and which tells its meaning.

A priest went forth in the early dawn. The sky was clear. The grass and wild flowers waved in the breeze that rose as the sun threw its first beams over the earth. Birds of all kinds vied with one another as they sang their joy on that beautiful morning. The priest stood listening. Suddenly, off at one side, he heard a trill that rose higher and clearer than all the rest. He moved toward the place whence the song came that he might see what manner of bird it was that could send farther than all the others its happy, laughing notes. As he came near he beheld a tiny brown bird with open bill, the feathers on its throat rippling with the fervor of its song. It was the wren, the smallest, the least powerful of birds, that seemed to be most glad and to pour out in ringing melody to the rising sun its delight in life.

As the priest looked he thought: "Here is a teaching for my people. Everyone can be happy; even the most insignificant can have his song of thanks."

So he made the story of the wren and sang it; and it has been handed down from that day, a day so long ago that no man can remember the time.

COYOTE AND THE CHOKE-CHERRIES*

Coyote was going along, and it was snowing very hard. He came to a ravine, and here he found many choke-cherries on the trees. So he began to eat, and ate the cherries, until his belly became swollen. Then he went on until he came to a plain, and as he travelled along the plain, had a desire to relieve himself. There were no hollows or ravines where he could go, therefore he sat on the open plain. As he relieved himself the faeces froze so fast that Coyote was soon raised high into the air. The excrement parted at the top, and as he was at a height above the ground, Coyote fell, in such manner that his nose struck the bottom of his own frozen excrement, and he was killed.

*From George A. Dorsey, *Traditions of the Skidi Pawnee*, p. 272.

I AM LIKE A BEAR*

I am like a bear,
I hold my hands waiting for the sun to rise.

SPRING IS OPENING*

Spring is opening,
I can smell the different perfumes of the white weeds used in the dance.

THE HEAVENS ARE SPEAKING*

I stood here, I stood there,
The clouds are speaking,
I say, "You are the ruling power,
I do not understand, I only know what I am told,
You are the ruling power, you are now speaking,
This power is yours, O heavens."

OUR HEARTS ARE SET IN THE HEAVENS*

It is there that our hearts are set,
In the expanse of the heavens.

WINNEBAGO

THE ORIGIN OF THE BUFFALO CLAN**

"LISTEN, my grandson. Those who originated from the buffaloes and the way in which they originated, they have heretofore told one another thus. This it is. Whenever one asked about it, they would tell him, but

*From Frances Densmore, *Pawnee Music*, pp. 43, 49, 88, 90.
**From Paul Radin, *The Winnebago Tribe*, pp. 243-245.

they would never tell him unless he brought some present. Even when they had a child whom they loved very much (and for whom they were accustomed to do everything), even to such a one they would not tell it unless he brought them gifts. Thus they would not even say the least thing about the story of their origin merely because they loved some one. It is really essential to make a gift. And if some one came, carrying a gift, the old man would ask him what he wanted and what he would like to know, as this was not the only thing gifts were made for. Then he would announce his desire. However, he would not be told in public but when he was alone. Then the old man who had the right to tell the origin myth would announce subsequently at some feast that he had told so-and-so the story of the origin of their clan and that if anyone wished to be told of the same he should in the future, when he himself had died, go to this young man and ask him in the proper way. Remember, he would add, that before everything else it is the duty of an individual to try and learn of the origin of his clan.

"Father, this I give you, a full suit of clothes. This I am giving you." "Thanks, my son. What do you wish? What do you wish to hear?" "Father, what did we originate from?" "My son, you have done well. My son, he who makes the most gifts obtains life therewith." "Well, then, father, you need not tell me now, but later, when I have made a sufficient number of gifts, then you may tell me." "My son, you have spoken well and if you do as you say, you will travel unharmed along the road of life." "Father, these also I give you, some beads and a blanket." "Thanks, my son, it is good. Now, my son, what I told you was true. I did not tell it to you because I coveted anything of yours, but truly because it is true—this, that we must make a sufficient number of presents. Whoever does as you have done will obtain the possibility of a good life for himself." "Now again, father, I give you these gifts. There is enough food for you in it." "My son, you have done well, very well indeed, for the life that I am to give you is holy; and as you know, even if one was loved very much they would not tell him this merely because they loved him, as it is holy." "Father, this I give you as a gift, a horse, as I desire to know what we originated from." "Now, then, my son, you have done well. This is what I meant when I said it is holy. Therefore, my son, you have done well. Come and sit down here. Listen very carefully so that if afterwards anyone should ask you for this story you will be able to tell it well."

"My son, we first originated in human form at Bad Lake (*de cicik*). From four buffalo spirits who are there, did we originate. The youngest one was clever and from him did we originate. The buffaloes asked one another what they were to do, and they then began to exert their powers, and the youngest one obtained the knowledge that there was to be a gathering of all the animals. So they all landed at a place called Red Banks. So it is said. And to the elk was given the charge of the seating arrangements.

"Thus did we originate. And then they counciled with one another as to how they should travel along the road of life. And as they arrived at Red Banks, each one would ask the other to do some work. And there they made a sacred (covenant)—that they would never fail to grant one another's requests. Likewise they agreed that when they died they would bury one another. The Buffalo clan and the Water-spirit clan were to bury one another, and they were to ask one another to work."

THE ORIGIN OF THE WARRIOR CLAN*

In the beginning, Earthmaker made four men. Then he sent them to the earth. Within Lake, there, they landed and they alit on the branch of a tree. There were four branches and each one alit on one branch. And then on the earth they jumped and started walking toward the east. There they erected a camping place. There they started the fire. It was the principal fire. Then they started to look for food, but they were unable to find any. So the second brother was sent, but he was not able to get any animal, but he brought a man. Because he brought it, for that reason, the first male child we have shall be called *He-who-eats-humans*. Then the second one, him whom they called the warrior, was sent. Thus it was. And then all of them went toward the chief's lodge. They walked as chiefs, all four of them. The four of them went there. The chief's lodge was an oval lodge, and there they entered.

The Snake clansman was the one appointed to get the food. He went after the food. It was an Eagle-people feast. Two fish the Snake clansman brought, and with these the Eagle chief gave a feast. The Deer clan acted as attendants. Thus they ate the fish. And when they were finished with the eating, on either side, they left the head and the tail of the fish. This they left of their meal. "And if we have a dog we will call him *Leaves-fish-on-both-ends*," they said. Then they sat down. As they were sitting some one peeped in. It was the dog. Only his nose stuck in. Then

*From Paul Radin, *The Winnebago Tribe*, pp. 219-220.

they said, "Whose nose does it look like?" So the chief spoke. "If we ever have a dog and if we wish to keep it permanently, *Whose-nose-does-it-look-like,* we will call it."

Then all of a sudden their bodies began to be different and their feathers began to look as if they were worn off. They were about to enter the chief's lodge. Then the chief passed the fire to the Deer clan and when they were through the lodge was purified with the incense of smoking cedar leaves. Then again into the very long lodge they entered. This was at Red Banks. Then the upper people taught the lower people the things to make them good. Thus Earthmaker ordained everything, and as he ordered, so it was. That is the way they were. Holy they were. And all (of my clan?) lived as chiefs. This is all that I was taught.

FUNERAL SPEECH OF THE BUFFALO CLAN*

To-day when you ceased to breathe we were aware of it. Therefore relatives who are present, I greet you. Here my brother's life has ended, and for the last time I will talk to him about the road he is to take.

Hanho, my brother, the place at which we originated was called Bad Lake. There were four buffaloes there and from the youngest one are we descended. They lived holy lives, and we hope you will walk in their path. That you may strike everything (you meet on your journey) you must take along with you a war club. You shall walk armed with sharp teeth; and it will be impossible for bad spirits to walk back and forth across your path. And your sight shall be holy as you walk.

HOW WEGI'CEKA TRIED TO SEE EARTHMAKER**

Once there was a Winnebago whose name was Wegi'ceka. As soon as he was grown up his father begged him to fast. The old man told his son that Earthmaker, when he created this earth, made many good spirits and that he put each one of them in control of powers with which they could bless human beings. Some he placed in control of war powers. If these spirits bless an individual, he will always be victorious on the warpath. Earthmaker told the human beings to fast for these powers and

*From Paul Radin, *The Winnebago Tribe,* p. 154.
**From Paul Radin, *The Winnebago Tribe,* pp. 291-293.

then they would be rich and powerful. Now, my son, if Earthmaker has put all these spirits in charge of something, he himself must be in charge of much more power. Thus the old man reasoned and the son thought the same. So he tried to "dream" of Earthmaker. "I wonder what sort of blessings Earthmaker bestows on people," he thought to himself.

None of the spirits blessed Wegi′ceka during his fastings. He was always thinking of Earthmaker and asking him to bless him. Wegi′ceka made himself "pitiable" and wept. He could not stop. "Perhaps I will be able to see Earthmaker if I weep," he thought to himself. "Indeed, if Earthmaker does not bless me I will die during my fast."

He fasted continuously without stopping. Verily, he fasted for Earthmaker. First he fasted for 4 nights, and then for 6 nights, and then for 8 nights, for 10, and finally for 12 nights. Yet he received no blessing of any kind. After fasting 12 nights he stopped and ate something. He kept fasting on until he had grown to be a fully developed man. Then he stopped and married and, accompanied by his wife, he moved away from his village to some uninhabited place. There he lived alone with his wife. There again he fasted and his wife helped him. As before, he tried to have Earthmaker bestow a blessing upon him. This time he made up his mind once and for all that if Earthmaker did not bless him he would die during his fast. "It is true," he said to himself, "that no one has ever heard of anyone being blessed by Earthmaker, but nevertheless I will either obtain a blessing from him or die in the attempt."

As time passed on his wife gave birth to a male child. Then the man said, "We will offer up our son to Earthmaker," and the woman consented. So they sacrificed their son to Earthmaker. Then they placed the body of the child on a scaffold and wept bitterly. "Surely," he said to himself, "Earthmaker will bless us to-night." And indeed during the night he came to him. Wegi′ceka felt positive that it was he. He wore a soldier's uniform and a cocked hat and he was pleasing to the sight. Wegi′ceka looked and wondered whether it was really Earthmaker. Then this person took a step forward toward Wegi′ceka. "Indeed it must be," he thought. Then he took another step in his direction and uttered something. Wegi′ceka looked and saw that it was not Earthmaker but a pigeon. The spirits had fooled him. His heart ached, but, undaunted, he again fasted, and after a while Earthmaker seemed to come to him and say, "Man, I bless you. For a long time you have wept and made yourself pitiable. I am indeed Earthmaker." When Wegi′ceka looked again he beheld something pleasing to the sight and he liked it. The clothing the man wore was pleasing and Wegi'ceka now felt certain that this person was Earthmaker. He looked at him again and it seemed to him as if Earthmaker was getting smaller and smaller, and as he looked for the fourth time he saw that he had been looking at a little bird all the time. Then his heart ached all the more, and he cried even more bitterly than before. Then for the third time Earthmaker blessed him and spoke to him. "You have tried to 'dream' of Earthmaker and you have worried yourself to death. Behold, I am Earthmaker and I will bless you and you will never be in want of anything. You will be able to understand the language spoken by strange tribes and you will never be wanting in the goods of life." Then he looked up for the first time, but when he saw the individual who had spoken to him he thought that there was something wrong. Soon he saw that the one who had spoken to him was a bird.

Then for the last time he tried to "dream" of Earthmaker. He did not eat anything and positively resolved to die if Earthmaker did not appear to him. He felt bad, for he thought that all the bad birds (spirits) were laughing at him.

He fasted, and soon Earthmaker, far above, heard his voice and said, "Wegi'ceka, you are weeping bitterly. For your sake, I will come to the earth." Then Earthmaker told Wegi'ceka that when he (Wegi'ceka) looked at him he would see a ray of light extending from above far down to his camp. That far it would reach. "Only thus, Wegi'ceka, can you see me. What you ask of me (to see me face to face) I cannot grant you. But, nevertheless, you may tell (your fellowmen) that you saw me." Thus he spoke to him. He did not bless him with war powers. Only with life did he bless him.

Then Wegi'ceka tried to draw a picture of the flash of light extending from the heavens to his camp, just as he had seen it, upon a cane. To that cane he sacrificed. The descendants of Wegi'ceka are using cane even to the present day.

HOW A BEAR BLESSED A MAN*

Once a band of Winnebagoes used to give a feast to the bears. A bear had blessed one of their number with life and victory on the warpath.

It was a spirit-bear that had blessed him. The man was fasting and

*From Paul Radin, *The Winnebago Tribe*, pp. 301-302.

the spirit blessed him and said, "Human, I bless you. In war you will be able to do as you wish (i.e., you will be able to kill an enemy whenever you desire). The first time you go on the warpath you will come back with the fourth war honor; the second time you go on a warpath you will return with the third war honor; the third time you will return with the second war honor, and the fourth time you will return with the first war honor and receive the first prize, which you are to give to your sister." This is what the man "dreamed." He believed it and was happy. Then the spirit-bear said again, "Human, I said that I blessed you and I really mean it. Earthmaker created me and gave me control of many things. Human, I bless you. As many years as Earthmaker bestowed upon you, that number I also bless you with. You will reach the limit of the years that were granted you. With my body I also bless you. Whenever you are hungry and wish to kill a bear, pour a pipeful of tobacco for me. If then you go out hunting, you will be successful. Don't abuse the bears. I am the chief of the bears. I bless you. Never before have I blessed a human being, as long as I have lived here. As long as your descendants live on this earth, so long will this blessing last. Should your descendants perform the feasts in my honor well, I will bless them with life and victory on the warpath. Whenever you offer me tobacco I will smoke it. If you put on a kettle of food for me I will be thankful to you. When you put this kettle of food on the fire and offer me tobacco see to it that you keep away menstruating women. . . ."

INSTRUCTIONS TO A SON*

My son, when you grow up you should see to it that you are of some benefit to your fellowmen. There is only one way in which you can begin to be of any aid to them, and that is to fast. So, my son, see to it that you fast. Our grandfather, the fire, who stands at all times in the center of our dwelling, sends forth all kinds of blessings. Be sure that you make an attempt to obtain his blessings.

My son, do you remember to have our grandfathers, the war chiefs, bless you. See to it that they pity you. Some day when you go on the warpath their blessings will enable you to have specific foreknowledge of all that will happen to you on that occasion. This will likewise enable

*From Paul Radin, *The Winnebago Tribe*, pp. 166-169.

you to accomplish what you desire without the danger of anything inter-
fering with your plans: Without the slightest trouble you will then be able
to obtain the prizes of war. Without any trouble you will be able to obtain
these and in addition glory and the war honors. If, in truth, you thirst
yourself to death, our grandfathers who are in control of wars—to whom
all the war powers that exist in this world belong—they will assuredly
bless you.

My son, if you do not wear out your feet through ceaseless activity (in
fasting), if you do not blacken your face for fasting, it will be all in vain
that you inflict sufferings upon yourself. Blessings are not obtained
through mere desire alone; they are not obtained without making the
proper sacrifices or without putting yourself time and again in proper
mental condition. Indeed, my son, they are not to be obtained without
effort on your part. So see to it that, of all those spirits whom Earthmaker
created, one at least has pity upon you and blesses you. Whatever such a
spirit says to you that will unquestionably happen.

Now, my son, if you do not obtain a spirit to strengthen you, you will
not amount to anything in the estimation of your fellowmen. They will
show you little respect. Perhaps they will make fun of you.

Do not die in the village. It is not good to die there. Whenever a
person is grown up that is what is told him. Nor is it good, my son, to let
women journey ahead of you from amidst the village. It is not good thus
to let women die before you. Therefore, in order to prevent this, our
ancestors encouraged one another to fast. Some day you will travel in a
difficult road; there will be some crisis in your life, and then when it is
too late you will begin to reproach yourself for not having fasted at the
proper time. So that you may not have occasion to blame yourself at such
a time I counsel you to fast. If you do not obtain a blessing when the
other women are dividing the war prizes brought home from the warpath
by their brothers, your sisters will stand aside envying them. If, however,
you are blessed by the spirits in control of war power, and if you then
return victorious, how proud your sisters will be to receive the war honors and to wear them around their necks and participate with them in the
victory dance! And in this way your sisters likewise will be strengthened
by your war deeds. You will keep well, in health.

My son, it will indeed be good if you obtain war powers, but our
ancestors say it is difficult. Especially difficult is it to be leader on the
warpath. So they say. If you do not become an individual warranted to
lead a war party, yet mistaking yourself for one although really an ordinary warrior, you "throw away a man," your act will be considered

most disgraceful. A mourner might harm you in revenge for the fact that you have caused him to mourn, and burn you with embers. Your people will all be sad, both on account of your disgrace and on account of the pain inflicted upon you.

My son, not with the blessing of one of the spirits merely, nor with the blessing of twenty, for that matter, can you go on the warpath. You must have the blessing of all the spirits above the earth, and of all those on the earth, and of all those who are pierced through the earth; of all those under the earth; of all those who are under the water; of all those that are on the sides of the earth, i.e., all the four winds; of the Disease-giver; of the Sun; of the Daylight; of the Moon; of the Earth; and of all those who are in control of war powers—with the blessings of all these deities must you be provided before you can lead a successful war party.

My son, if you cast off dress men will be benefited by your deeds. You will be an aid to all your people. If your people honor you, it will be good. And they will like you even the more if you obtain a limb.* They will indeed like you very much if you obtain a limb, or, even better, two or three. If you do thus, wherever people boil an animal with a head‡ you will always be able to eat.

If on account of your bravery you are permitted to tell of your war exploits during the Four Nights' Wake for the benefit of the soul of the deceased, do not try to add to your glory by exaggerating any exploit, for by so doing you will cause the soul to stumble on its journey to the spirit land. If you do this and add an untruth to the account of your war exploit, you will die soon after. The war spirits always hear you. Tell a little less. The old men say it is wise.

My son, it is good to die in war. If you die in war, your soul will not be unconscious. You will have complete disposal of your soul and it will always be happy. If you should ever desire to return to this earth and live here again, you will be able to do so. A second life as a human being you may live, or, if you prefer, as an inhabitant of the air (a bird) you may live, or you may roam the earth as an animal. Thus it is to him who dies in battle.

My son, fast for an honorable place among your fellowmen. Fast, so that when you are married you may have plenty of food; that you may be happy and that you may not have to worry about your children. If

*To obtain a limb is the same as to count coup.
‡In other words, give a feast.

in your fastings you have a vision of your future home, the members of your family will be lacking in nothing during their life. Fast for the food that you may need. If you fast a sufficiently large number of times, when in after life you have children and they cry for food you will be able to offer a piece of deer or moose meat without any difficulty. Your children will never be hungry.

INSTRUCTIONS TO A DAUGHTER*

This is the way the old men used to speak to the little girls:

My daughter, as you go along the path of life, always listen to your parents. Do not permit your mother to work. Attend to your father's wants. All the work in the house belongs to you. Never be idle. Chop the wood, carry it home, look after the vegetables and gather them, and cook the food. When in the spring of the year you move back to your permanent settlements, plant your fields immediately. Never get lazy. Earthmaker created you for these tasks.

When you have your menses, do not ask those in your lodge to give you any food, but leave the lodge and fast and do not begin eating until you return to your own lodge. Thus will you help yourself. If you always fast, when you marry, even if your husband had amounted to nothing before, he will become an excellent hunter. It will be on account of your fasting that he will have changed so much. You will never fail in anything and you will always be well and happy. If, on the contrary, you do not do as I tell you—that is, if you do not fast—when you marry he will become very weak, and this will be due to you. Finally he will get very sick.

My daughter, do not use medicine. If you marry a man and place medicine on his head he will become very weak and will not amount to anything. It may be that you do not want to have your husband leave you and this may induce you to use medicine to keep him. Do not do that, however, for it is not good. You will be ruining a man. It is the same as killing him. Do not do it, for it is forbidden. If you marry a man and you want to be certain of always retaining him, work for him. With work you will always be able to retain your hold on men. If you do your work to the satisfaction of your husband, he will never leave you. I say again, it is not proper to use medicine. Above all, do not use medicine until you have

*From Paul Radin, *The Winnebago Tribe*, pp. 177-180.

passed your youth. You will otherwise merely make yourself weak. You will lead a weak life. It may even happen that you will cause yourself to become foolish.

Do not use a medicine in order to marry. If you marry remain faithful to your husband. Do not act as though you are married to a number of men at the same time. Lead a chaste life. If you do not listen to what I am telling you and you are unfaithful to your husband, all the men will jeer at you. They will say whatever they wish to (and no one will interfere). Every man will treat you as though he were on the "joking relationship" with you. If you do not listen to me, therefore, you will injure yourself.

Thus the old people used to talk to one another. Thus they would warn one another against certain actions. They used to instruct the young girls as they grew up (just as I am doing to you now). That is why I am telling of these things now.

My daughter, as you grow older and grow up to be a young woman, the young men will begin to court you. Never strike a man, my daughter. It is forbidden. If you dislike a man very much, tell him gently to go away. If you do not do this and instead strike him, remember that it frequently happens that men know of medicines; or if they themselves have none they may know from whom to get them. If you make a man feel bad by striking him, he may use this medicine and cause you to run away with him and become a bad woman. It is for this reason that the old men used to warn the young girls not to strike the men who are courting them, but whom they dislike. Pray with all your heart that you do not become such a woman.

Do not act haughtily to your husband. Whatever he tells you to do, do it. Kindness will be returned to you if you obey your husband, for he will treat you in the same manner.

If you ever have a child, do not strike it. In the olden times when a child misbehaved the parents did not strike it, but they made it fast. When a child gets hungry, he will soon see the error of his ways. If you hit a child, you will be merely knocking the wickedness into him. Women should likewise never scold the children because children are merely made wicked by scoldings. If your husband scolds the children, do not take their part, for that will merely make them bad. In the same way, if a stranger makes your children cry, do not say anything to the stranger in the presence of the children, nor take their part in his presence. If you wish to prevent a stranger from scolding your children, keep them home and teach them how to behave by setting them a good example. Do not imagine that you do the best for your children by taking their part, or that you love them if you talk merely about loving them. Show them that you love them by your actions. Let them see that you are generous with donations. In such actions they will see your good work and then they will be able to judge for themselves whether your actions equal your words.

My daughter, do not show your love for other children so that strangers notice it. You may, of course, love other children, but love them with a different love from that which you bestow on your own children. The children of other people are different from your own children, and if you were to take them to some other place after you had been lavishing so much love upon them they would not act as your children would under the same circumstances. You can always depend upon your own children. They are of your own body. Love them, therefore. This is what our ancestors taught us to do.

If a wife has no real interest in her husband's welfare and possessions she will be to him no more than any other woman, and the world will ridicule her. If, on the other hand, you pay more attention to your husband than to your parents, your parents will leave you. Let your husband likewise take care of your parents, for they depend on him. Your parents were instrumental in getting you your husband, so remember that they expect some recompense for it, as likewise for the fact that they raised you.

My daughter, the old people used to teach us never to hurt the feelings of our relatives. If you hurt their feelings, you will cause your brothers-in-law to feel ashamed of themselves. Do not ever wish for any other man but your husband. It is enough to have one husband. Do not let anyone have the right to call you a prostitute.

Do not hit your relatives at any time. For if you did that or if you were on bad terms with one of them, it may chance that he will die, and then the people will say that you are glad that he is dead. Then, indeed, you will feel sad at heart and you will think to yourself, "What can I best do" (to make up for my conduct). Even if you were to give a Medicine Dance in his honor or donate gifts for the Four Nights' Wake, many people will still say, "She used to be partial and jealous when he was alive. Now that he is dead she loves him. Why does she act this way? She is wasting her wealth. (She really does not love him and therefore), and she ought not to spend so much money upon him now." Then, indeed, my daughter, will your heart ache; then, indeed, will you get angry. That is why the old people would tell their children to love one another. If you love a person and that person dies, then you will have a right to mourn for him, and everyone will think that your mourning is sincere. Not only will your own relatives love you, but everyone else will love you likewise. If, then, in the course of your life you come to a crisis of some kind, all these people will turn their hearts toward you.

My daughter, all that I am trying to tell you relates to your behavior (when you grow up). In your own home the women all understand the work belonging to the household and that relating to camping and hunting. If you understand these and afterwards visit your husband's relatives, you will know what to do and not find yourself in a dilemma from which you can not extricate yourself. When you visit your husband's people do not go around with a haughty air or act as if you considered yourself far above them. Try to get them to like you. If they like you, they will place you in charge of the camp you happen to be visiting. If you are goodnatured, you will be placed in charge of the home at which you happen to be visiting. Then your parents-in-law will tell your husband that their daughter-in-law is acting nicely to them.

Plains

THE BOY WHO CAUGHT THE SUN*

AN orphan boy and his sister were living together. The boy had a sinew string. During the daytime he was never home. "What do you do during the day?" his sister asked. "I am trying to ensnare the sun with my sinew." One day he caught him and there was no daylight. The girl asked, "What is the matter? Why is there no light?" "I have caught the sun." "You had better release him; if we don't see the daylight, we shall die." The boy approached the sun, but it got too hot for him. He returned to his sister, and said, "I cannot free him, he is too hot." At last, he sent a small mouse to gnaw up the sinew. The mouse went close. All its hair was burnt up, nevertheless it gnawed the sinew in two. Then the sun was free, and there was daylight once more.

MORNING-STAR**

A man and his wife were camping by themselves. She was pregnant. While her husband was away, another man would come and embrace her. Her lover wished to elope with her, but he did not like to take her with the baby in her womb. So he once entered her lodge and said, "I want to eat food from your belly." She asked, "How shall I sit?" "Lie down on your back, and place the dish on your belly." She obeyed. When he was done eating, he stuck a knife into her, and took out the child, which he left in the lodge.

*From Robert H. Lowie, *The Assiniboine*, p. 140.
**From Robert H. Lowie, *The Assiniboine*, p. 176.

Then the lovers fled underground, entering the earth under the fire-place. When the woman's husband returned, he found the child's body, and saw that his wife was gone. He split trees and dried up the creeks where he thought she might have fled. When the lovers came above ground again, he tracked them. They turned into snakes and crawled into a hollow tree. He followed in pursuit, and saw the snakes, but did not recognize them as the fugitives. He thought the lovers had gone up the tree. He climbed up, but could not find them. At last he climbed higher still, reached the sky, and became the Morning Star.

DUNG SUITOR*

A young woman refused to marry any of her suitors. She always ate a little whitish meat from the flesh of a buffalo neck. Whenever she defecated, her faeces were white. She never grew fat. Her mother said, "If you will continue to eat just from one piece, you will starve. Eat the tongue, that's a good piece to eat." Then the girl ate of the tongue, and her excrements were black. She was angry, scolding them "bad excrements." She went home, and was angry at her mother.

In the spring the camp moved. The black excrements were angry at being called names. They began to talk, summoning the faeces of other people. They agreed to gather together in a heap as large as a man. When the people had moved, this pile marched after them in human guise. Wherever the dung-man caught sight of a little piece of cloth or skin on the ground, he picked it up and shook it, saying, "I want a bigger one." He found a small weasel-skin, shook it, and said, "This is a small legging." The skin became larger, and he had a pair of leggings. Then he found a small otter-skin, which he transformed into gloves. He found some blanket cloth and changed it into a new robe. He found a little paint, put it on his face, and soon had the appearance of a handsome Indian.

The dung-man continued to track the people. After a long time he caught sight of their camp. He stood there watching them for a while. At length they saw him and said, "He must have come from another camp." The girl's father invited him to his tent. The girl herself was confined in a menstrual hut, but she could hear the people speaking of the arrival of a handsome young man, and looked outside. The old chief gave

*From Robert H. Lowie, *The Assiniboine*, pp. 162-164.

the visitor some soup of animal blood. It was hot, and the dung-man, who was frozen stiff, knew what would happen if he drank it. The chief asked him, "Where do you come from?" "From far away." "How many people live there?" "A great many." "What are their names?" "One of the chiefs is called Standing-Hat, another Lie-down-on-the-ground, a third is called Quick and another Big-Ball." As the dung-man was sitting in the camp, he got heated and softened. He could not stay within, so he excused himself, saying, "I will go out to chase some elk now." In going away, he passed the girl's hut, threw a little stick at its cover, and walked off. When the girl looked outside, he ran back and spoke to her. The girl said to her mother, "This young man has asked me to go home with him." She put all her belongings in a little sack, put it under her arm, and ran after her lover. Looking back, the dung-man could see her following. A warm mountain wind came, and he began to melt. The girl, tracking him, found one of his otter-skin gloves on the ground, put it on, and found it filled with dung. "This young man's gloves are full of excrements," she said to herself. She found his moccasins in the same condition. At last, she caught up to her suitor. He was lying on the ground with his face down, all melted by the heat. His clothes were fine, but they only covered dung. The girl went home crying. When she got near her camp, she began to sing, "I have followed my own excrements."

THE OLD HUSBAND AND THE YOUNG LOVER*

An old woman's grandson desired to steal the youngest of another man's four wives. The old man was a great dreamer. The boy went to his camp at night and eloped with the woman coveted. The husband dreamt what was happening, woke up, and gave chase. When he got close to the fugitives, they suddenly disappeared, having changed into ants. After looking for them everywhere, the old man went home. When asleep, he again saw them walking, woke up, and pursued them. They disappeared, changing into tall grass. The next time they turned into cottonwoods. When the old man could not find them, he went home again. The lovers went to their old grandmother. The boy was combing his mistress's hair. When the old man saw this in a dream, he was furious and gave chase once more. They fled. Before going, the youth gave his grandmother

*From Robert H. Lowie, *The Assiniboine*, pp. 166-167.

some tobacco, bidding her offer it to the old man. When the cuckold arrived, she offered him the tobacco, and while pursuing the lovers he smoked it. For a month he pursued them without overtaking them. The young man, in the meantime found many horses and made many fine things. He killed a porcupine and ordered his wife to make porcupine garments. Out of the animal's skull-bones he made himself a pipe. One day they heard the sound of shooting and moved towards the marksman, but could not find him. The next morning the boy said, "It is your brother. I have dreamt of him, and we shall see him." They moved camp and found the woman's brother by a lake. The boy lent his brother-in-law a horse, and the latter went to his camp and told the people whom he had met. He returned, saying, "That old man is there, he may kill you." Nevertheless, they accompanied him to the camp, and the woman went to her father's lodge.

The old husband invited both the elopers to his tent, but only his rival went there. He wore his porcupine clothing. The old man filled his pipe, and they smoked. The old man thought he would kill his rival while asleep, but the young man had mysterious power and knew his thoughts. Finally, the old husband said, "I shall give you plenty of food, but if you don't eat it all up, I will kill you." He gathered plenty of food, cooked it, and set it before his guest. All his friends were there, while his opponent only had his brother-in-law with him. "To-day we will have a hot sun," said the youth, snatching up his porcupine garments. Before beginning to eat, he smoked his porcupine pipe. Then he went outside and called all the animals to come in and eat. A big bear, a mountain-lion, a wolf, a coyote and a lynx came into the lodge. The old man was terrified. They ate up all the food and walked out again. Then the youth caught the sunbeams and pulled them down like a rope. It was getting hotter all the time. The old man was perspiring. He jumped into the water, but it was boiling hot. The youth told his wife and her brother to put on porcupine clothes. Thus they escaped injury, but the old man and his friends were all burnt up.

SHARPENED-LEG*

Two young men were living together. One day one of them heard his comrade chopping outside the lodge. He saw that the other man was

*From Robert H. Lowie, *The Assiniboine*, p. 186.

sharpening his leg to a point, after having chopped off his feet. He was frightened and fled, running for a night and a day. He arrived at some high trees, and climbed up one of them. Sharpened-Leg pursued him. When he got to the tree, he espied his comrade, and fell to kicking the trunk. With a dozen kicks he split the tree, so that it tumbled down. He looked for his former comrade, whom he found lying on the ground. "Why did you run away? We used to play together." He kicked his comrade with the point of his leg, and killed him. Then he walked away to some other trees. He began kicking these also, but his leg stuck fast, and he died in this position. When the two men did not return to camp, the father of the one slain went to look for them. He got to their lodge, and then followed their tracks until he reached the corpse of his son and the tree where Sharpened-Leg was caught.

Sharpened-Leg was named Canska (Ground-Hog), and his comrade Umbis'ka (Eagle).

FROG*

Some people were camping; Frog lived near-by. One of the men in the tribe had many good-looking children, while all of Frog's children were ugly. While the children were all playing together one day, Frog stole the youngest of the good-looking children, which was just beginning to walk. He raised it. "How is this?" asked one of Frog's children; "this child is handsome, and all the rest of us are ugly." "Oh, I washed him in red water, that is why he is handsome." At last, the man whose child had been stolen recaptured the kidnapped boy. He was very angry at Frog. Frog was scared and went into the water. That is why frogs live there now.

BLACKFOOT

THE ORDER OF LIFE AND DEATH**

THERE was once a time when there were but two persons in the world, Old Man and Old Woman. One time, when they were travelling about,

---

*From Robert H. Lowie, *The Assiniboine*, p. 201.
**From C. Wissler and D.C. Duvall, *Mythology of the Blackfoot Indians*, pp. 19-21.

Old Man met Old Woman, who said, "Now, let us come to an agreement of some kind; let us decide how the people shall live." "Well," said Old Man, "I am to have the first say in everything." To this Old Woman agreed, provided she had the second say.

Then Old Man began, "The women are to tan the hides. When they do this, they are to rub brains on them to make them soft; they are to scrape them well with scraping-tools, etc. But all this they are to do very quickly, for it will not be very hard work." "No. I will not agree to this," said Old Woman. "They must tan the hide in the way you say; but it must be made very hard work, and take a long time, so that the good workers may be found out."

"Well," said Old Man, "let the people have eyes and mouths in their faces; but they shall be straight up and down." "No," said Old Woman, "we will not have them that way. We will have the eyes and mouth in the faces, as you say; but they shall all be set crosswise."

"Well," said Old Man, "the people shall have ten fingers on each hand." "Oh, no!" said Old Woman, "that will be too many. They will be in the way. There shall be four fingers and one thumb on each hand."

"Well," said Old Man, "we shall beget children. The genitals shall be at our navels." "No," said Old Woman, "that will make child-bearing too easy; the people will not care for their children. The genitals shall be at the pubes."

So they went on until they had provided for everything in the lives of the people that were to be. Then Old Woman asked what they should do about life and death; should the people always live, or should they die? They had some difficulty in agreeing on this; but finally Old Man said, "I will tell you what I will do. I will throw a buffalo-chip into the water, and, if it floats, the people die for four days and live again; but, if it sinks, they will die forever." So he threw it in, and it floated. "No," said Old Woman, "we will not decide in that way. I will throw in this rock. If it floats, the people will die for four days: if it sinks, the people will die forever." Then Old Woman threw the rock out into the water, and it sank to the bottom. "There," said she, "it is better for the people to die forever; for, if they did not die forever, they would never feel sorry for each other, and there would be no sympathy in the world." "Well," said Old Man, "let it be that way."

After a time Old Woman had a daughter, who died. She was very sorry now that it had been fixed so that people died forever. So she said to Old Man, "Let us have our say over again." "No," said he, "we fixed it once."

THE FIXED STAR*

One summer night when it was very hot inside the lodge, two young women went outside to sleep. They woke up before daylight and were looking up at the sky, when one of them saw the Morning Star. She said to her companion. "That is a very bright star. I should like him for a husband." She soon forgot what she had said. In a few days these two young women went out from the camp to gather wood. When they had made up their packs and were drawing them up on their shoulders with the pack-straps, the strap broke that belonged to the girl who said she wished the Morning Star for her husband. Every time she made up her bundle and raised it to her back, the strap would break. Her companion, who was standing by her side with her pack on her shoulders, began to grow weary. She said, "I shall go on with my load: you can follow."

When the young woman was left alone, and had made up her bundle again, a handsome young man came out of the brush. He wore a fine robe made of beaver-skins, and had an eagle-plume in his hair. When the young woman started to go on, he stepped in front of her. Whichever way she turned, he headed her off. Finally she said to him, "Why do you head me off?" The young man replied, "You said you would take me for your husband." "No," said the young woman, "you must be mistaken. I never had anything to do with you. I do not know you." "I am the Morning Star," said the stranger, "and one night, when you looked up at me, you said that you wished me for a husband. Now I have come for you." "Yes, I did say that," said the young woman. So she consented to go away with him. Then Morning Star put an eagle plume in her hair, and told her to shut her eyes. Then they went up into the sky.

Now the Sun was the father of the Morning Star and the Moon was his mother. When they came into the lodge, Morning Star said to his parents, "I have brought a wife with me." The parents were pleased with what their son had done. Moon gave the young wife four berries and a few drops of water in a little shell. These were given to her to eat and to drink. Though the young woman was very hungry, she could neither eat all of the berries nor drink all of the water, because these berries were all the food there was in the world and the shell contained all the water there was in the ocean.

After a time, Moon said to her daughter-in-law, "Now I shall give

*From C. Wissler and D.C. Duvall, *Mythology of the Blackfoot Indians*, pp. 58-61.

you a root-digger, and you may go out to dig roots; but you are not to dig that big turnip there, because it is medicine [nātōji′wā].'' So the young woman went about the sky country digging roots for their food. She often looked at that fine large turnip growing there, and was curious to know why she was forbidden to dig it up. In course of time she gave birth to a child. One day, when it was old enough to sit alone, she said to herself as she went out to dig roots, ''Now no one will know about it if I do dig it up.'' So she stuck her digging-stick into the ground under the turnip; but, when she tried to raise it, the stick would not move. When she found that she could not get the stick out, she began to cry. Then two large white cranes flew down; one was a male and the other a female. The young woman prayed to them for help to get her root-digger out of the ground. Then the Crane-Woman said, ''When I married I was true to my vow. I never had anything to do with any other man than my husband. It is because of this that I have power to help you. Your mother gave you this digging-stick. Now I shall teach you the songs that go with it.'' Then Crane-Woman made a smudge, took the hands of the woman into her own, and, while she sang the songs, placed them upon the digging-stick. Then Crane-Woman pulled out the stick, and, marching around in the direction of the sun, made three movements toward the turnip, and with the fourth dug it out. Now the young woman took the digging-stick and the turnip home with her. When they saw what she had, they reprimanded her. Morning Star said to her, ''What did you see when you dug out this turnip?'' The woman replied, ''I looked down through the hole and saw the earth, the trees, the rivers, and the lodges of my people.''

''Now,'' said Morning Star, ''I cannot keep you any longer. You must take the boy with you and go back to your people; but when you get there you must not let him touch the ground for two-seven [fourteen] days. If he should touch the ground before that time, he will become a puff-ball [a fungus], go up as a star, and fit into the hole from which you dug the turnip. He will never move from that place, like the other stars, but will always be still.''

Sun said to her, ''I shall call in a man to help you down to the earth.'' After a while a man came with a strong spider-web, to one end of which he tied the woman and the boy, and let them down through the hole from which the turnip was taken. The woman came down over the camp of her own people. The young men of the camp were playing at the wheel-game. One of them happened to look up into the sky, where he saw something coming down. Now this young man had very poor eyes, and, when he told his companions that something was coming down from the sky, they looked, and, seeing nothing, made sport of him. As he still insisted, they, in derision, threw dirt into his eyes. But after a while they, too, saw something coming down from the sky. As the woman reached the ground in the center of the camp, some one, recognizing her, called out, "Here is the woman who never came back with her wood." Then all her friends came out to meet her, and her mother took her home.

Now, before the woman left the sky, Morning Star told her, that, since she had made one mistake in digging up the turnip, she would no doubt make another mistake, and allow the child to touch the ground before the time was up. So he advised her to make the sign of the Morning Star on the back of her lodge, so that she might be reminded daily of her duty. (The doors of the lodges at that time faced the sun, and the sign of the Morning Star was to be made upon the back of the lodge, because he always travels on the other side from the sun.)

The young woman kept careful watch over the boy for thirteen days. On this day her mother sent her out for water. Before going out, the young woman cautioned her mother to keep the child upon the bed, and not allow him to touch the ground. Now the grandmother was not so careful, because she did not understand the reason for watching the child; and while her back was turned he crawled out upon the ground. When she saw him, she caught him, putting him back on the bed as quickly as she could. This seemed to make the child angry, for he pulled the robe up over himself. The grandmother paid no further attention to him.

Now, when the boy's mother came back, she looked around, and said, "Where is my child?" "Oh, he covered himself up with a robe," said the grandmother. The young mother rushed to the bed, pulled back the robe, and found nothing but a puff-ball [fungus]. She caught this up, and carried it in her bosom all the time.

That evening when the stars came out, she looked up into the sky. A new star stuck in the hole from which she pulled the turnip. Then she knew what had become of her child.

This is the way the Fixed Star came to be.

After this the woman painted circles around the bottom of her lodge to represent the puff-ball, or the Fallen Star [the one that came down]. She had already painted the Morning Star on the back of her lodge. This is why the people paint their lodges in the way that you see them. Also this woman brought down the turnip and the digging-stick. Crane-Woman taught her songs that go with them and their use in the sun-dance. This was the beginning of the medicine-woman [leader in the sun-dance].

Many years after, this woman, while holding the sun-dance, made another mistake. She took some of the offerings from the sun lodge. When she did this, she died.

THE SEVEN STARS*

Once there was a young woman with many suitors; but she refused to marry. She had seven brothers and one little sister. Their mother had been dead many years and they had no relatives, but lived alone with their father. Every day the six brothers went out hunting with their father. It seems that the young woman had a bear for her lover, and, as she did not want any one to know this, she would meet him when she went out after wood. She always went after wood as soon as her father and brothers went out to hunt, leaving her little sister alone in the lodge. As soon as she was out of sight in the brush, she would run to the place where the bear lived.

As the little sister grew older, she began to be curious as to why her older sister spent so much time getting wood. So one day she followed her. She saw the young woman meet the bear and saw that they were lovers. When she found this out, she ran home as quickly as she could, and when her father returned she told him what she had seen. When he heard the story he said, "So, my elder daughter has a bear for a husband. Now I know why she does not want to marry." Then he went about the camp, telling all his people that they had a bear for a brother-in-law, and that he wished all the men to go out with him to kill this bear. So they went, found the bear, and killed him.

When the young woman found out what had been done, and that her little sister had told on her, she was very angry. She scolded her little sister vigorously, then ordered her to go out to the dead bear, and bring some flesh from his paws. The little sister began to cry, and said she was afraid to go out of the lodge, because a dog with young pups had tried to bite her. "Oh, do not be afraid!" said the young woman. "I will paint your face like that of a bear, with black marks across the eyes and at the corners of the mouth; then no one will touch you." So she went for the meat.

*From C. Wissler and D.C. Duvall, *Mythology of the Blackfoot Indians*, pp. 68-70.

Now the older sister was a powerful medicine-woman. She could tan hides in a new way. She could take up a hide, strike it four times with her skin-scraper and it would be tanned.

The little sister had a younger brother that she carried on her back. As their mother was dead, she took care of him. One day the little sister said to the older sister, "Now you be a bear and we will go out into the brush to play." The older sister agreed to this, but said, "Little sister, you must not touch me over my kidneys." So the big sister acted as a bear, and they played in the brush. While they were playing, the little sister forgot what she had been told, and touched her older sister in the wrong place. At once she turned into a real bear, ran into the camp, and killed many of the people. After she had killed a large number, she turned back into her former self. Now, when the little sister saw the older run away as a real bear, she became frightened, took up her little brother, and ran into their lodge. Here they waited, badly frightened, but were very glad to see their older sister return after a time as her true self.

Now the older brothers were out hunting, as usual. As the little sister was going down for water with her little brother on her back, she met her six brothers returning. The brothers noted how quiet and deserted the camp seemed to be. So they said to their little sister, "Where are all our people?" Then the little sister explained how she and her sister were playing, when the elder turned into a bear, ran through the camp, and killed many people. She told her brothers that they were in great danger, as their sister would surely kill them when they came home. So the six brothers decided to go into the brush. One of them had killed a jack-rabbit. He said to the little sister, "You take this rabbit home with you. When it is dark, we will scatter prickly-pears all around the lodge, except in one place. When you come out, you must look for that place, and pass through."

When the little sister came back to the lodge, the elder sister said, "Where have you been all this time?" "Oh, my little brother mussed himself and I had to clean him," replied the little sister. "Where did you get that rabbit?" she asked. "I killed it with a sharp stick," said the little sister. "That is a lie. Let me see you do it," said the older sister. Then the little sister took up a stick lying near her, threw it at the rabbit, and it stuck in the wound in his body. "Well, all right," said the elder sister. Then the little sister dressed the rabbit and cooked it. She offered some of it to her older sister, but it was refused: so the little sister and her brother ate all of it. When the elder sister saw that the rabbit had all been eaten, she became very angry, and said, "Now I have a mind to kill you." So the little sister arose quickly, took her little brother on her back, and said, "I am going out to look for wood." As she went out, she followed the narrow trail through the prickly-pears and met her six brothers in the brush. Then they decided to leave the country, and started off as fast as they could go.

The older sister, being a powerful medicine-woman, knew at once what they were doing. She became very angry and turned herself into a bear to pursue them. Soon she was about to overtake them, when one of the boys tried his power. He took a little water in the hollow of his hand and sprinkled it around. At once it became a great lake between them and the bear. Then the children hurried on while the bear went around. After a while the bear caught up with them again, when another brother threw a porcupine-tail [a hairbrush] on the ground. This became a great thicket; but the bear forced its way through, and again overtook the children. This time they all climbed a high tree. The bear came to the foot of the tree, and, looking up at them, said, "Now I shall kill you all." So she took a stick from the ground, threw it into the tree and knocked down four of the brothers. While she was doing this, a little bird flew around the tree, calling out to the children, "Shoot her in the head! Shoot her in the head!" Then one of the boys shot an arrow into the head of the bear, and at once she fell dead. Then they came down from the tree.

Now the four brothers were dead. The little brother took an arrow, shot it straight up into the air, and when it fell one of the dead brothers came to life. This he repeated until all were alive again. Then they held a council, and said to each other, "Where shall we go? Our people have all been killed, and we are a long way from home. We have no relatives living in the world." Finally they decided that they preferred to live in the sky. Then the little brother said, "Shut your eyes." As they did so, they all went up. Now you can see them every night. The little brother is the North Star (?). The six brothers and the little sister are seen in the Great Dipper. The little sister and the eldest brother are in a line with the North Star, the little sister being nearest it because she used to carry her little brother on her back. The other brothers are arranged in order of their age, beginning with the eldest. This is how the seven stars [Ursa major] came to be.

THE WOMAN WHO MARRIED FILTH*

Once there was a young woman very much sought by young men. She was quite a belle. One day as she went out for wood, she saw some human excrement. It was most extraordinary. "Bah!" she said. "That is a pile. I wonder who could have done it." This was in the fall. It was frozen hard.

Next day when she went after wood, she smelled something sweet and pleasant, and as she was looking around she saw a handsome young man. He wore a white buffalo-robe. She fell in love with him at once and thought to herself, "I shall marry him." So she asked him to stop. "Why?" said he, but kept on going. Every time she said this, he repeated the question, without stopping. She ran after him, caught hold of him, and began to embrace and kiss him. All this time she was saying, "I will marry you. I like a handsome man." (At first sight of him she was nauseated.) "All right," said the man. She went home alone and told her father and mother to go out of the lodge, for, she said, "I am married to a man. I shall bring him here. He suits me: at last I have found one that will do."

The next day all the men of the camp went in to see her husband. They thought him very fine indeed. They congratulated her. She lived with him all winter and kissed him all the time. When spring came, he complained of not feeling well. Now she was frightened, and wished to call in a medicine-man, but he would not consent. He said that it would be of no use, because he was going to die. While they were talking, a man in the camp saw a black cloud in the west, and called out, "Ho-o-o-o-! We shall have a big Chinook." When the husband heard this, he kissed his wife farewell, telling her that he must die. They had a child: it was a boy, and still in her womb. He said to her, "Let us go out to walk, away from the camp." As they went along he caressed her, telling her to take good care of the child he should never see. When they were out from the camp he said, "I shall go into the brush." The woman called after him. She said, "I want to see you again." He turned back to look. As she hurried up, she said, "I love you, I cannot let you go," etc. She tried to kiss him, but he smelled bad. Then he ran. He was thawing out. The woman pursued him. After a while, she saw him fall. Now it was thawing. There was water everywhere. When she got to the spot there was nothing but

*From C. Wissler and D.C. Duvall, *Mythology of the Blackfoot Indians*, pp. 151-152.

excrement. The child became a chief. His name was Excrement Chief.

THE WATER-BULL*

This is a story of the water-buffalo. There was a girl who lived in the water, and it was the time when the Blackfoot got the painted buffalo-lodge. This girl was rich, for her father was a chief. One time the girl went down to the river to bathe with the others, but when they returned they noticed that she was missing. The chief sent some one about the camp to look for her, but the last place at which she was seen was the bathing-place. Now the chief told all the people that when the time came for them to move camp, he would stay until the water was low so that he might find her body. So he stayed.

One day the children who were playing near the stream saw the girl put her head out of the water. She called to them, "Tell my father that I shall come ashore to-night." Now, when they told the chief, he did not believe them, but in the evening they heard a noise down by the river. There was a great roaring, and a voice called out asking them to make a smudge. So they made a smudge in the chief's lodge. Then the girl came in. They offered her food, but she refused, saying, "I cannot eat that food now, as I am used to other food." She then told them that her husband lived in the water. So her father gave her all her clothes and other property. "Now," said the girl, "my husband will give you food. The buffalo, he will drown them for you, but they will be of two colors, brown and white. Of these the white must be given back to him. I will visit you every time you camp here." Now they watched her as she went out and saw her go down into the water. That night while the buffalo were crossing the river a great many were drowned and thrown upon the shore. The people found them of two colors. So they butchered them and fixed up the robes.

Now the chief said to a boy, "Go to the camp of our people and invite them to come back." When they came in, he told them what had happened, and that they all must give something to his daughter. They must throw the gifts into the water. This they did. That night the girl came out of the water again and called all the people together. They

*From C. Wissler and D.C. Duvall, *Mythology of the Blackfoot Indians*, pp. 128-129.

gathered around and looked into the lodge where she sat. She invited one of her friends to go down into the water with her. This friend and another went down. She gave them a black rock to hold so that they would not float. When they were in the water, the girl said, "Now shut your eyes and do not look until you hear some one say, 'Oki'!" So they went down. Some one said, "Oki!" and upon looking round they found themselves in a lodge. They were not wet and did not seem to be in the water. It was a fine place. There was a man in the lodge who sang them a medicine-song, and explained to them that whenever crossing a stream they should throw something into the water as an offering to the water-people.

When the women returned, they told what had happened, and to this day our people still throw things into the water.

WHY DOGS DO NOT TALK*

Once a man owned a very large dog. One day when his wife went out to gather wood, the dog followed her into the brush. Now it seems that this woman had a lover who often met her when she went after wood. The dog saw what was going on. That night, when the woman's husband returned, the dog told him what he had seen. This made the dog's master so angry that he beat his wife, finally knocking her down with a piece of wood. Then he went away. After a while the woman got up and began to scold the dog. Then she beat him, and heaped all manner of abuse upon him. She took up human excrement and made him eat it. She was a medicine-woman, and used her power in such a way, that, after this, dogs could not talk. They still have the power to understand some words, but not many.

NEVER-SITS-DOWN'S SHIELD**

Somewhere on the other side of the mountains a Piegan was sleeping in lonely places. One night he slept in a buffalo-wallow and had a dream. Next day he returned to his people and entered his father's lodge. The next day he asked his father to cut a piece of skin from the belly of

*From C. Wissler and D.C. Duvall, *Mythology of the Blackfoot Indians,* p. 133.
**From C. Wissler and D.C. Duvall, *Mythology of the Blackfoot Indians,* pp. 102-103.

a bull and shrink it by heating over a fire. This done, he was to cut it round like the sun, and paint the picture of a bull and a cow on one side; also to put a fringe across the middle of the shield to represent the beard of the bull. In the center of the piece he was to tie the head of a jack-rabbit. Then he was to take a piece of elk-horn, bend it into a hook, and tie it across the middle. Wristlets were to be made from the skin of the buffalo's nose, and dew-claws were to be tied to them. Armlets were to be made from the skin taken from the throat where the hair is long. A strip of skin from the buffalo's mane was to be taken for a necklace. Finally his father was requested to get a white horse with red ears, and to bob his tail like that of the rabbit. The horse should be made to look as much like the rabbit as possible. A whistle was to be used to imitate the noise made by the rabbit.

When the boy's father had done all this, he was directed by his son to hang the shield upon a pole on the back of the lodge, then to ride round the camp and tell all the people to stake down their lodges. "When this is done," said the boy. "I shall sing a song, and if nothing happens, we shall destroy this shield." So the boy's father rode round the camp, calling out to all the people and telling them to stake down their lodges and send a swift runner to assist his son. The whole camp knew that some powerful medicine was about to work. The women hurried out to stake down their lodges. When the father returned to his lodge, the boy dug up some dirt at the side of his bed, and scattered some light-colored dust in the hole. "This," said he, "is to represent the place where the buffalo do their pawing." The young man directed the runner to go out by the left side of the lodge and run around very fast, take the shield down from the pole as he ran, and bring it into the lodge without stopping. While the runner was doing this, the boy sang a song. He was sitting down with a buffalo-robe, hairside out, drawn around him. When the runner came in with the shield, the boy put it on by putting his feet through the carrying-strap and pulling it over his shoulders. Then he fell over into the hole he had dug, rolled in the dust he had scattered there, and grunted like the buffalo. Then he got up and shook himself. Immediately a great storm came. It blew the dust the boy shook from himself straight up into the air. It did not blow down the lodge in which the shield was; but every other lodge in the camp was blown over, notwithstanding the fact that they had been staked down very tight. In this way, the great medicine-power of this shield became known to the people.

Once, a long time after this, the enemy attacked the camp, and the

Piegan were driven back among their lodges. The boy who owned the shield sat quietly in his lodge and let them fight. His people called him to come out, but he sat still. Finally he sent for a number of young men, and when they arrived he requested them to get a number of young cottonwood-trees and put them against his lodge. While the young men were bringing the trees, the boy had his horse brought in. The young men soon came back, and brought so many trees that they almost broke down the lodge. Then the boy put on his wristlets, his armlets, his necklace, took the shield, sang a song, rolled in the dust and shook himself, as before. This time, however, he shot straight up in the air and came out at the top of the lodge, breaking some of the cottonwood-trees, and came down astride his horse. The horse jumped four times, like a rabbit. All this time the enemy were shooting at him. As the horse jumped the fourth time, the enemy ran. The boy pursued them, striking them with the hook of elk-horn that hung upon the shield, and every man struck fell dead.

The shield takes its name from its owner, who always sat down; but the people speak of him, according to their way, as he who never-sits-down.

CHEYENNE

THE ORIGIN OF THE BUFFALO AND OF CORN*

WHEN the Cheyenne were still in the north they camped in a large circle. At the entrance of the camp-circle there was a deep spring of water rapidly flowing from out the hillside. They camped near this spring so that they might get their water easily. One bright day they were playing the game of ring and javelin in the center of the circle. The game consisted of a hoop painted red and black all over, and four throwing sticks which were to be thrown at the hoop when it was rolled. Two of the sticks were painted red, and two were painted black. The sticks were three or four feet long, and were tied together in pairs. The hoop was rolled along the ground, and as it rolled the red or the black sticks were

*From George A. Dorsey, *The Cheyenne*, pp. 39-40.

thrown at it, and the contestants won accordingly as the black or red portion of the ring fell upon the black or red sticks as it stopped. The owner of the stick which matched the color of that portion of the ring that fell on it won. There was a large crowd of Cheyenne gathered in the middle of the camp, watching the game. As the players contested there came from the south side of the camp-circle a certain young man to witness the game. He stood outside of the crowd to look on. He wore a buffalo robe with the hair side turned out, his body was painted yellow, and a yellow painted eagle breath-feather stuck up on top of his head. Soon there came from the north side of the camp-circle another young man to see the game, and he was dressed exactly like the man who came from the south side. He also stood outside of the crowd, and opposite the first man, to view the game. When they saw each other they went inside the crowd and met face to face and asked each other questions. They were unacquainted with each other, and were surprised when they saw that they were dressed alike. The crowd stopped playing the game, and stood around to hear what the two young men said. The man from the south said to the man from the north, "My friend, you are imitating my manner of dress. Why do you do it?" Then the man from the north said, "Why do you imitate my manner of dress?" At last each told the other the reason for his manner of dress on that day. Each claimed to have entered the spring that flowed out from the hillside at the entrance to the camp-circle, where he had been instructed to dress after this fashion. They then told the great crowd that they were going to enter the spring again, and that they would soon come out. The crowd watched them as they approached the spring. The man from the south side reached the spring, covered his head with his buffalo robe, and entered. The other young man did the same thing. They splashed the water as they went, and soon found themselves in a large cave. Near the entrance sat an old woman cooking some buffalo meat and corn in two separate earthen pots. The woman welcomed them thus: "Grandchildren, you have come. I have been expecting you, and am cooking for you. Come and sit down beside me." They sat down, one on each side of her, and told her that their people were hungry, and that they had come to her for their relief. The woman gave them corn from one pot and meat from the other. They ate, and were filled, and when they were through the pots were as full as when they began. Then the old woman told the young men to look toward the south. They looked, and they saw the land to the south covered with buffalo. She then told them to look to the west. They looked and saw all manner of animals, large and small, and there were ponies, but they knew nothing of ponies in those days, for they never had seen any. She then told them to look toward the north. They looked to the north, and saw everywhere growing corn. Then said the old woman to them, "All this that you have seen shall in the future be yours for food. This night I cause the buffalo to be restored to you. When you leave this place the buffalo shall follow you, and you and your people shall see them coming from this place before sunset. Take in your robes this un-cooked corn. Every spring-time plant it in low, moist ground, where it will grow. After it matures you will feed upon it. Take also this meat and corn which I have cooked, and when you have returned to your people, ask them all to sit down in the following order, to eat out of these two pots: first, all males, from the youngest to the oldest, with the exception of one orphan boy; second, all females, from the oldest to the youngest, with the exception of one orphan girl. When all are through eating, the contents of the pots are to be eaten by the orphan boy and the orphan girl."

The two young men went out and obeyed the old woman. When they passed out of the spring they saw that their entire bodies were painted red, and the breath-feathers of their heads were painted red instead of yellow. They went to their people, and they ate as directed of the corn and the meat, and there was enough for all; and the contents of the pots was not diminished until it came time for the two orphan children, who ate all the food. Toward sunset the people went to their lodges and began watching the spring closely, and in a short time they saw a buffalo jump from the spring. It jumped and played and rolled, and then returned to the spring. In a little while another buffalo jumped out, then another, and another, and finally they came out so fast that the Cheyenne were no longer able to count them. The buffalo continued to come out until dark, and all night and the following day the whole country out in the distance was covered with buffalo. The buffalo scented the great camp, for they left a long, narrow space where the wind went from the camp. The next day the Cheyenne surrounded the buffalo. Though they were on foot they ran very fast. For a time they had an abundance of buffalo meat. In the spring-time they moved their camp to low, swampy land, where they planted the corn they had received from the medicine spring. It grew rapidly, and every grain they planted brought forth strong stalks, and on each stalk grew from two to four ears of corn. The Cheyenne planted corn every year after this.

One spring, after the planting of their corn, the Cheyenne went on a buffalo hunt. When they had enough meat to dry to last them for a considerable time, they returned to their corn-fields. To their surprise they found that their corn had been stolen by a neighboring tribe. Nothing but the stalks remained, not even a kernel for seed; so it was a long time before the Cheyenne planted any more corn. They trailed the footprints of the enemy for several days from their fields, though the thieves had visited them about one moon before. They fought with two or three tribes of Indians, but could not trace the thieves, nor could they learn anything regarding the stolen corn.

COMANCHE

WHY THE BEAR WADDLES WHEN HE WALKS*

IN the beginning days, nobody knew what to do with the sun. It would come up and shine for a long time. Then it would go away for a long time, and everything would be dark.

The daytime animals naturally wanted the sun to shine all the time, so they could live their lives without being interrupted by the dark. The nighttime animals wanted the sun to go away forever, so they could live the way they wanted to.

At last they all got together, to talk things over.

Old Man Coyote said, "Let's see what we can do about that sun. One of us ought to have it, or the other side ought to get rid of it."

"How will we do that?" Scissor-tailed Flycatcher asked. "Nobody can tell the sun what to do. He's more powerful than anyone else in the world."

"Why don't we play hand game for it?" Bear asked. "The winning side can keep the sun or throw it away, depending on who wins and what they want to do with it."

So they got out the guessing bones to hide in their hands, and they got out the crow-feathered wands for the guessers to point with, and they got out the twenty painted dogwood sticks for the umpires to keep score

*From A. Marriott and C. K. Rachlin, *American Indian Mythology,* pp. 128-130.

with. Coyote was the umpire for the day side, and nighttime umpire was Owl.

The umpires got a flat rock, like a table, and laid out their counting sticks on that. Then the two teams brought legs, and lined them up facing one another, with the umpires and their flat rock at one end, between the two teams.

That was a long hand game. The day side held the bones first, and they were so quick and skillful passing them from hand to hand behind their backs and waving them in the guessers' faces that it seemed surely they must win. Then Mole, who was guessing for the night side, caught both Scissor-tail and Hawk at the same time, and the bones went to the night side, and the day people began to guess.

Time and again the luck went back and forth, each team seeming to be about to beat the other. Time and again the luck changed, and the winning team became the losing one.

The game went on and on. Finally the sun, waiting on the other side of the world to find out what was going to happen to him, got tired of it all.

The game was so long that Bear got tired, too. He was playing on the night side. He got cramped sitting on the log, and his legs began to ache. Bear took off his moccasins to rest his feet, and still the game went on and on.

At last the sun was so bored that he decided to go and see for himself what was happening. He yawned and stretched and crawled out of his bed on the underneath side of the world. He started to climb up his notched log ladder to the top side, to find out what was happening.

As the sun climbed the light grew stronger, and the night people began to be afraid. The game was still even; nobody had won. But the sun was coming and coming, and the night animals had to run away. Bear jumped up in such a hurry that he put his right foot in his left moccasin, and his left foot in his right moccasin.

The sun was full up now, and all the other night animals were gone. Bear went after them as fast as he could in his wrong moccasins, rocking and waddling from side to side, and shouting, "Wait for me! Wait for me!"

But nobody stopped or waited, and Bear had to go waddling along, just the way he has done ever since.

And because nobody won the game, the day and night took turns from that time on. Everybody had the same time to come out and live his life the way he wanted to as everybody else.

CROW

THE DIPPER*

THE Seven Stars were once living on this earth. They got angry about something. They had a younger sister, who owned a little dog. "What shall we turn into so as to live forever?" One of them said, "Let us be the earth." They refused. "The earth caves in," they said. Then one of them said, "Let us be trees." "Trees are chopped down," they said and would not do it. "We'll be stones," said one of them. "Stones are broken off," they said. That, too, they would not do. "Let us be mountains." "The rocks cave in." They would not do it. One of them said, "Let us be stars." "They also fall down," they said. They did not do it. One of them said, "You are crazy, we'll be the Dipper." Then they became stars. They did not fall down, they remained above. This is what we have heard.

DAKOTA

INCEST**

THERE was a tribal camp. And in it lived a young man who was the only son of his parents, and was greatly loved; so they had him live by himself in a special tipi in the manner of a boy-beloved. He had two younger sisters who lived with their parents. The entire tribe loved this young man, and the plan was to make him a chief some day. And it happened that one night as he lay sleeping, a woman entered his tipi and lay down beside his bed. This she did to tempt him. But of course it was dark, so he could not tell what woman it was. In the morning he did not tell his father; he simply said, "Father, this evening I want you to set a dish of red face paint near my bed."—"What does he mean?" the father thought, but was reluctant to ask him. The next night, the woman

*From Robert H. Lowie, *Myths and Traditions of the Crow Indians,* p. 211.
**From Ella Deloria, *Dakota Texts,* (Franz Boas, ed.), pp. 175-180.

entered again and bothered him, so he secretly dipped his hand in the paint and applied it over her dress as thoroughly as he could. The next morning he said, "Father, I wish all the women in the camp to engage in a shinny game."—"What does my son mean?" he thought, but he was reluctant to ask him; so he went without a word to the council tent where he told the boy-beloved's wish. Immediately a shinny game was arranged for the women. But he could not tell whether the woman who visited him nightly was in the game or not; because she could change her clothing for other before taking part. Again she came (the next night), so this time he covered her entire face with the paint, and sent her out. Next day he ordered another shinny game, and it was arranged through the council tent. In time, all the women assembled in the center of the enclosure, and now they ran. Out of all the players there was one who unbraided her hair and left it hanging loosely about her face. As she played, with her face thus hidden, he studied her to make sure, and it shocked him to realize that she was the elder of his own two younger sisters! Her face was as if dipped in blood. That is why she hid it as she played. It came over him then that one of his own sisters was tempting him, and he was filled with anger and shame. As he was retiring he said, "Father, get an iron rod and heat it thoroughly, and wait near the tipi. When I clear my throat, slide it in to me." Why he should request this was not at all clear, but the father did what his son commanded. And now, once again the woman entered and came and lay down beside his bed. But that instant, he cleared his throat, and his father, who sat immediately outside the tipi, slid the heated iron in to him, under the base of the tipi. With the iron he branded the woman's face all over, and then sent her out. Now that he was aware that this was his own sister he was very much ashamed, and angry. After she left he slept; and on waking, he felt something move under him, so he looked down and saw that he was standing attached, as if glued, to a tree which was rapidly growing taller; of course, since he was part of the tree, he was rising higher all the time, too. Until now he was rising out of the tipi through the smoke-vent. So the people below took down the tipi in haste. Then the tree grew even faster, elevating the young man higher and higher. The people were frightened by the miracle, and because of fear they moved away and disappeared from the scene. Only the good little sister of the young man stayed at the base of the tree and wept. It did not disturb her that the people had left her behind, and as she stood weeping, suddenly, from the wood near by, the wicked sister looked out, and called tauntingly, "There's someone loves her brother very much; but I have caused him to grow onto the tree!'' And the young man called down to his good sister, ''Reply this to her, little sister. 'There is someone who tempted her own brother, but he caused her face to be branded with a hot iron!' So the girl called back as her brother had taught her, and straightway the one in the wood called back, ''Oh, that's the thing I resent!'' and a deer ran back into the wood amid rustling leaves. From then on, the girl, who was very weary, slept, until a man came from somewhere, and said, ''Young girl, roast this for your brother,'' and he threw her a piece of deer meat. So she rose and cooked it and tossed it up to her brother, though by now he stood very high. Her brother ate it. Then the man said to her, ''Now, I have something for you to decide. If it pleases you that we two shall live together, I can cause your brother to come down.'' So she told her brother what the man had said to her; and the brother said, ''Do it, sister; I want to come down; I am so thirsty.'' So the girl consented to become the wife of the stranger, and he said, ''In that case, lie down under here.'' She did so, and he covered her with a blanket, and pegged down the four corners so securely that she was imprisoned underneath. Thus it was that she did not see how her husband worked his magic, and was unable to tell it. He was actually a Thunder man, though they did not know at first. For the Thunder man opened his eyes (lightning), and repeatedly he roared (thunder), and the tree was split in two, and fell broken to the ground so that the young man stepped off. Then the man took out the tipi-base pegs and removed the blanket, and helped the girl to her feet. So she greeted her brother. Because he was thunder he killed many buffaloes, and with his bare hands he ground the meat and bones, and made a cake of pemmican which he handed to his brother-in-law. ''Now, go to your tribe, and invite them back to this camp-site they have abandoned,'' he said. So he went to his people and called them together. Then he gave every one a piece of the pemmican, in very small amounts. He was distributing it in that manner when a very greedy woman who was in the company complained at the smallness of her share, and threw it all into her mouth at once. Then she chewed; but it gradually increased in amount until finally her mouth could not hold it all; and she was choking on it. So they took a knife, and cut out piece by piece until she was relieved. Despite the smallness of the cake, the quantity continued to increase, until they were able to fill many containers with it. Then the young man invited the people to their old camp ground. So they followed him back, and on their arrival, they found at each individual site, great quantities of meat, jerked, and drying on poles. "That is our camp-site!" was heard on all sides as families identified their places and proceeded to set up their homes again; and they were very well provisioned. From then on, that people no longer knew want, they say. Then the Thunder man told his wife this, "Now, young girl, you whose love for your brother was so big that you consented to be my wife for his sake, I am going home. It is enough, for I have now given you aid." And so he went away, somewhere, wherever it is that the thunders abide. That is all.

A DOG'S REVENGE*

There was a dog; and there was an old woman who had a pack of dried meat laid away. This the dog knew; and, when he supposed the old woman was asleep, he went there at night. But the old woman was aware of his coming and so kept watch, and, as the dog thrust his head under the tent, she struck him across the face and made a great gash, which swelled greatly.

The next morning a companion dog came and attempted to talk with him. But the dog was sullen and silent. The visitor said: "Tell me what makes you so heart-sick." To which he replied: "Be still, an old woman has treated me badly." "What did she do to you?" He answered: "An old woman had a pack of dried meat; this I saw and went for it; and when it was now far in the night, and I supposed she was asleep, I went there and poked my head under the tent. But she was lying awake and cried out: 'Shoo! what are you doing here?' and struck me on the head and wounded me as you see."

Whereupon the other dog said: "Alas! Alas! she has treated you badly, verily we will eat up her pack of meat. Call an assembly: call *Water-mist* (*i.e.*, rain); call *Bite-off-silently;* call *Strong-neck;* call *Sharp-knife.*" So he invited them all. And when they had all arrived, he said: "Come on! an old woman has treated this friend badly; bestir yourselves; before the night is past, the pack of dried meat which she prizes so much, and on account of which she has thus dealt with our friend, that we will eat all up."

*From Reverend Stephen Return Riggs, "Illustration of the Method of Recording Indian Languages," pp. 58-59.

Then the one who is called *Rain-mist* caused it to rain, and it rained all the day through until dark; and the tent was all drenched, and the holes of the tent-pins were thoroughly softened. Then *Bite-off-silently* bit off all the lower tent-fastenings, but he did it so quietly that the old woman knew nothing of it. Then *Strong-neck* came and seized the pack with his mouth, and carried it far away. Whereupon *Sharp-knife* came and ripped the pack through the middle; and so, while it was yet night, they ate up the old woman's pack of dried meat.

Moral—A common thief becomes worse and worse by attaching himself to more daring companions. This is the myth.

If the moral appended to this tale appears to be something of a *non sequitur*, it should alert the reader to the dual nature of myth. To be sure, bad companions do encourage worse behavior, but there is no punishment meted out for the behavior. Can this moral neutrality be accidental? Or are the thieves not punished because they are stealing from an old woman who has refused to share food? Like many other myths, this one allows expression to several forbidden impulses even as it piously inveighs against improper behavior.

Southwest

Jicarilla (Eastern) Apache

THE MONSTER FISH*

A MONSTER fish which lived in a lake swallowed anyone coming near it. Naiyenesgani came there and was swallowed by the fish which swam to the center of the lake and lay in deep water. Naiyenesgani, sitting inside of the fish, began singing ceremonial songs, that the fish might move to the shore of the lake. When he had finished his songs, he cut off the heart of the fish which raced with him toward the shore, throwing the smaller fish and water far away. It fell with him at the shore of the lake. Naiyenesgani, with his obsidian knife, cut openings in the neck of the fish through which he went out, carrying the heart in his hand. He gave it to the sun, saying, "Here, carry this where he cannot get it again." That is why a fish has a series of openings on the sides of his neck. He went home to his grandmother, Yolgaiisdzan. The firedrill had blazed up and then died down again.

San Carlos (Western) Apache

SECURING FIRE**

THEY say long ago there was no fire. The people ate their food

*From Pliny Earle Goddard, *Jicarilla Apache Texts*, pp. 201-202.
**From Pliny Earle Goddard, *Myths and Tales of the San Carlos Apache*, p. 43.

uncooked. There were only two men who had fire. They could see it in the tops of a very tall pine tree which stood there.

Coyote proposed that a large company of people be invited to come together for a dance. He also suggested that a letter be sent to those who had fire asking them to bring some as they wished to gamble with the guessing game.

Coyote told his companions to tie dry grass around his tail. When it was daybreak Coyote danced by himself. "I will dance over the fire," he said. "Your tail is afire," they called to him. "Why do you say my tail is burning?" he asked. "Your tail is burning," they called to him again. He went around the fire four times and then jumped over them. He ran away with the fire. Those who owned the fire ran after him and put out what fire they found. They caught Coyote after he had run a long distance and pulled out his nose so it is long and spread his mouth apart so it is wide.

Then another man was running away beyond with the fire. It was Night Hawk. They caught him after a long chase. They pushed the crown of his head down hard and spread his mouth open.

Another person was running with the fire. It was Turkey Buzzard. They caught him a long distance away and pulled the hair out of his head. He had given the fire to Humming Bird. A large mountain was standing in the distance. Fire was coming out from the top of this mountain. The people had been without fire but came to have plenty of it because of Coyote. The fire went inside of the trees and became plentiful.

SONGS OF THE DEER COMPANY*

1

They went on a hunting trip.

Here to the east,
Where he made a mountain ridge of jet,
Where he made lie the head of the mountain of jet.

Here to the south,
Where he made a mountain ridge of bailgaiye,
Where he made lie the head of the mountain of bailgaiye.

*From Pliny Earle Goddard, *Myths and Tales of the San Carlos Apache*, pp. 56-62.

Here to the west,
Where he made a mountain ridge of coral.
Where he made lie the head of the mountain of coral.

Here to the north,
Where he made a mountain ridge of turquoise,
Where he made lie the head of the mountain of turquoise,
One horn stands up at the four places in the sky where he made its head
    lie.

They went on a hunting trip.

II

He placed a house here where there was none.
He covered it with the black skin of the deer which come from the east.
He covered it with the white skin of the deer which come from the south.
He covered it with the yellow skin of the deer which come from the
    west.
He covered it with the white skin of the deer which come from the north.
He caused the black deer horns to alight one after the other on the top
    of his house.
He placed a house there.
He alights there.

III

At the east where he made a spring with black red water,
He alights there.

At the south where he made a spring of white red water,
He alights there.

At the west where he made a spring of the yellow colored slobberings
    of red water,
He alights there.

At the north where he made a spring of the blue colored slobberings
    of red water,
He alights there.

He caused two black deer horns to come together.
He made pillows under them as the two arrived.
He caused two fawns to alight at his feet.
He made holes inside through his house in four directions with mouth
    blood.
Here where he made a moving bed,
He alighted.

IV

I go after it on the earth.
Panther boy they call me,
    I go after it.
With dark mouth blood lying under my soles,
With dark mouth blood making a black strip between my toes
    I go after it.
With mouth blood making stripes on me,
    I go after it.
With mouth blood making stripes running out from each other on my
face,
    I go after it.

V

Send word for me
Where I am going.
Send word for me
Who am called Panther Boy.

XVII

Where the rising sun looks,
Walk out, they tell me.
When I went there, she who walks on the water was wild.
Her walk was wild, her eye was wild,
I came as she brought me some.

With a bone medicine belt not wild, I came to her.
With wind's footprints not wild, I came near her.
With a yellow spotted belt not wild, I came near her.
With a bone medicine shirt not wild, I came near her.

Mescalero (Western) Apache

A SONG OF GOTAL*

The black turkey-gobbler, under the East, the middle of his tail;
toward us it is about to dawn.
The black turkey-gobbler, the tips of his beautiful tail; above us
the dawn whitens.
The black turkey gobbler, the tips of his beautiful tail; above us
the dawn becomes yellow.
The sunbeams stream forward, dawn boys, with shimmering shoes of
yellow;
On top of the sunbeams that stream toward us they are dancing.
At the East the rainbow moves forward, dawn maidens, with shimmering
shoes and shirts of yellow, dance over us.
Beautifully over us it is dawning.
Above us among the mountains the herbs are becoming green;
Above us on the tops of the mountains the herbs are becoming
yellow.
Above us among the mountains, with shoes of yellow, I go around
the fruits and herbs that shimmer.
Above us among the mountains, the shimmering fruits with shoes
and shirts of yellow are bent toward him.
On the beautiful mountains above it is daylight.

Part of a ceremony celebrating the creation and re-creation of the world, "A Song of Gotal," like many Indian poems, utilizes an animal metaphor—in this case, the turkey—to symbolize sunrise and the process of creation and rebirth.

*From Pliny Earle Goddard, *Putnam Anniversary Volume,* p. 17.

HAVASUPAI

SUN, MY RELATIVE: A WORK POEM*

Sun, my relative
Be good coming out
Do something good for us

Make me work
So I can plant anything in the garden
I hoe, I plant corn, I irrigate

You, sun be good going down at sunset
We lay down to sleep I want to feel good

While I sleep you come up.
Go on your course many times
Make good things for us men

Make me always the same as I am now.

An emphasis on things as they are, on the virtue of work characterizes the life and
literature of many of the sedentary southwest Indians.

HOPI

THE HAWK AND THE CHILD**

A long time ago some Navaho lived east of Oraíbi. They had stolen, as
occasionally happened, a little Hopi boy. They were very hard on him,
making him work constantly and giving him very little to eat, so that
he became very much emaciated. Somewhere north of this Navaho

*From Leslie Spier, *Havasupai Ethnography*, p. 203.
**From H. R. Voth, *The Traditions of the Hopi*, pp. 167-168.

camp there was a high bluff on which a large Hawk lived. This Hawk was often flying around and frequently saw this little boy and pitied him. One time the Navaho had a great gathering at one place not far from this camp where the little boy was, leaving the little orphan behind. When the Hawk found this out he flew to the camp, flying around above the little boy. The latter was afraid and begged the Hawk not to hurt him. The Hawk at once sat down beside the boy and said to him: "I am not going to hurt you, but I pity you and we shall go to my house. You come and sit on my back and I shall carry you there." The child at once mounted on the back of the Hawk, holding himself to the wings, and the Hawk then flew away with him.

When passing the place where the Navaho were gathered, the latter noticed that the Hawk was carrying away the boy and were very much astonished at it. They had never thought of such a thing. After the Hawk had deposited the little son on the bluff he said to him, "I am going to borrow some clothes for you. You are naked, and you want to be clothed." Immediately he swooped down upon the Navaho camp, singled out a little son of a wealthy Navaho, grabbed him and flew back to the bluff. While he was flying he tore off all the clothes from the child and then dropped the body to the earth. The assembled Navaho were very much frightened and screamed.

At that time the Navaho still wore long buckskin leggings with yellow buttons on the sides, also buckskin shirts, and such a costume the Hawk brought to the little boy. The Hawk soon after flew down again, grabbed another little Navaho boy and carried him upward, the head of the child hanging down, pulled off his moccasins, dropped the body, and brought the moccasins to the little child. The Navaho were very much frightened and dispersed in all directions. This confusion the Hawk made use of and came down several times, taking away from several of the Navaho articles of clothing and ornaments, bringing them back to the little child. The Hawk then said to the little boy: "But you are not used to this raw food that I am eating." "No," the little boy said, "I never ate that before." So the Hawk got him some firewood and even fire, and some rabbit meat, and the boy roasted some meat and ate it. He stayed there four days in the house of the Hawk. At the end of the four days the Hawk said to him: "In the morning I am going to take you to your home in Oraíbi." So the boy mounted his back again and the Hawk flew first down to the Navaho camp where he circled around a number of times, showing himself to the Navaho, who were very much astonished, and then flew on to the village of Oraibi returning the child to his home, where he lived forever afterwards.

THE COYOTE AND THE BLUE JAYS*

Haliksai! A long time ago the people lived in Oraíbi. West of the village, at Ishmovala, lived the Coyote and his wife. They had six children and the Coyote used to go and hunt rabbits for his children. One day he went hunting again and found a little cottontail rabbit, which he chased. The rabbit ran into the hole, which the Coyote could not enter. "How shall I get this rabbit out now?" he thought to himself; then somebody came along; it was the Badger. "You get this out for me here," the Coyote said, "I want this rabbit for my children to eat." So the Coyote sat down and waited while the Badger scratched a hole until he reached the rabbit, whereupon he pulled the latter out. The Coyote was very happy. "Thus," he said, "on your account my children will have something to eat." Then the Coyote took the rabbit in his mouth and ran home with it, being very happy. When he arrived in his home the little Coyotes wrangled over the rabbit, tore it to pieces and devoured it, some of them getting something, others not, so they remained hungry.

The next morning both the Coyote and his wife went out in search of food again, the latter ascending up to the village, and ran past the village on the west side, then by the north side, turning northward over the mesas. Not finding anything, she finally entered the woods north of the village. All at once she heard something in the trees, and, looking up, she saw some Blue Jays in the tree. The Blue Jays were dancing in the tree and she coveted them. They said to the Coyote: "We are having a dance here, you come and be with us and assist us." "I would like to," the Coyote said, "but how shall I get up there?" "Why, we shall lend you some of our wings, tails, and feathers," the Blue Jay said. "All right," she said. So they took off some of their wings, tails, and feathers and put them on her legs. They then told her that she must dance and sing just the same as they did, and then they again began to sing.

The Coyote now having wings ascended and danced with them. When they had finished the song they all flew away, the Coyote with them,

*From H. R. Voth, *The Traditions of the Hopi*, pp. 196-197.

and alighted on some other tree. This they repeated in all three times. They then flew up high into the air, the Coyote with them, and when they were very high up they all surrounded the Coyote, each one saying: "This is my tail, this is my wing, these are my feathers," and then tore out all the feathers that they had loaned the Coyote. When they had torn out all the feathers the Coyote began to fall downward to the earth. When she reached it she was dead.

Her children still had nothing to eat. When the Coyote father saw that his wife was not coming home he concluded that he would go and hunt her. Following her tracks, he ascended to the village, passed the village on the west side, and when he reached the north side of the village the dogs of the village noticed him and pursued him. He at once left the footprints of his wife and ran back to his children. So after that the little Coyotes had no mother. The Coyote then afterwards hunted food alone for his children, and that is the reason why so many Coyotes have to look out for their food alone.

WHY THE ANTS ARE SO THIN*

Ishyaoi! East of Tcöokávü lived a great many Ants. One time the chief of the Ants said to them that they were going to have a Katcina initiation in four days. On the fourth day two of the Ants dressed themselves up as Hū Katcinas; one as Angwúshnacomtaka, just the same as is being done today when children are initiated into a Katcina society. They dressed up at Koritvi, a short distance northwest of the village. Some of the Ants also made a sand picture on the floor of the kiva; then the Ants began to bring their children that were to be initiated into the kiva.

When the children had all been put in, the Katcina priest of the Ants related the story in the same manner as the Katcina priest now relates it at the Katcina initiation. Four little Kóyemsis then had their performance. One of the Ants was in the meanwhile sitting on a rock outside, and when they were through in the kiva this Ant swung one forefoot vigorously as a signal for the Katcinas to come. The Katcinas at once came running to the kiva, circled around the kiva several times, and then entered it, taking places opposite the sand picture. They then flogged the little Ant chil-

*From H. R. Voth, *The Traditions of the Hopi*, p. 239.

dren. They flogged them so hard that they almost cut them through in the middle of their body. When they were through all the Katcinas left the kiva and ran away. And that is the reason why the ants are now so thin in the middle of their bodies, because they were almost cut in two on that occasion.

THE COYOTE AND HIS PREY*

Haliksai! At Hohóyapi the people were living. The Coyote had children somewhere. So he was hunting some food for them and had killed a rabbit and he did not want to eat it alone, so he mounted a bluff and called it out in the way Coyotes bark. So from the north came a yellow Coyote, from the west a blue one, from the south a red one, from the east a white, from the north-east a black, and from the south-east a gray one. "This here I killed," he said to them, "and because I do not want to eat it alone I have called you. We shall eat it together." So they tore it to pieces and devoured it there very quickly, and that is the reason why a coyote never eats any prey that he has found alone, but always calls out when he has found something.

In order to set stories off from ordinary discourse, Hopi Indians—and many others—frequently utilized an expression like "Haliksai." Also common in Hopi literature and an indication of the importance of the village in Hopi life, is an initial reference to the place in which the action is supposed to have taken place.

BIG HEAD AND GOAT HORN**

Haliksai! In Oraibi they were living. East of the Kwan kiva a youth lived, by the name of Big Head (Wuyákqötö). Away south are the Hopi Buttes, and on the westernmost butte lived Goat Horn (Chiwákala). These two were friends, but as they lived so far apart they did not visit each other often; but one time Goat Horn visited his friend in Oraibi. After they had eaten and talked together, towards evening Goat Horn wanted to return home. "My friend," he said to Big Head. "What is it?" the latter replied. "You must come and visit me sometime, too," Goat Horn said; whereupon he went home. After a while Big Head vis-

---

*From H. R. Voth, The Traditions of the Hopi, p. 216.
**From H. R. Voth, The Traditions of the Hopi, p. 153.

ited his friend, and stayed all night there. In the morning Goat Horn killed a goat for his friend, cut it in two, and gave him one-half, which Big Head took with him to the village; and that is the reason why Hopi, when they kill a goat, cut it up.

THE SHONOGOPAVI MAIDEN WHO TURNED INTO A DOG*

Haliksai! In Shonogópavi they were living, and a youth there was very handsome, and all the maidens were coveting him. And one maiden was young yet, had small hair whorls; she was dirty, and a bad looking maiden. The maidens owned the chiro birds, and one of the maidens ground coarse meal (hakwúshkwi) for them and put it into a tray, and when she had put in she lifted it up, and while she was singing she threw it away. She sang: "Póta, póta, póta, Yóa íni, yóa ini," and then scattered it to the birds. Now the chiros darted towards it and ate of it, and when they had eaten they dispersed again, whistling, and were flying around somewhere in the field. When it was evening they again assembled at the mána's house. In the morning she again made hakwúshkwi for them and fed them, and after that the mána always fed them.

Now that youth also made a tray. When he was done with it the maidens assembled. He handed that tray to them, and when he had handed it to them he said: "Now then, who opens this shall get me." Now one when she had loosened it could not untie it. She handed it to another one, who could not untie it, and thus one after the other tried to loosen and untie it, and not one could open it. Now then when it came to that bad looking maiden she also tried it. Now the old grandmother (Spider Woman) informed her, "When you will sing this you will open it." Thus she informed her. So the maiden, while she was secretly singing, opened it. When she had opened it, singing secretly, she opened it as her song ended. When she had opened it all she owned the youth. Then those pretty maidens were very sad and were angry.

Now the youth took her to his house, where the mother of the youth bathed her entirely, whereupon she became a pretty maiden. She now remained there a bride. Then they made a bridal costume for her whereupon she went home. When she went home the youth followed her. Now she slept there in their house twice, and when she slept there

*From H. R. Voth, *The Traditions of the Hopi*, p. 150.

the second time she did not get up. At last when they were eating they would still not get up, so the mother of the maiden went up to them and looked at them and they were still sleeping, but that maiden had turned into something; she had turned into a dog. Now the mother said to them, "Get up, please." The dog got up at once and rushed out right away and jumped down as a dog, and at once ran away somewhere, and is still going around somewhere.

THE BLIND MAN AND THE LAME MAN*

A long time ago there was an earthquake at Oraíbi. It was a very nice day; people had eaten their breakfast as usual, and were happy. Then towards noon the earth and the houses began to move and to tremble, and very soon there was a great noise like thunder, but nothing could be seen and the people did not know where it came from. They ran to their houses and everywhere to see what was the matter. Sometime in the afternoon the earth trembled very much, and a large piece of ground sank down at Skeleton gulch (Másvövee), so called because at one time a great many slain people were thrown there. This is situated about half a mile northeast of Oraibi; the piece that sank down reached nearly to the village of Oraibi. There was also a very large crack right on the public square or plaza of the village.

By this time the people got frightened very much, and all left the village, running toward the north. In the village there lived in one of the houses a blind man, and in another house a cripple who could not walk. When these noticed that some serious disturbance was taking place, they got very much frightened, and the blind man called over to the cripple asking for information. The latter answered that the earth had been trembling and the village had been in motion, and that all the people had left the village. The cripple then asked the blind man to come over to his house. The blind man asked the cripple to come over to his house, but after a while the cripple prevailed, and the blind man, taking a stick and feeling his way before himself, tried to reach the house of the cripple, the latter directing him which way to go. When he had arrived at the house the cripple said: "Let us also flee. You carry me on your back, and I shall show you the way." This they did, the cripple turning the head of

*From H. R. Voth, *The Traditions of the Hopi,* pp. 151-152.

the blind man in the direction in which he wanted him to turn and to go. Thus they left the village, also in a northerly direction, following the others.

A short distance north of the village a large elk met them, coming from the north. "Oh my! what is that?" the cripple said, on the back of the blind man. "What is it?" the latter asked. "Something very large. It is nearly black, and yet it is not quite black." The blind man, who had been a great hunter in his youth, when he still had his eyesight, at once suspected what it might be, and asked for details, and soon concluded that it must be an elk. Before leaving the village the blind man had suggested that they take a bow and arrows along, so that, in case they needed some food, they could kill some game. When they had come opposite the elk the cripple suggested that the blind man shoot the elk, as his own hands were also somewhat crippled, and he was unable to handle a bow. He put an arrow on the bow, and the blind man got the bow ready, the cripple doing the aiming for him. The elk was now standing west of them, and at the proper time the cripple told the blind man to shoot. He shot and killed the elk.

They were now very anxious to roast some of the meat, but had nothing to skin the animal or cut the meat with; so they went there and with one of their arrows they dug out the eyes of the elk. The blind man then, being directed by the lame man, gathered some sticks of wood and they built a fire, starting the fire by rubbing wood and fire sticks together. They placed the two eyes on the fire and waited. When the eyes got very hot they burst with a great report. "Hihiyá!" the men exclaimed, and both jumped up, the lame man finding that he could walk, and the blind man finding his eyes opened. "Ishuti," the blind man said. "What is it (hinti)?" "My eyes are open." "Yes, and I can walk," the other man replied. By this time it had become evening. "Now let us remain awake all night," the man who had been blind said, "because if we go to sleep my eyes might stick together again." "Yes, if I lie down I might find that I cannot walk again in the morning," the other one replied. So the first one handed the other a small twig of öcvi (Ephedra), saying to him, "If you see that I go to sleep, you prick my eyes so that I awake." The other one handed the blind man, as we shall call him for brevity's sake, also some prickly weed, saying: "If you see me sit down you prick my body so that I remain standing." Thus they remained awake all night watching each other.

Early in the morning they concluded that they would follow the tracks of the inhabitants of the village who had fled. They finally found them in a timber quite a distance to the north. "What has happened to you?" they said. "Why, you were blind and lame, and now you can see and walk." "Yes," they said, "something has happened to us; and now let us go back again to the village. There is nothing the matter there any more." So the people all returned to the village, these two taking the lead, and that is the reason why Oraíbi is again inhabited. If these two had not brought the people back they would never have returned.

The value placed on interdependency is explicit here and is one of the most salient and recurrent themes in Pueblo literature.

YELLOW BUTTERFLIES*

Yellow butterflies
Over the blossoming, virgin corn,
With pollen spotted faces
Chase one another in brilliant throng.

Blue butterflies
Over the blossoming, virgin beans
With pollen painted faces
Chase one another in brilliant throng.

Over the blossoming corn,
Over the virgin corn
Wild bees hum;
Over the blossoming beans
Over the virgin beans
Wild bees hum.

Over your field of growing corn,
All day shall hang the thundercloud.
Over your field of growing beans
All day shall come the rousing rain!

*From Natalie Curtis, *The Indian Book,* p. 304

Keres (Acoma)

THE HUNTING SONG*

Deer-youth, the one who is four times ahead,
That is the one of whom I am thinking,
It is the kind of robe and the kind of face, the whole body and the kind
    of health he has,
That is the one I am thinking about.
Antelope-youth, the one who is four times ahead,
That is the one of whom I am thinking,
It is the kind of robe and the kind of face, the whole body and the kind
    of health he has,
That is the one I am thinking about.
Somewhere along the edge, under a pine tree,
There you are looking for me, you are waiting for me,
Now I shall follow where you have gone.
Somewhere out on the plain, somewhere among the sages,
There you are looking for me, you are waiting for me,
Now I shall follow where you have gone.

THE RAIN CLOUDS ARE CARING FOR
THE LITTLE CORN PLANTS**

Nicely, nicely, nicely, nicely, there away in the east,
The rain clouds are caring for the little corn plants as a mother takes
    care of her baby.

THE SUN-YOUTH HAS RISEN IN THE EAST**

There in the east, there in the east,
The sun-youth has risen and has sent out his breath so that the leaves
    and all vegetation is in gentle motion.

*From Frances Densmore, *Music of Acoma, Isleta, Cochiti and Zuñi Pueblos*, p. 22.
**From Frances Densmore, *Music of Acoma, Isleta, Cochiti and Zuñi Pueblos*.

The sun-youth has risen and has sent out his breath so that the leaves
    and all vegetation is in gentle motion,
The corn maidens and the vine maidens are also in motion with this
    breeze.

SONG ADDRESSED TO A NEW CHIEF*

I wonder if somewhere in an eastern village a new chief has arisen for
    the year,
This is what I said,
I wonder if somewhere in an eastern village a new chief has arisen for
    the year,
This is what I said.
From the north direction it has rained,
From the west direction the water comes in streams,
In front of the streams of water.
Down toward the east the lightnings come down and strike the earth.
All of us receive life.
Now, chief, for this life-giving rain, you must love the earth and the
    sky.
We all receive the benefit from the rain,
It is the duty of the chief to look after his people,
This is what I ask you to do.
From the south it is raining,
From the east the water is coming in streams,
In front of the streams of water toward the west,
From there westward the lightning strikes the earth,
All of us receive crops.
Now here, chief, are crops. With this you may love your people.
This I ask of you.

*From Frances Densmore, *Music of Acoma, Isleta, Cochiti and Zūni Pueblos*, pp. 33,
43, 53.

KERES (SIA)

THE COYOTE AND THE RATTLESNAKE*

THE coyote's house was near the house of the rattlesnake. The coyote said to the snake, "Let us walk together," and while walking he said to the snake, "To-morrow come to my house." In the morning the snake went to the house of the coyote and moved along slowly on the floor, shaking his rattle. The coyote sat to one side, much afraid; he became frightened after watching the movements of the snake and hearing the noise of the rattle. The coyote had a pot of rabbit meat cooking on the fire, which he placed in front of the snake, inviting him to eat, saying, "Companion, eat." "No, companion, I will not eat your meat; I do not understand your food," said the snake. "What food do you eat?" asked the coyote. "I eat the yellow flowers of the corn," was the reply, and the coyote immediately began to look around for some, and when he found the pollen, the snake said, "Put some on the top of my head that I may eat it," and the coyote, standing as far off as possible, dropped a little on the snake's head. The snake said, "Come nearer and put enough on my head that I may find it." He was very much afraid, but after a while he came close to the snake and put the pollen on his head, and after eating the pollen the snake thanked the coyote saying, "I will go now and pass about," but before leaving he invited the coyote to his house: "Companion, to-morrow you come to my house," "Very well," said the coyote, "to-morrow I will go to your house." The coyote thought much what the snake would do on the morrow. He made a small rattle (by placing tiny pebbles in a gourd) and attached it to the end of his tail, and, testing it, he was well satsified and said: "This is well;" he then proceeded to the house of the snake. When he was near the house he shook his tail and said to himself, "This is good; I guess when I go into the house the snake will be very much afraid of me." He did not walk into the house, but moved like a snake. The coyote could not shake the rattle as the snake did his; he had to hold his tail in his hand. When he shook his rattle the snake appeared afraid and said, "Companion, I am much afraid of you." The snake had a stew of rats on the fire, which he placed before the coyote and invited him to eat, saying, "Companion, eat

*From Mathilde Cox Stevenson, The Sia, pp. 156-157.

some of my food," and the coyote replied, "I do not understand your food; I cannot eat it, because I do not understand it." The snake insisted upon his eating, but the coyote continued to refuse, saying, "If you will put some of the flower of the corn on my head I will eat; I understand that food." The snake quickly procured some corn pollen, but he pretended to be afraid to go too near the coyote, and stood off a distance. The coyote told him to come nearer and put it well on the top of his head; but the snake replied, "I am afraid of you." The coyote said, "Come nearer to me; I am not bad," and the snake came closer and put the pollen on the coyote's head and the coyote tried to eat the pollen; but he had not the tongue of the snake, so could not take it from his head. He made many attempts to reach the top of his head, putting his tongue first on one side of his nose and then on the other, but he could only reach either side of his nose. His repeated failures made the snake laugh heartily. The snake put his hand over his mouth, so that the coyote should not see him laugh; he really hid his head in his body. The coyote was not aware that the snake discovered that he could not obtain the food. As he left the snake's house he held his tail in his hand and shook the rattle; and the snake cried, "Oh companion! I am so afraid of you," but in reality the snake shook with laughter. The coyote, returning to his house, said to himself, "I was such a fool; the snake had much food to eat and I would not take it. Now I am very hungry," and he went out in search of food.

All men fear the powers of nature and those of the supernatural, and all cultures attempt to control these unpredictable and dangerous forces. In this tale, Coyote and Snake are symbols for nature and the supernatural respectively. The snake, because he sheds his skin, is often believed to possess eternal life and extraordinary powers. Old Man Coyote, on the other hand, is generally used to symbolize the natural world as it existed before man made rules by which to order it. Old Man Coyote can often be dangerous, he is sometimes helpful, and he is often portrayed as a fool ignorant of the rules that govern proper human behavior. This narrative gives voice to the human fear of both natural and supernatural forces even as it suggests that culture mediates between them. Neither nature nor the supernatural triumphs here because both Coyote and Rattlesnake are incapable of sharing a cooked communal meal. The message is clear: Human cooperation—expressed through the sharing of cooked food by two enemies—is the method by which man may evade the unpredictability of nature and the power of the supernatural.

A RAIN SONG*

—WHITE floating clouds. Clouds like the plains come and water the earth. Sun embrace the earth that she may be fruitful. Moon, lion of the north, bear of the west, badger of the south, wolf of the east, eagle of the heavens, shrew of the earth, elder war hero, younger war hero, warriors of the six mountains of the world, intercede with the cloud people for us, that they may water the earth. Medicine bowl, cloud bowl, and water vase give us your hearts, that the earth may be watered. I make the ancient road of meal, that my song may pass straight over it—the ancient road. White shell bead woman who lives where the sun goes down, mother whirlwind, father Sûs'sistinnako, mother Ya'ya, creator of good thoughts, yellow woman of the north, blue woman of the west, red woman of the south, white woman of the east, slightly yellow woman of the zenith, and dark woman of the nadir, I ask your intercession with the cloud people.

MOJAVE

DREAM TALE**

THE first were Sky and Earth, male and female, who touched far in the west, across the sea. Then were born from them Matavilya, the oldest; Frog, his daughter, who was to cause his death; his younger brother or son Mastamho, his successor and greater than he; and all men and beings. In four strides Matavilya led them upward to Aba'-av'ulypo, "house-post water," in Eldorado Canyon on the Colorado, above Mohave land; the center of the earth, as he found by stretching his arms. There he made his "dark round," the first house. With an unwitting indecency he offended his daughter, and plotting against him, she swallowed his voidings, and he knew that he should die, and told the people. Coyote, always suspected, was sent away for fire, and then Fly, a

*From Mathilde Cox Stevenson, *The Sia,* p. 130.
**From A.L. Kroeber, *Handbook of the Indians of California,* pp. 770-771.

woman, rubbed it on her thigh. Coyote raced back, leaped over Badger, the short man in the ring of people, snatched the god's heart from the pyre, and escaped with it. Mastamho directed the mourning, and, Han'ava, the cicada, first taught how to wail. Korokorapa, also called Hiko or Haiko, "white man," alone had sat unmoved as Matavilya lay dying, now sank into the ground with noise, and returned westward to Pi'in, the place of universal origin.

Matavilya's ashes offended, and wind, hail, and rain failed to obliterate them. In four steps Mastamho strode far north, plunged his cane of breath and spittle into the earth, and the river flowed out. Entering a boat, Mastamho journeyed with mankind to the sea, twisting and tilting the boat or letting it run straight as he wished wide bottom lands or sharp canyons to frame the river. He returned with the people on his arms, surmounted the rising waters to the mountain Akokahumi, trod the water down, and took his followers upstream to the northern end of what was to be the Mohave country. Here he heaped up the great pointed peak Avikwame—more exactly Avikwa'ame—Newberry or Dead Mountain as the Americans call it, where he, too, built himself a house. It is of this house that shamans dream, for here their shadows were as little boys in the face of Mastamho, and received from him their ordained powers, confirmed by tests on the spot. Here, too, Mastamho made the people shout, and the fourth time day and sun and moon appeared.

Then he plotted the death of "sky-rattlesnake," Kammay-aveta, also called Umas-ereha, a great power far south in the sea. Message after message was sent him; he knew that the sickness which he was summoned to cure was pretended; but at last he came, amid rain and thunder, stretching his vast length from ocean to mountain. As his head entered the great house it was cut off. It rolled back to the sea in the hope of reconstituting its living body, but became only an ocean monster; while from his blood and sweat and juices came rattlesnakes and noxious insects whose powers some shamans combat. This was the first shaman killed in the world.

Now Mastamho's work was nearly done. To Walapai, Yavapai, Chemehuevi, Yuma, and Kamia he gave each their land and mountains, their foods, and their speech, and sent them off. The youngest, the Mohave, he taught to farm, to cook in pottery, to speak and count as was best fit for them, and to stay in the country. Then, meditating as to his own end, he stretched his arms, grew into *saksak* the fish eagle, and flew off, without power or recollection, ignorant and infested with vermin.

Navajo

THE CREATION OF THE HORSE*

Something was spread over it. It moved and became alive. It whimpered. Woman-who-changes began to sing:—

Changing Woman I am, I hear.
In the center of my house behind the fire, I hear.
Sitting on jewels spread wide, I hear.
In a jet basket, in a jet house, there now it lies.
Vegetation with its dew in it, it lies.
Over there,
It increases, not hurting the house now with it it lies,
      inside it lies.

THE CORN GROWS UP**

The corn grows up.
The waters of the dark clouds drop, drop.
The rain descends.
The waters from the corn leaves drop, drop.
The rain descends.
The waters from the plants drop, drop.
The corn grows up.
The waters of the dark mists drop, drop.

Imitation of natural sounds was characteristic of much Indian poetry. Here the translator has succeeded quite well in preserving both the hypnotic quality of the poem and the onomatopoeic references to water.

*From Pliny Earle Goddard, *Navajo Texts,* p. 161.
**From Washington Matthews, ''Songs of Sequence,'' p. 191.

HUNTING SONG*

Comes the deer to my singing,
Comes the deer to my song,
Comes the deer to my singing.

He, the blackbird, he am I,
Bird beloved of the wild deer.
    Comes the deer to my singing.

From the Mountain Black
From the summit,
Down the trail, coming, coming now,
    Comes the deer to my singing.

Through the flower dewdrops
Through the flowers, coming, coming now,
  Comes the deer to my singing.

Through the pollen, flower pollen,
    Coming, coming now,
    Comes the deer to my singing.

Starting with his left fore-foot,
Stamping, turns the frightened deer,
    Comes the deer to my singing.

Quarry mine, blessed am I
In the luck of the chase.
    Comes the deer to my singing.

Comes the deer to my singing,
    Comes the deer to my song,
    Comes the deer to my singing.

*From Natalie Curtis, *The Indians' Book*, p. 64.

TSEGIHI: THE HOUSE MADE OF DAWN*

In Tsegihi (oh you who dwell!)
In the house made of the dawn,
In the house made of the evening twilight,
In the house made of the dark cloud,
In the house made of the he-rain,
In the house made of the dark mist,
In the house made of the she-rain,
In the house made of pollen,
In the house made of grasshoppers,
Where the dark mist curtains the doorway,
The path to which is on the rainbow,
Where the zigzag lightning stands high on top,
Where the he-rain stands high on top,
Oh, male divinity!
With your moccasins of dark cloud, come to us.
With your leggings of dark cloud, come to us.
With your shirt of dark cloud, come to us.
With your headdress of dark cloud, come to us.
With your mind enveloped in dark cloud, come to us.
With the dark thunder above you, come to us soaring.
With the shapen cloud at your feet, come to us soaring.
With the far darkness made of the dark cloud over your head, come
    to us soaring.
With the far darkness made of the he-rain over your head, come to us
    soaring.
With the far darkness made of the dark mist over your head, come to
    us soaring.
With the far darkness made of the she-rain over your head, come to
    us soaring.
With the zigzag lightning flung out on high over your head, come to
    us soaring.
With the rainbow hanging high over your head, come to us soaring.
With the far darkness made of the dark cloud on the ends of your wings,
    come to us soaring.
With the far darkness made of the he-rain on the ends of your wings,
    come to us soaring.

*From *Memoirs of the American Folk-Lore Society*, Volume V (1897) pp. 273-275.

With the far darkness made of the dark mist on the ends of your wings,
    come to us soaring.
With the far darkness made of the she-rain on the ends of your wings,
    come to us soaring.
With the zigzag lightning out on high on the ends of your wings,
    come to us soaring.
With the rainbow hanging high on the ends of your wings, come to us
    soaring.
With the near darkness made of the dark cloud, of the he-rain, of the
    dark mist, and of the she-rain, come to us.
With the darkness on the earth, come to us.
With these I wish the foam floating on the flowing water over the roots
    of the great corn.
I have made your sacrifice.
I have prepared a smoke for you.
My feet restore for me.
My limbs restore for me.
My body restore for me.
My mind restore for me.
My voice restore for me.
To-day, take out your spell for me.
To-day, take away your spell for me.
Away from me you have taken it.
Far off from me it is taken.
Far off you have done it.
Happily I recover.
Happily my interior becomes cool.
Happily my limbs regain their power.
Happily my head becomes cool.
Happily my limbs regain their power.
Happily I hear again.
Happily for me (the spell) is taken off.
Happily I walk.
Impervious to pain, I walk.
Feeling light within, I walk.
With lively feelings, I walk.
Happily (or in beauty) abundant dark clouds I desire.
Happily abundant dark mists I desire.
Happily abundant passing showers I desire.
Happily an abundance of vegetation I desire.

Happily an abundance of pollen I desire.

Happily abundant dew I desire.

Happily may fair white corn, to the ends of the earth, come with you.

Happily may fair yellow corn, to the ends of the earth, come with you.

Happily may fair blue corn, to the ends of the earth, come with you.

Happily may fair corn of all kinds, to the ends of the earth, come with you.

Happily may fair plants of all kinds, to the ends of the earth, come with you.

Happily may fair goods of all kinds, to the ends of the earth, come with you.

Happily may fair jewels of all kinds, to the ends of the earth, come with you.

With these before you, happily may they come with you.

With these behind you, happily may they come with you.

With these below you, happily may they come with you.

With these above you, happily may they come with you.

With these all around you, happily may they come with you.

Thus happily you accomplish your tasks.

Happily the old men will regard you.

Happily the old women will regard you.

Happily the young men will regard you.

Happily the young women will regard you.

Happily the boys will regard you.

Happily the girls will regard you.

Happily the children will regard you.

Happily the chiefs will regard you.

Happily, as they scatter in different directions, they will regard you.

Happily, as they approach their homes, they will regard you.

Happily may their roads home be on the trail of pollen (peace).

Happily may they all get back.

In beauty (happily) I walk.

With beauty before me, I walk.

With beauty behind me, I walk.

With beauty below me, I walk.

With beauty above me, I walk.

With beauty all around me, I walk.

It is finished (again) in beauty,

It is finished in beauty,

It is finished in beauty,
It is finished in beauty.

THE BEAVER'S SONG*

I follow the river
In quest of a young beaver.
Up the river I go
Through the cut willow path I go
In quest of a young beaver.

THE BEAR'S SONG*

A foot,
A foot with toes,
A foot with toes came.
He came with a foot with toes.
Aging as he came with a foot with toes.

THE OWL'S SONG*

I am the owl.
I sit on the spruce tree.
My coat is gray.
I have big eyes.
My head has two points.
The white smoke from my tobacco can be seen
As I sit on the spruce tree.
The little rabbit comes in sight,
Nearby where I sit on the spruce tree.
I think soon my claws will get into its back,
As I sit on the spruce tree.
Now it is dawn, now it is dawn.
The old man owl's head has two points.

*From Aileen O'Bryan, *The Diné: Origin Myths of the Navaho Indians,* pp. 66, 67.

He has big, yellowish eyes.
We see white smoke from his tobacco.
Ho, ho! Ho, ho! Ho, ho!

WHITE CORN BOY*

I am the White Corn Boy.
I walk in sight of my home.
I walk in plain sight of my home.
I walk on the straight path which is towards my home.
I walk to the entrance of my home.
I arrive at the beautiful goods curtain which hangs at the doorway.
I arrive at the entrance of my home.
I am in the middle of my home.
I am at the back of my home.
I am on top of the pollen foot print.
I am on top of the pollen seed print.
I am like the Most High Power Whose Ways Are Beautiful.
Before me it is beautiful,
Behind me it is beautiful,
Under me it is beautiful,
Above me it is beautiful,
All around me it is beautiful.

PAPAGO**

A WHITE WIND FROM THE WEST

From the west a white wind is coming out.
Stand there and look, it is not near,
It is beside the ocean, there you will see it.
By the reflected light of the sun you will see it.

*From Aileen O'Bryan, *The Diné: Origin Myths of the Navaho Indians,* p. 156.
**The following poems are from Frances Densmore, *Papago Music*, pp. 86, 110, 114, 141, 142, 165, 173.

SONG CONCERNING THE BLACK SNAKE

A black snake goes toward the west,
It travels erect on its tail,
It sings as it goes toward the west, and coils
    around a mountain.

THE SUNSET

The sun is slowly departing,
It is slower in its setting,
Black bats will be swooping when the sun is gone,
  That is all.

The spirit children are beneath,
They are moving back and forth,
They roll in play among tufts of white eagle down,
    That is all.

WE ARE SINGING IN THE NIGHT

Now as the night is over us we are singing the songs that were given
    to us.
You see the clouds beginning to form on top of the mountains.
They look like little white feathers.
You will see them shake like feathers in a wind.
Soon the raindrops will fall and make our country beautiful.

I AM RUNNING TOWARD THE EDGE OF THE WORLD

I am on my way running,
I am on my way running,
Looking toward me is the edge of the world,
I am trying to reach it,
The edge of the world does not look far away,
To that I am on my way running.

THE WIND BLOWS FROM THE SEA

By the sandy water I breathe in the odor of the sea,
From there the wind comes and blows over the world,
By the sandy water I breathe in the odor of the sea,
From there the clouds come and rain falls over the world.

CLOUDS ARE APPROACHING

Clouds are standing in the east, they are approaching,
It rains in the distance,
Now it is raining here and the thunder rolls.

Green rock mountains are thundering with clouds.
With this thunder the Akim village is shaking.
The water will come down the arroyo and I will float on the water.
Afterwards the corn will ripen in the fields.

Close to the west the great ocean is singing.
The waves are rolling toward me, covered with many clouds.
Even here I catch the sound.
The earth is shaking beneath me and I hear the deep rumbling.

A cloud on top of Evergreen Trees Mountain is singing,
A cloud on top of Evergreen Trees Mountain is standing still,
It is raining and thundering up there,
It is raining here,
Under the mountain the corn tassels are shaking,
Under the mountain the horns of the child corn are glistening.

PICURIS

THE WOMAN AND THE WOLF*

ONCE upon a time the people were dwelling at Picuris. The women, after it got dark, were to remain inside their houses.

And one woman in the night had no water. She took the water jar and went down to Painon to get water. As she was pouring the water with her gourd, a Wolf came to her. "What are you doing?" he said. "I am pouring water," the woman said to the Wolf. "Get on my back, then," the Wolf said to her. "I am already about to take the water to my house," said the woman. "Get on my back, I said to you, or I will eat you up right here." The woman got afraid, left the water jar, and got on the Wolf's back.

And the Wolf took the woman up to the mountains. When he had brought her to the mountain top, the Wolf went northeast, northwest, southwest, and southeast, to call the other wolves. The woman then climbed a tall pinyon tree.

Her husband, when his wife did not come up from below quickly, yelled as a signal from the top of the house. And shortly men with their weapons arrived.

When the Old Wolf arrived from his summoning [the other wolves], the woman was sitting in the top of the pinyon tree.

The men all gathered for search. And then at about midnight one man found the woman. Then the man gave a yell. After the rest came they took the woman home again. The woman was scolded very much by the men. And this is why the women, after it gets dark, do not go forth from inside the houses alone, for something might happen to them.

THE ANTS**

Once upon a time at Komaithotha dwelt the Ants. No birds came around there, and so they lived without fear. They went wherever they pleased without fear, for there was not even a little Hummingbird around near where they lived.

*From J.P. Harrington and Helen H. Roberts, *Picuris Children's Stories*, p. 355.
**From J.P. Harrington and Helen H. Roberts, *Picuris Children's Stories with Texts and Songs*, p. 357.

One day their leader told them at a meeting: "My people, in four days from to-day we are going to dance here in this land of ours; we will entertain the other people. So you must be looking for such things as red paint, beads, war bonnets, and whatever dress you may need. And we will call the flying animals of all kinds here to look on." As their leader instructed them thus, they said: "It seems all right the way you say, we will get ready to dance four days from to-day." And the Ants were getting ready within that time. They went around borrowing things from their neighbors whom they knew.

On the fourth day the leader assembled them in their estufa. And they then were told: "My people, to-morrow the day arrives on which we are to dance, so the flying animals of every kind are to come here to our home to look on. And so you must all do your best."

The next morning as the sun was rising the Ants gathered in their estufa. After they were all assembled, both men and women, all dressed up nicely, emerged from the estufa. When they looked around at the trees, there were birds of every kind sitting there.

They were only dancing a little while when all the Eagles, who were sitting looking on, flew to the ground where the Ants were dancing, and being hungry, began to eat the Ants up. After they had enough, they flew away to their homes. The leader of the Ants said to the people: "Dance your best, my people, for there are many people looking on."

When he had hardly finished saying thus, the Redtail Hawks, from where they were sitting looking on, flew down to where the Ants were dancing, and began to eat up the Ants. When they got enough, they all flew away to their homes. The leader of the Ants said to them: "My people, dance your best, for there are many people looking on."

When he had hardly finished saying thus, the Buzzards, from where they were sitting looking on, flew down to where the Ants were dancing, and began to eat the Ants. When they got enough, they all flew away to their homes. By that time there were very few of the Ants left, but they would not quit dancing. They danced all the more. Their leader said to them: "My people, dance your best, for there are still many people looking on."

When he had hardly finished saying thus, the Turkeys, from where they were sitting looking on, flew down to where the Ants were dancing, and began to eat the Ants up. When they got enough, they all flew away to their homes. By that time there were but few of the Ants left. But they danced their best. Their leader said to them: "My people, dance your best, for there are still many people who are looking on."

When he had hardly finished saying thus, the Bluebirds, from where they were sitting in the trees looking on, flew down to where the Ants were dancing, and ate the Ants that were left, together with their leader. And then the Bluebirds all flew away to their homes.

And the other birds who were looking on flew away. Because there were no more Ants left for them, they all said: "Since the other birds have not left us any Ants, let us also go and look for some." When the birds who were sitting looking on said thus, they all scattered to look for Ants.

So this is the reason that the birds to-day hunt around for ants, and also the reason that birds like ants, because they ate the ants at that time.

THE SPHYNX MOTH AND THE OLD COYOTE*

There once lived at Picuris Pueblo a Sphynx Moth and his grandmother. The Sphynx Moth was a great believer; he believed everything concerning the customs of the people. And he was very obedient to his grandmother; he would go wherever his grandmother would tell him, without talking back.

Once his grandmother said to him: "My grandson, you must make plumeros to-night and take them to Kan'in'ai, to the southeast, early to-morrow morning. The Picuris youths and even Picuris maidens take their plumeros there and supplicate. So early to-morrow morning you must carry these plumeros and go there to supplicate." So that night the Sphynx Moth made plumeros the way his grandmother had told him.

Early the next morning, carrying the plumeros, he set out for Kan'in'ai, to the southeast. As he went along through the fields, he met Old Coyote, who was hunting around. "Good morning, where are you going?" the Old Coyote said to the Sphynx Moth. "I am going over southeast to Kan'in'ai," said the Sphynx Moth. "What is it that you are carrying?" said the Old Coyote to the Sphynx Moth. Then the Sphynx Moth said: "I am carrying my dead grandmother over southeast to Kan'in'ai." Then the Old Coyote said: "Then wait here for me, for I am going to get my grandmother."

As Old Coyote told the Sphynx Moth thus, he ran toward Teiuthotha where his own grandmother was. When he arrived there he hunted for

*From J.P. Harrington and Helen H. Roberts, *Picuris Children's Stories with Texts and Songs*, pp. 363-365.

a bag and went inside the house where his grandmother was toasting corn meal. And he said to his grandmother: "Grandmother, get into this bag!" But the grandmother would not get into it. "Get in here, I tell you," said Old Coyote to his grandmother. But his grandmother would not get in. The Old Coyote said: "If you do not get in, I will hit you on the head with a fire poker and then put you in this bag." The Old Coyote told his grandmother thus several times, but he soon got disgusted and, taking the fire poker which was lying by the fireplace, he struck his grandmother, where she was sitting toasting the corn meal, and then putting her into the bag and carrying her, he brought his grandmother over to where the Sphynx Moth was waiting for him. "Now we shall both take our grandmothers over southeast to Kan'in'ai," said the Old Coyote to the Sphynx Moth. The Sphynx Moth assented.

Then they both started off to Kan'in'ai, to the southeast. As they went along talking on the road they reached Kan'in'ai. There in a rocky place the Sphynx Moth dug, and laid his plumeros. When the Old Coyote noticed what the Sphynx Moth was doing, he discovered that instead of a dead grandmother it was plumeros that he was laying under a rock. And the Old Coyote said to himself: "This Sphynx Moth has told me a lie. Instead of having a dead grandmother in his bag, he is putting the plumeros under the rock. Now, I will go over there where he is and bite him." As the Sphynx Moth heard him saying thus, he flew away. Then the Old Coyote was very angry, and he said to himself: "That accursed Sphynx Moth, it is on account of him that I have killed my grandmother." As the Sphynx Moth disappeared as soon as he flew, the Old Coyote did not know what to do. Again he packed his grandmother on his back, and started for home. He was crying as he went along the road.

As he reached home, his children heard him crying from where they were playing, and said to each other: "But why is it that our father is so happy? He is coming along the road singing. Let us all go to meet him." As they said thus, the little Coyotes went to meet their father. When they met him, they asked him: "Our father, why are you so happy? Why are you coming along singing so loud?" Then their father told them: "My children, I am not coming along singing, but I am coming along crying. It is on account of that accursed Sphynx Moth that I have killed my grandmother by hitting her on the head, because he told me a lie. If I had known this, I would have bitten him while I had a chance." As their father told the little Coyotes thus, they all joined crying. The

Old Coyote carried his grandmother into the house and set her down again at the fireplace where she had sat toasting corn meal, and gave her the corn meal toasting sticks and told her, although she was dead: "Now, grandmother, finish toasting your corn meal!" As he would set her down she would topple over again, and at last the Old Coyote got more angry, and he took the fire poker and struck his grandmother again on the head, to be sure that she had been killed. Then he put her on his back and took her to the arroyo to bury her.

So this is the reason that coyotes nowadays are smart, because they learned this kind of work long ago; this is the reason that the coyotes are smarter than any other four-footed animal.

You have a tale.

PIMA

HOW TURQUOISES WERE OBTAINED BY
CHIEF MORNING GREEN*

ONE day, long ago, the women and girls of Casa Grande were playing an ancient game called *toka,* formerly much in vogue at Casa Grande, but now no longer played by Pima. During the progress of the game a blue-tailed lizard was noticed descending into the earth at a spot where the stones were green. The fact was so strange that it was reported to Morning Green, who immediately ordered excavation to be made. Here they eventually discovered many turquoises, with which they made, among other things, a mosaic covering for a chair that used to stand in one of the rooms of Casa Grande. This chair was carried away many years ago and buried, no one knows where.

Morning Green also distributed so many turquoises among his people that the fame of these precious stones reached the ears of the Sun, in the East, who sent the bird with bright plumage (parrot?) to obtain them. When Parrot approached within a short distance of Casa Grande he was met by one of the daughters of the chief, who returned to the town and announced to her father the arrival of a visitor from the Sun. The father said, "Take this small stick, which is charmed, and when Parrot puts the

*From Jesse Walter Fewkes, *Casa Grande, Arizona,* pp. 46-47.

stick into his mouth, you lead him to me.'' But Parrot was not charmed by the stick and refused to take it into his mouth and the girl reported her failure. The chief answered, ''Perhaps the strange bird would eat pumpkin seed,'' and told his daughter to offer these to him. She made the attempt without result and, returning, reported that the bird refused pumpkin seed. The father then said, ''Put the seed into a blanket and spread it before the bird; then perhaps you may capture him.'' Still Parrot would not eat, and the father thereupon suggested watermelon seeds. But Parrot was not tempted by these nor by seeds of cat's claw, nor was he charmed by charcoal.

The chief of Casa Grande then told his daughter to tempt Parrot with corn well cooked and soaked in water, in a new food-bowl. Parrot was obdurate and would not taste it, but, noticing a turquoise bead of blue-green color, he swallowed it; when the two daughters of the chief saw this they brought to him a number of blue stones, which the bird greedily devoured. Then the girls brought valuable turquoise beads, which Parrot ate; then he flew away. The girls tried to capture him, but without success. He made his way through the air to the home of the Sun in the East, where he drank an emetic and vomited the turquoises, which the Sun god distributed among that people which reside near his house of rising, beyond the eastern mountains. This is the reason, it is said, why these people have many stone ornaments made of this material.

But when the chief of Casa Grande heard that Parrot had been sent to steal his turquoises, he was greatly vexed and caused a violent rain to fall that extinguished all fires in the East. His magic power over the Rain god was so great that he was able even to extinguish the light of the Sun, making it very cold. Then the old priests gathered in council and debated what they should do. Man-Fox was first sent by them into the East to get fire, but he failed to obtain it, and then Road-runner was commissioned to visit Thunder, the only one that possessed fire, and steal his lighted torch. But when Thunder saw him running off with the torch he shot an arrow at the thief and sparks of fire were scattered around, setting afire every tree, bush, and other inflammable object, from which it happens that there is fire in everything.

In the legends of the Hopi turquoises were believed to be the excrement of reptiles. Charcoal is regarded by the fire priests as possessing most powerful magic in healing diseases, especially those of the skin in which there is a burning sensation.

HOW MORNING GREEN LOST HIS POWERS OVER THE WIND GODS AND THE RAIN GODS*

Morning Green is reputed to have had special magic power over two supernatural beings, known as Wind-man and Rain-man. It happened at one time that many people were playing a game with canes in the main plaza of Morning Green's settlement [Casa Grande], on the south side of the compound; among these were Rain-man and Wind-man. The latter laid a wager that if he lost, his opponent should look on the charms of a certain maid. When Wind-man lost, in revenge he sent a great wind that blew aside her blanket, at which indignity she cried and complained of Wind-man to Morning Green, who was so angry that he made Rain-man blind, obliging him to be led about by his servant, the wind; he also banished both from Casa Grande. They went to the San Bernardino Mountains in what is now California and lived at Eagle Mountain, near the present town of Wadsworth, where as a consequence it rains continually.

After the banishment of these two the rain ceased at Casa Grande for four years, and Morning Green sent Humming-bird to the mountains where Wind-man and Rain-man resided. Humming-bird carried with him a white feather, which he held aloft to detect the presence of the wind. Three times he thus tried to discover Wind-man by the movement of this feather, but was not successful. When at last Humming-bird came to a place where there was much green grass he again held up the feather to see whether it showed any movement of the air. It responded by indicating a slight wind, and later he came to the spot where Wind-man and Rain-man were, but found them asleep.

Humming-bird dropped a little medicine on the breasts of Wind-man and Rain-man, which caused them after a time to move and later to awake. When they had risen from their sleep Humming-bird informed them that Morning Green had sent him to ask them to return and again take up their abode with him at Casa Grande. Rain-man, who had no desire to return, answered, "Why did Morning Green send us away?" and Wind-man said, "Return to Morning Green and tell him to cut off his daughter's hair and make from it a rope. Bring this rope to me and I will tie it about my loins that Rain-man, who is blind, may catch hold of it while I am leading him. But advise all in Casa Grande to take the precaution to repair the roofs of their houses so they will not leak, for when we arrive it will rain violently." Humming-bird delivered the mes-

*From Jesse Walter Fewkes, *Casa Grande, Arizona*, pp. 47-48.

sage to the chief of Casa Grande and later brought back the twisted rope of human hair. Wind-man and Rain-man had barely started for Casa Grande when it began to rain, and for four days the downpour was so great that every roof leaked. Morning Green vainly used all his power to stop the rain, but the magic availed but little.

THE BIRTH OF HOK*

Long ago the Sun god sent a messenger on an errand to the settlement now called Casa Grande. As this messenger proceeded on his way he occupied himself in kicking a stone ball, and on approaching Casa Grande he gave the ball so violent a kick that it landed near a maiden who sat on the housetop making pottery. Seeing the object, the girl picked it up and hid it under her belt. When the man sought the stone it was nowhere to be found; he asked the girl if she knew where it fell, but she would not divulge what had become of it. Discouraged in his quest, the man was about to return to the Sun god, but the girl urged him not to depart but to search more diligently for the ball. She also sought for it, but it was no longer under her belt; it had disappeared. Later she was with child and in due time gave birth to a girl baby, which, instead of feet and hands, had claws like a bear or a mountain lion. As this strange child grew older and played with other boys and girls she scratched them so often with her claws that they were afraid of her, and ran away whenever she appeared. The brothers of the girl were hunters of rabbits, but were unsuccessful. When their sister grew older she followed them to the hunt and their luck changed, so that thenceforth they killed plenty of game. As she matured, however, she outgrew all restraint and became a wild woman. She was then called Hok, and developed into a cannibal monster, who captured her victims wherever she went and carried them in a basket on her back until she wished to devour them. Hok once met two youths, whom she tried to capture, but they ran swiftly away and when she made another attempt they blinded her by throwing sand in her eyes. This monster terrorized the whole country to such an extent that the ancients sought her life, but in vain. The culture-hero, Tchuhu, endeavored to kill Hok. He turned himself into a snake and

*From Jesse Walter Fewkes, *Casa Grande, Arizona*, pp. 48-49.

furnished the children with rattles; when Hok approached them they shook these rattles and frightened her. Hok first retired to a distant cave in the Santa Catalina Mountains, but later went south to Poso Verde. The people living there were also oppressed by Hok and desired to kill her. Tcuhu sent word to his uncle that there was to be a dance at Casa Grande and asked him to invite Hok to attend. This was a kind of ceremonial dance in which men and women participate, forming a circle and alternating with each other. Several invitations were sent to Hok, but she did not accept; at last she promised to attend the dance and to be there at sunset. Tcuhu danced and smoked with Hok, and the festivities lasted four days and nights. While she was absent the women gathered wood and made a fire in the cave where Hok lived. When she discovered what had taken place she flew to the top of her cave and entered it through a crack open to the sky. At the opening Tcuhu stood so as to prevent Hok's escape and slew her as she emerged.

A CREATION LEGEND*

In the beginning all was dark and there was neither earth nor sky. Earth Doctor (Tcuwut Marka) was the only being then living.

Earth Doctor took a particle of sweat from his body and made from it a small disk, which he held in his hand and started to go to the west. When he stopped, the sweat showed signs of life, for it trembled; he proceeded and still the material moved. He halted four times in his course and as he stopped the fourth time the disk, which was the nucleus of the earth, became stable, and neither trembled nor wavered. He then knew he was at the middle point of the universe. Earth Doctor then made a bush and created small ants to feed on it. He took a louse from his breast and put it at the root of the bush. This insect found a ring of soil that kept growing larger and larger as Earth Doctor danced near it, until it became the earth. In the same way the solid sky was formed. Earth Doctor pounded "medicine" in a bowl and shortly afterward there appeared over the surface a transparent substance resembling ice. Earth Doctor threw this substance toward the north, where it fell but shortly afterward rose again and then sank below the horizon. He then cast another fragment to the west and it fell below the horizon, never to rise again. He threw another frag-

*From Jesse Walter Fewkes, *Casa Grande, Arizona*, p. 49.

ment into the south; this struck the earth or sky and bounded back, whereupon he picked it up and again threw it to the south. This time it rose and passed over the sky. These fragments became the sun and the moon, both formed in the same way. Earth Doctor spurted a mouthful of medicine-water into the sky and created the stars, first the larger and then the smaller, the last of all being nebulae like the Milky Way. Having formed the celestial bodies, he made seeds of all good used by man, after which he created men and women from a particle of sweat or grease from his body.

Buzzard Doctor lives in the Underworld, where there are many people similar to those who inhabit the earth. The entrance [*sipapu*] to this underworld is in the east.

As soon as men and women had been created they began to quarrel; this angered Earth Doctor and he put them to death. After he had killed all human beings, Earth Doctor and Buzzard emerged together from the Underworld and the former begged the latter to help him re-create men and women. The result was men who were gray-haired at birth. Earth Doctor again destroyed man because he smoked too much, but on the fourth trial there emerged from the earth four men who later became great medicine-men—Land, Buzzard, Tcuhu, and Tohouse.

The youth Tcuhu became a great warrior and married many women, whom he deserted before children were born.

SKULL AND HIS MAGIC*

Once there was a pretty girl who was unwilling to marry anyone. All the young men brought presents of game to her parents, but none found favor in the eyes of the critical maiden. At last to the surprise of neighbors and kinsmen she chose for her husband one who was a man by night and a skull by day. Then all laughed at the marriage, saying, "One man in this valley has a bone for a son-in-law."

One morning the crier of the village made this proclamation: "To-day we hunt deer in the mountains to the northward!" Skull went ahead of the party and hid in a defile in the mountains. When the hunters came driving the game before them the deer all fell dead at the sight of gruesome Skull; so the people had an abundance of venison without the trouble of trailing and killing. Thus it was that Skull rose in their regard and ridicule was no longer heaped upon him.

*From Frank Russell, *The Pima Indians*, p. 241.

The next day had been appointed for the foot race in which the runners would kick the ball. Skull entered as one of the contestants, though his neighbors laughed and said: "How can one ball manage another?" But when he reached the goal a winner the last voice of contumely was silenced.

THE NAUGHTY GRANDCHILDREN*

An old woman had two bright grandchildren. She ground wheat and corn every morning to make porridge for them. One day as she put the olla on the fire outside the house, she told the children not to fight for fear they would upset the water. But they soon began quarreling, for they did not mind as well as they should, and so spilled the water, and the grandmother had to whip them. They became angry and said they were going away. She tried to make them understand why she had to whip them, but they would not listen and ran away. She ran after them, but could not catch up. She heard them whistling and followed the sound from place to place, until finally the oldest boy said, "I will turn into a saguaro, so I shall last forever, and bear fruit every summer." And the younger said, "Well, I will turn into a palo verde and stand there forever. These mountains are so bare and have nothing on them but rocks, so I will make them green." The old woman heard the cactus whistling and recognized the voice of her grandson; so she went up to it and tried to take it into her arms, and the thorns killed her.

And that is how the saguaro and palo verde came to be.

THE CREATION OF THE EARTH**

Earth Magician shapes this world.
　　Behold what he can do!
Round and smooth he molds it.
　　Behold what he can do!
Earth Magician makes the mountains.
　　Heed what he has to say!

*From Frank Russell, *The Pima Indians*, p. 247.
**From Frank Russell, *The Pima Indians*, p. 285.

He it is that makes the mesas.
    Heed what he has to say.
Earth Magician shapes this world;
Earth Magician makes its mountains;
Makes all larger, larger, larger.
    Into the earth the Magician glances;
Into its mountains he may see.

GOPHER SONG: I STIR THE AIR*

In the reddish glow of nightfall,
    In the reddish glow of nightfall
I return to my burrow,
    About which the flowers bloom.

With the four eagle feathers,
    With the four eagle feathers
I stir the air. When I turn
    My magic power is crossed.

AT THE TIME OF THE WHITE DAWN**

At the time of the White Dawn;
At the time of the White Dawn;
I arose and went away.
At Blue Nightfall I went away.

I ate the thorn apple leaves
And the leaves made me dizzy.
I drank the thorn apple flowers
And the drink made me stagger.

The hunter, Bow-Remaining,
He overtook and killed me,
Cut and threw my horse away.

*From Frank Russell, *The Pima Indians,* p. 319.
**From Frank Russell, *The Pima Indians,* pp. 299-300.

The hunter, Reed-Remaining,
He overtook and killed me,
Cut and threw my feet away.

Now the flies become crazy
     And they drop with flapping wings.
The drunken butterflies sit
     With open and shutting wings.

BLACK MOCKING BIRD*

Is it in this condition that we are sitting here, understanding the advice of our forefathers? There is an unknown house in which lies the magic brand; toward this we point the ceremonial cigarette and smoke, thus acquiring an insight that shall enable us to speak wisely.

When the earth was new it was shaking and rough. As you know, Black Mocking Bird lives in the west. I had considered my relationship to him and guessed what should be the right manner in which to address him. Because of my entreaty he was disposed to be friendly toward me.

Yes, Black Mocking Bird, if your plans for controlling the earth have failed, go far hence and leave the black wind and the black clouds behind you. Your people will henceforth entreat your assistance from a distance.

When the land was new I knew of a Blue Mocking Bird in the south, and I called on him also for help, and he came. He gave commands to control the hills, mountains, trees, everything. But still the earth continued shaking.

Yes, Blue Mocking Bird, if your plans have failed, go hence and leave the blue wind and blue clouds behind you. Your people will henceforth entreat your assistance from a distance.

Then I knew the White Mocking Bird in the east, and I called on him for help, and he came, bringing commands that would control the hills, mountains, trees, everything. But the earth continued shaking.

Yes, White Mocking Bird, if your plans for controlling the earth have failed, go hence and leave the white winds and the white clouds behind you. Your people will henceforth entreat your assistance from a distance.

Then, above me enveloped in darkness lived the magician Kuvik, on whom I called for help. He came in a friendly spirit, with commands

*From Frank Russell, *The Pima Indians*, pp. 347-352.

that would control the hills, mountains, trees, everything. The earth became much quieter, but still moved somewhat.

Then, there was a Gray Spider in the west. I called on him for assistance. He was friendly to me and came in answer to my appeal. He took bundles of sticks, which he placed in the edges of the land and sewed them firmly together. He pulled the black corner at the west, where stands the house of the Rain god of the west. He firmly enveloped the earth with his black power. He pulled the blue corner at the south, where stands the house of the Rain god of the south. He firmly enveloped the earth with his blue power. He pulled the white corner at the east, where stands the house of the Rain god of the east. He firmly enveloped the earth with his white power, and with that the earth became quieter.

Then, in the west there was a Black Measuring Worm that was friendly to me and came in answer to my entreaty. He came in four strides and in short broken lengths stood up as crotched posts. In the south there was a Blue Measuring Worm that was friendly to me and came in answer to my entreaty. He came in four strides and in short broken lengths formed the joists to lie upon the posts. In the east there was a White Measuring Worm that was friendly to me and he came in four strides in answer to my entreaty. He in short broken lengths covered the joists with a layer of small poles. In the north there was a Reddish Measuring Worm that was friendly to me and came in four strides in answer to my entreaty. He in short broken lengths covered the other parts in a curved outer layer, thus finishing the framework.

Then, in the west there was a Blue Gopher who came with plenty of brush which he placed layer above layer around the house, covering it as with thin clouds. Around the house were four gopher hills with which he covered it with earth in a thin, even layer, as snow covers the ground. Looking around the earth I selected one to take me up like a little boy and place me in the house. He placed a brand of fire down before me and a cigarette also. Lighting the cigarette he puffed smoke toward the east in a great white arch. The shadow of the arch crept across the earth beneath. A grassy carpet covers the earth. Scattering seed, he caused the corn with the large stalk, large leaf, full tassel, good ears to grow and ripen. Then he took it and stored it away. As the sun's rays extend to the plants, so our thoughts reached out to the time when we would enjoy the life-giving corn. With gladness we cooked and ate the corn and, free from hunger and want, were happy. Your worthy sons and daughters, knowing nothing of the starvation periods, have been happy. The old men and the old women will have their lives prolonged yet day after day by the possession of corn.

People must unite in desiring rain. If it rains their land shall be as a garden, and they will not be as poor as they have been.

TEWA

LONG SASH AND HIS PEOPLE*

THE bright star that rises in the east soon after autumn sunset is Long Sash, who guided the ancestors of the Pueblos from the north to their present home. He was a famous warrior, and the people followed him because they knew he could lead them in defense against their enemies. Someone was always attacking the villages, and wrecking the fields. The enemies captured women and children for slaves, and killed many of the men, until Long Sash came to the rescue.

"Take us away from here," the people begged him. "Lead us to a new land, where we can live peacefully."

"My children," Long Sash said, "are you sure you want to leave? Life is hard here, I know, but it will not be easy anywhere. There will be dangers on the way if you travel. Some will be sick; many will be hungry and thirsty; perhaps some of you may die. Think, and be sure you want to take that risk."

"We will face any hardships," the people promised him. "Only lead us away from this dark country, to a place where we may have light and life of our own."

So Long Sash started out, and the people followed him. They set their feet on the Endless Trail that stretches like a white band across the sky. This was the road they were going to follow until they found a place of their own.

As the people traveled along the Endless Trail with Long Sash, they began to grow tired and discouraged. Some of them quarreled with one another. They had little clothing and less food. Long Sash had to teach

*From Alice Marriot and C. K. Rachlin, *American Indian Mythology*, pp. 59-62.

his followers how to hunt for food, and how to make clothing from feathers. At last he led them to a country that was so new that even Long Sash had never been there before.

In this new country there was no darkness, it was daylight all the time. The people walked and walked, and when they were too tired to go on they rested. Children were born and old people died and still they journeyed.

The quarrels grew more bitter, and the people began to fight among themselves, exchanging blows and inflicting wounds. At last Long Sash said to them, "This must stop. You are hurting yourselves worse than your enemies hurt you. If you are to come to the place of your own, there can never be violence among you. Now you must decide. We will stop here and rest. Many of the women are ready to have their babies. We will wait until the children are delivered and the mothers are strong. Then you must make your own decision, whether you will follow me or take another trail."

There where the two very bright stars are north of Long Sash in the sky, the people rested and made up their minds. Those two bright stars became known as the Place of Decision, and people look up to them for help today, when they come to the turning points in their lives. We all have decisions to make as long as we are on the earth: good or bad forward or backward, kind or unkind. Those stars can tell us what to do.

When the people had rested and felt stronger, they were ready to go ahead with Long Sash. They told him so, and everybody went forward again. Long Sash watched, to be sure that his children traveled with good hearts and love toward each other.

But Long Sash himself was growing tired, and his own heart was empty and doubting. He heard strange voices speaking in his mind, and could not tell who spoke, or what they were trying to say to him. At last he decided to answer the voices. As he spoke to the unseens, his own people gathered around him to listen.

"Show me a sign to tell me who you are, fathers and mothers," Long Sash began. "My people are tired and I am growing old. Give me a word to tell me we are on the right path and will soon reach our home."

Then while his people watched him, frightened, Long Sash appeared to go to sleep. He dropped down where he had been sitting and his eyes were closed. He lay without moving while the people stayed beside him, because they did not know what to do. They grew more and more afraid.

At last Long Sash opened his eyes. He looked at the people who had gathered around him while he slept. "Don't be frightened," Long Sash told them. "I have been given many signs and promises. The worst part of your journey is over, and we will soon reach its end."

"That's good. Thank you," all the people said.

"Many people will reach this Place of Doubt in their lives," Long Sash went on. "When that happens, you should pray to the Above Persons, your fathers and mothers, for help and for guidance. In order to remind you of that, I will leave my headdress here, where people can look up and see it."

He laid his headdress down, and it became a bright, comforting cluster of stars.

And so the people went on traveling, and all the story of their journey is told in the stars above. Where there are three bright stars close together, they represent two young men who made a drag and fastened their load on it. Then, because there were two of them, they could add an old woman's load to the other two, and go on, pulling three loads on the drag. Those stars are a reminder of the helpfulness of the young men, and of their thoughtfulness of other people.

At last the people came to the end of their journey, and to the Middle Place which was to be their home forever.

SONG OF THE SKY LOOM*

O Our Mother the Earth, O Our Father the Sky
Your children are we and with tired backs
We bring you the gifts you love.
Then weave for us a garment of brightness
May the warp be the white light of morning
May the weft be the red light of evening
May the fringes be the falling rain
May the border be the standing rainbow.
Thus weave for us a garment of brightness
That we may walk fittingly where grass is green
O Our Mother the Earth, O Our Father the Sky.

*From Herbert J. Spinden, *Songs of the Tewa*, p. 6.

ZUNI

CREATION MYTH*

IN the beginning A'wonawil'ona with the Sun Father and Moon Mother existed above, and Shi'wanni and Shi'wano'kia, his wife, below. Shi'wanni and Shi'wano'kia were superhuman beings who labored not with hands but with hearts and minds. The rain priests of Zuñi are called A'shiwanni and the Priestess of Fecundity is called Shi'wano'kia, to indicate that they do no secular work; they give their minds and hearts to higher thoughts in order that their bodies be so purified they may enter into communion with the gods.

All was shi'pololo (fog), rising like steam. With the breath from his heart A'wonawil'ona created clouds and the great waters of the world. He-She is the blue vault of the firmament. The breath clouds of the gods are tinted with the yellow of the north, the blue-green of the west, the red of the south, and the silver of the east of A'wonawil'ona. The smoke clouds of white and black became a part of A´wonawil´ona; they are himself, as he is the air itself; and when the air takes on the form of a bird it is but a part of himself—is himself. Through the light, clouds, and air he becomes the essence and creator of vegetation. The Zuñi conception of A'wonawil'ona is similar to that of the Greeks of Athena.

It is not strange, therefore, that the A'shiwi cover their altars with symbols of cumulus and nimbus clouds, with "the flame of the cloud crest," and "the blue of the deep wells of the sky," and use all these, woven into plumes, to waft their prayers to the gods, and have as their symbol of life, embracing all the mysterious life-securing properties, including mystery medicine, an ear of corn clothed in beautiful plumage; for the spirit of A'wonawil'ona is "put into and upon this created form." The name of this symbol, mi'li, is but another word for corn, and the et'tone, the most sacred fetish of the A'shiwanni, is another symbol of life, including rain and vegetation.

While every Zuñi is taught that in inhaling the sacred breath from his fetishes or in breathing upon the plumes he offers to the gods he is receiving from A'wonawil'ona the breath of life or is wafting his own breath

*From Mathilde Cox Stevenson, *The Zuñi Indians,* pp. 23-31.

prayers to his gods, only the few have any conception of all that is implied in their observances or fully appreciate the poetic nature of their myths.

After A'wonawil'ona created the clouds and the great waters of the world, Shi'wanni said to Shi'wano'kia: "I, too, will make something beautiful, which will give light at night when the Moon Mother sleeps." Spitting in the palm of his left hand, he patted the spittle with the fingers of his right hand, and the spittle foamed like yucca suds and then formed into bubbles of many colors, which he blew upward; and thus he created the fixed stars and constellations. And Shi'wanni was well pleased with his creation. Then Shi'wano'kia said, "See what I can do," and she expectorated into the palm of her left hand and slapped the saliva with the fingers of her right, and the spittle foamed like yucca suds, running over her hand and flowing everywhere; and thus she created A'witelin 'Si'ta (Earth Mother).

Creation of the A'shiwi and Their Coming to the Outer World

Shi'wanni and Shi'wano'kia were the parents of the A'shiwi, who were created in the undermost world, being born as infants; not, however, at long intervals, but in rapid succession, until many were born.

Yätokia (Sun Father) created two sons, Kow'wituma and Wats'usi, by impregnating two bits of foam with his rays. These Divine Ones ascended to their Sun Father over a road of meal, which they made by throwing the meal upward.

The Sun Father, wishing to bring his children from the undermost world to his presence, provided each of the Divine Ones with an a'mitolan pi'"länne (rainbow), wil'lolonanne sho'liwe (lightning arrows), and a 'kia'alänne (cloud shield), and directed them to go to the undermost world and bring his children to his presence. They rent the earth with their lightning arrows and descended into A'witente'hula (fourth world).

When the A'shiwi inquired of the Divine Ones "Who are you? Whence did you come?" they replied "A'chi ana pi'akoa" ("The two come down").

The undermost world was so dark that the people could not see one another, and they trod upon one another's toes. Their houses were but holes in the earth, and their food was seed grass. In order to see the people Kow'wituma laid dry grass upon the ground and placed his bow on the grass, and by rubbing his arrow, with a rotary motion, upon the bow he produced fire, and lighted the grass, using it as a torch to carry about among the people. Many could not look on the fire, for their eyes were not good for light, while others fell back crazed with fear. Kow'wituma said: "You have but few people." The elder ones replied "We have many," and they called those who were absent.

The Divine Ones, throwing out a line of meal, produced light, which guided them to the north, where they cut an ä'shekia (pine tree of the north, Pinus ponderosa var. scapulorum) with stone knives, and returning, planted it for the people to ascend to the third world, A'wishote'hula (water-moss world). Here the Divine Ones threw out meal to the west, which produced light to guide them thither; and there they cut a kia'lä'silo (spruce of the west, Pseudotsuga douglassii), and returning, they planted it for the people to ascend to the second world, Pä'nanula te'hula (mud world). Here the Divine Ones, led by the line of meal which they threw out, went to the south and cut a 'hlan'ilkoha (aspen of the south, the quaking aspen, Populus tremuloides) and returning, they planted it for the people to ascend to the first world, La'tow'te'hua (wing world; from yä'tokia la'towwe, sun's wings, the rays of the sun being referred to as wings). It was in this world that the A'shiwi first saw the faintest light of day; hence the name. Throwing out a line of meal to the east, the Divine Ones visited this direction, where they cut a lo'kwimo (spruce of the east, silver spruce, Picca pungens), and returning, they planted it for the people to ascend and then returned to the painting and, taking their seats resumed their prayers. At this time Mo'yächun'hlan'na (Great Star, the morning star), the first warrior to the Sun Father, could be seen, but faintly at first through the delicate showers. When the people saw the star they exclaimed "Our Father comes," but the Divine Ones declared "He is not your Sun Father, but his warrior who comes before." Later, when the sun appeared, the people fell on their faces in fear; but the Divine Ones cried: "Be not afraid; it is your Sun Father."

At this time the Kia'kwemosi went over the eastern road and, planting te'likinawe (prayer plumes) which the Sun Father had sent him by the Divine Ones, prayed, saying: "My Sun Father, my Moon Mother. I give to you te'likinawe."

Te'hula refers only to underworlds. Unl'onannē is the term for the outer world, or this world. The undermost world bears several other names: An'nociyan te'hula (world of utter darkness, blackness of soot world); Lu'hote kía'pínna; lu'hote (fine earth or dust); kía'pínna (uncooked, not hardened by fire).

PRAYER OF WAR*

He lived and grew to maturity,
By virtue of the corn priests' rain
      prayers
(He becomes valuable;)
Indeed, the enemy,
Though in his life
He was a person given to falsehood,

He has become one to foretell
How the world will be,
How the days will be.
That during his time,
We may have good days,
Beautiful days,

Hoping for this;
We shall keep his days.
Indeed, if we are lucky,
During the enemy's time
Fine rain caressing the earth,
Heavy rain caressing the earth,
(We shall win.)
When the enemy's days are in
      progress,
The enemy's waters,
We shall win,
His seeds we shall win,
His riches we shall win,
His power,
His strong spirit,
His long life,
His old age,
In order to win these,

Tirelessly, unwearied,
We shall pass his days.
Now, indeed, the enemy,
Even one who thought himself a
      man,
In a shower of arrows,

*From Ruth L. Bunzel, *Zuñi Origin Myths,* p. 680.

In a shower of war clubs,
With bloody head,
The enemy,
Reaching the end of his life,
Added to the flesh of our earth
     mother.

Although the Zuñi were not particularly warlike, they too invented chants glorifying the warpath and asking the aid of powerful forces in their battles. Here the death of the enemy is seen as a form of enrichment for the Zuñi, an offering to the earth that will, hopefully, be rewarded.

PRAYER AT SUNRISE*

Now this day,
My sun father,
Now that you have come out stand-
    ing to your sacred place,
That from which we draw the water
    of life,
Prayer meal,
Here I give to you.
Your long life,
Your old age,
Your waters,
Your seeds,
Your riches,
Your power,
Your strong spirit,
All these to me may you grant.

PRESENTING AN INFANT TO THE SUN*

Now this is the day.
Our child,
Into the daylight
You will go out standing.

*From Ruth Bunzel, *Zuñi Origin Myths,* pp. 635.

Preparing for your day,
We have passed our days.
When all your days were at an end,
When eight days were past,
Our sun father
Went in to sit down at his sacred
    place.
And our night fathers
Having come out standing to their
    sacred place,
Passing a blessed night
We came to day.
Now this day
Our fathers,
Dawn priests,
Have come out standing to their
    sacred place.

Great Basin

THE THEFT OF PINE NUTS*

THE people in this country had no pine nuts. They talked about going off toward the north to get some.

They started off toward the northeast. Coyote was among them. They went to a big camp where there were many people gathering pine nuts. Soon after they arrived, they began to play the hand game against these people. But the next day, they did not know whether they had lost or won. They went on to another place where there were also people who had pine nuts. Here they played a game of shooting at a small round target with a bow and arrow. They bet their lives in this game; the losers were to be killed by the winners. When one side missed the target, its opponents took its arrow. Crow was shooting and had only two arrows left. Coyote watched him. When Coyote saw him losing, he walked around and shouted and wondered what to do. Crow was about to shoot at the target again. Coyote said to him, "Why don't you hit the target?" Crow shot and missed. He had only one arrow now. When he shot this one, he hit the target. Then he began to win. He won back everything they had lost and then won everything the other people owned. Finally, their opponents even bet their pine nuts, and lost them.

The people did not want to give up their pine nuts. They hung them on a tall tree which had no branches, so that no one could climb up. During the night they slept under the tree to prevent anyone getting the pine nuts. Cottontail began to play his flute, "tu hu du du du . . ." Some old women who were helping to protect the nuts knew that they were

*From Julian H. Steward, *Some Western Shoshoni Myths,* p. 256-257.

132

going to lose them and began to cry for help. Early in the morning, while the people under the tree were still asleep, Coyote and the others started to get the pine nuts. Coyote said, "What do these old women make a noise for? Why don't they go to sleep?" He poked their eyes with a stick and blinded them. Woodpecker (a red woodpecker) flew up in the tree and took the pine nuts.

When Woodpecker brought the pine nuts down, Coyote and the people took them and began to run for home. The others pursued them and caught those who became tired while they were running. They killed every one they caught. Although many people started out, nearly all were killed before they got home.

When nearly all the people were dead, Woodpecker gave the pine nuts to Crow. Crow went on with them. He hid them under his feathers, behind his ear, and in other parts of his body. The pursuers knew he would hide them this way and tried to hit him. They struck his leg and knocked it off. It went a long way through the air. Then they struck Crow and brought him to the ground. They said, "Now we will wait and take a rest."

After they had rested, they went on to where Crow had fallen and searched his body for the pine nuts. They found that Crow had left his feathers behind [i.e., shed his skin] and gone on, taking the pine nuts with him. They looked and a long way off saw where his leg had fallen, but Crow was far beyond, still carrying his pine nuts. They saw pine nut trees all over the mountains, where the nuts had fallen from Crow's leg when it was knocked through the air. They saw smoke coming up through the trees, where the people were already out picking the pine nuts. Crow was flying about crying, "Caw, caw, I have had my pine nuts with me all the time."

All this happened up by Lida.

Pine nuts provided the staple food of these Indians.

THE ORIGIN OF PEOPLE*

Coyote had a home. He hunted rabbits to make a rabbit-skin blanket. When he had a great many skins, he started to make the blanket in his house. While he was working on his blanket, he saw a shadow pass

*From Julian H. Steward, *Some Western Shoshoni Myths,* pp. 262-263.

the door. He went out of the door to see what it was, and saw a woman running. She had a rabbit's tail on her buttocks. He chased the woman, and she ran toward the west. Coyote ran fast, but could get no closer to her. He chased her to the ocean.

At the edge of the ocean the woman stopped and sat down. She said, "I will lie on my back and swim across and carry you over." They started across, the woman carrying him. When they had gone a little way, Coyote moved down on her. The woman dumped him off into the water. Coyote had already decided that, if she put him off into the water, he would turn himself into a water skate ("some little long-legged insect that runs on the water"). When she pushed him into the water, he turned into the skate and crossed the ocean. He reached the other side before the woman.

When Coyote got to the other side he found a tree and made himself a bow. He took green stringy stuff from the water, which he put on the back of his bow instead of sinew. He made the bow string of the same thing. Then he found some cane, made arrows, and began to shoot ducks. He took the ducks to the woman's house.

There were two women living at this house, the woman he had followed and her mother. The women were sitting outside their house. They told Coyote to go inside and sit down. When Coyote went in, he saw quivers made of fox skin hanging all over the wall.

The women started to cook the ducks. They ate the ducks; both women ate. Coyote was singing. He made a hole in the house and watched the women. After eating the meat, the women disposed of the bones. . . . Both of them did this.

They went into the house to sleep. Coyote made advances to the woman he had pursued. He was frustrated . . . In the morning, Coyote went out and got a hard stick. It was a kind of hard sage brush. He hid it by the house . . . The next morning, Coyote hunted mountain sheep. He killed a small one and took the bone from its neck. He put the neck bone by the house in the same place he had hidden the stick. . . . He made successful advances that night. . . .

In the morning, both women were large in the belly. The older one started to weave a basketry water jug. She finished making the jug. Both women put their babies in the jug. When they had finished, they told Coyote to go back home and to take the jug full of babies with him. Coyote started. When he came to the ocean, the old woman put a flat stick across it and Coyote walked over on it. He came toward his home. He went to Owens Valley.

While he was carrying the jug, he heard a noise. He wondered what it was. He pulled the stopper out of the jug. Indians came out; many Indians. When only a few were left inside the jug, he put the stopper back. The woman had told him to pull it out when he came to the middle of the world, but he had pulled it out when he heard the noise. He put the stopper in again and came on to Death Valley. In Death Valley he pulled it out again, and the remaining Indians came out. They stayed here. That is why there are Indians here now.

California

ORIGIN OF THINGS*

THE first were *Kyuvish*, "vacant," and *Atahvish*, "empty," male and female, brother and sister. Successively, these called themselves and became *Omai*, "not alive," and *Yamai*, "not in existence"; *Whaikut Piwkut*, "white pale," the Milky Way, and *Harurai Chatutai*, "boring lowering"; *Tukomit*, "night," with the implication of "sky," and *Tamayowut*, "earth." She lay with her feet to the north; he sat by her right side; and she spoke: "I am stretched, I am extended. I shake, I resound. I am diminished, I am earthquake. I revolve, I roll. I disappear." Then he answered: "I am night, I am inverted (the arch of the heavens). I cover. I rise, I ascend. I devour, I drain (as death). I seize, I send away (the souls of men). I cut, I sever (life)."

These attributes were not yet; but they would be. The four double existences were not successive generations: they were transitions, manifestations of continuing beings.

Then as the brother took hold of her and questioned, she named each part of her body, until they were united. He assisted the births with the sacred *paviut* stick, and the following came forth singly or in pairs, ceremonial objects, religious acts, and avenging animals:

Hair (symbolical of the spirit) and *Nahut* (the mystic
    wanawut figure?)
Rush basket and throwing stick.
Paint of rust from springs and paint of pond scum.
Water and mud.

*From A.L. Kroeber, *Handbook of the Indians of California*, pp. 677-679.

136

Rose and blackberry, which sting for Chungichnish.
Tussock grass and sedge, with which the sacred pits
  for girls were lined.
Salt grass (and grass?)
Bleeding and first periods.

These were human; and so were the next born, the mountains and rocks and things of wood now on the earth; and then followed the badger; Altair the buzzard; the feared meteor *Takwish*; the subterranean water monster *Chorwut; towish,* the spirit of man that survives the corpse; the black oak; "yellow-pine-canoe cottonwood" (a receptacle for feathers); *kimal chehenish,* the pole and offerings of the *Notush* mourning; the ash tree; the plant *isla*; the large brake fern; the black rattlesnake; the red rattlesnake; spider; tarantula hawk; raven; bear; sting ray; *tukmal*, the winnowing basket used in initiation; *shomkul papaiwish*, sea fish and urine for ceremonial sprinkling; *topal tamyush*, mortar and toloache mortar.

All these were the first people, touching one another in the obscurity, far in the north. They traveled to Darkening Dusk, where something high stopped them; then to Hill Climbing, the impassably narrow canyon; then to the lake at Elsinore; then to Temecula. There *Hainit Yunenkit* made the sun and the first people raised him in a net four times to the sky. There also Wiyot, bewitched by Frog, sickened and after long illness died. Under the direction of Kingbird, he was burned, but only after Coyote had stolen his heart. Kingbird announced his return: "Wiyot rises, Wiyot the moon," and all saw him in the west, soon to appear in the east. Eagle, knowing what was now in the world, went or sent his spirit north, east, south, west to escape, but finding *pi'mukvul,* death, everywhere, returned to Temecula, and, accepting his future fate of being danced with and killed, died. Deer, too, after a long evasion, resigned himself to death when he was told of the feathers that would wing the arrows sped after him. And last, Night, here at Temecula, divided the people, gave them the languages which they have now, and sent them to their fixed abodes.

Nahachish, "glutton, the disease consumption, old age, or male," a great man at Temecula, had the hook broken down on which he hung his abundance of food, and, starving, began to travel. Near Aguanga he was given gruel (which is light gray), so, saying "My stomach is *picha* (whitish)" he named the place Pichanga. On Palomar he was again fed, until his belly burned, and he uttered "My stomach is nettle, *shakishla,*" and the place became Shakishla. At Kayawahana he knelt and drank and left his footprints. Sovoyami he named because he was chilled, Pumai because he whistled, Yapichai for a feast witnessed, and Tomka because he was fed. Where he drank he called the place Pala, "water," and Pamai, "small water," and a muddy spot Yuhwamai. Below Pala, seeds were ground for him into meal too fine to handle, and he was poisoned. Perishing, he turned homeward, but died and became a rock just before he could arrive.

COUNSEL TO BOYS*

See these, these are alive, this is bear-mountain lion; these are going to catch you if you are not good and do not respect your elder relatives and grown-up people. And if you do not believe, these are going to kill you; but if you do believe, everybody is going to see your goodness and you then will kill bear-mountain lion. And you will gain fame and be praised, and your name will be heard everywhere.

See this, this is the raven, who will shoot you with bow and arrow if you do not put out your winnowing basket. Harken, do not be a dissembler, do not be heedless, do not eat food of overnight (i.e., do not secretly eat food left after the last meal of the day). Also you will not get angry when you eat, nor must you be angry with your elder relations.

The earth hears you, the sky and wood mountain see you. If you will believe this you will grow old. And you will see your sons and daughters, and you will counsel them in this manner, when you reach your old age. And if when hunting you should kill a hare or rabbit or deer, and an old man should ask you for it, you will hand it to him at once. Do not be angry when you give it, and do not throw it to him. And when he goes home he will praise you, and you will kill many, and you will be able to shoot straight with the bow. . . .

When you die your spirit will rise to the sky and people will blow (three times) and will make rise your spirit. And everywhere it will be heard that you have died. And you will drink bitter medicine, and will vomit, and your inside will be clean, and illness will pass you by, and you will grow old, if you heed this speech. This is what the people of long ago used to talk, that they used to counsel their sons and daughters. In this manner you will counsel your sons and daughters. . . .

This is the breaker; this will kill you. Heed this speech and you will

*From A.L. Kroeber, *Handbook of the Indians of California*, p. 684.

grow old. And they will say of you: He grew old because he heeded what he was told. And when you die you will be spoken of as those of the sky, like the stars. Those it is said were people, who went to the sky and escaped death. And like those will rise your soul (*towish*). . . .

COUNSEL TO GIRLS*

See, these are alive; these will think well of you if you believe; and if you do not believe, they are going to kill you; if you are heedless, a dissembler, or stingy. You must not look sideways, must not receive a person in your house with anger; it is not proper. You will drink hot water when you menstruate, and when you are pregnant you will drink bitter medicine.

This will cause you to have your child quickly, as your inside will be clean. And you will roast yourself at the fire (after childbirth), and then your son or daughter will grow up quickly, and sickness will not approach you. But if you are heedless you will not bear your child quickly, and people will speak of your heedlessness.

Your elder relatives you must think well of; you will also welcome your daughters-in-law and your brothers-in-law when they arrive at your house. Pay heed to this speech, and at some future time you will go to their house, and they are going to welcome you politely at their house. Do not rob food of overnight; if you have a child it will make him costive; it is also going to make your stomach swell; your eyes are also going to granulate. Pay attention to this speech; do not eat venison or jack rabbit, or your eyes will granulate, and people will know by your eyes what you have done. And as your son or daughter will grow up, you will bathe in water, and your hair will grow long, and you will not feel cold, and you will be fat, if you bathe in water. And after the adolescence rite you will not scratch yourself with your hands; you will scratch yourself with a stick; your body will have pimples if you scratch yourself with your hands. Do not neglect to paint yourself, and people will see, and you will grow old, if you pay attention to this speech, and you will see your sons and daughters.

See these old men and women; these are those who paid attention to this counsel, which is of the grown-up people, and they have already

*From A.L. Kroeber, *Handbook of the Indians of California*, p. 685.

reached old age. Do not forget this that I am telling you; pay heed to this speech, and when you are old like these old people, you will counsel your sons and daughters in like manner, and you will die old. And your spirit will rise northwards to the sky, like the stars, moon, and sun. Perhaps they will speak of you and will blow (three times) and (thereby) cause to rise your spirit and soul to the sky.

YOKUTS

A RATTLESNAKE CEREMONY SONG*

The king snake said to the rattlesnake:
Do not touch me!
You can do nothing with me.
Lying with your belly full,
Rattlesnake of the rock pile,
Do not touch me!
There is nothing you can do,
You rattlesnake with your belly full,
Lying where the ground-squirrel holes are thick.
Do not touch me!
What can you do to me?
Rattlesnake in the tree clump,
Stretched in the shade,
You can do nothing;
Do not touch me!
Rattlesnake of the plains,
You whose white eye
The sun shines on,
Do not touch me!

Where man cannot control his universe he often resorts to magic. This song hopes to impart to its singer the power of the king snake to successfully defy the venomous rattler. The human being, by using the same words employed by the king snake, hopes to assure his safety when he encounters a rattlesnake.

*From A.L. Kroeber, *Handbook of the Indians of California,* p. 506.

THREE PRAYERS*

At the Time of an Eclipse

Leave me a little of the sun!
Do not devour it altogether from me!
Leave me a little!

Before Drinking Strange Water

Let us live long in this world!
This is our water!

To the Dead

You are going to another land.
You will like that land.
You shall not stay here.

Short prayers in a fixed form are used on a variety of anxiety-provoking occasions.

*From A.L. Kroeber, *Handbook of the Indians of California*, p. 509.

Plateau

HOW THE WORLD WAS MADE*

KUMOKUMS was the one that made the world and everything that is in it. This is how he did it.

Kumokums sat down beside Tule Lake, on its east shore. He was not afraid, but he was interested, because there was nothing anywhere but Tule Lake.

That's a lot of water, Kumokums said to himself. I wonder how it would look if it had some land around it?

So he reached down, down, down, down, down, five times, to the bottom of Tule Lake, and the fifth time he reached, Kumokums drew up a handful of mud. He piled it up in front of him, like a hill, and patted it with the palm of his hand.

As Kumokums patted the mud, it began to spread beneath his hand, out and around him, until Tule Lake was completely surrounded by earth, and Kumokums was left sitting on a little island of mud in the middle of the water.

"Well!" said Kumokums. "I didn't know it would do that."

So he drew back some of the earth on the west and the north, to make the mountains. He cut grooves in the mountain sides with his fingernail, so the rivers could flow down to the lakes. That is why you should bury your fingernail parings, or throw them back into the water, so they will return to Kumokums.

Kumokums drew trees and plants out of the earth, and he put birds in the air, fish in the water, and animals on the land. He had shaped and decorated the world as a woman shapes and decorates a basket.

*From A. Marriott and C.K. Rachlin, *American Indian Mythology*, pp. 28-29.

Then Kumokums was tired. He had done everything he could think of to do, and winter was about to begin.

I will do what the bear does, Kumokums thought. I will make myself a hole where I will be safe, and sleep the winter through.

Kumokums dug himself a hole under the bottom of Tule Lake, with the hill where he had created the world to mark the spot. By now the hill had dried out and turned to solid rock, as it is today.

Just at the last moment, as he was about to go underground, Kumokums thought, I might want to look out sometime and see what is going on, without bothering to move around. So he scratched and scratched with his fingernail until he had made a hole in the rock, near its top, that was big enough to see through. It is still there, and people can climb the rock and look out through the hole, all around the country, for Tule Lake dried up and became planted land many years ago.

But some day Kumokums will surely wake up, and when he looks out and sees how his world has changed, perhaps he will bring the water back to the floor of Tule Lake, and things will again be as they were when Kumokums first made them.

HOW DEATH CAME INTO THE WORLD*

Kumokums was living by himself near the Sprague River, and he began to get lonesome. He called all the animals together, to talk to them.

"Let's build a village here," said Kumokums, "where we can all live together."

The animals liked the idea of a village, but some of them didn't like the place. "It's too cold here, and the grass is stubbly," remarked the deer. "I think we should go to Yainax."

"I like cold weather," Bear informed them. "That's when I can curl up and sleep as much as I want to. I'd rather stay here."

So they discussed the matter, without ever really quarreling, and at last Kumokums got tired of all the talking.

"Listen to me," he said. "I called this council and I am its chief. We will have two villages. In the summer we will all live in Yainax and in the winter we will live here on Sprague River. Then everybody will be satisfied."

*From A. Marriott and C.K. Rachlin, *American Indian Mythology*, pp. 190-193.

"How long is the summer and how long is the winter?" Porcupine asked.

"We ought to divide the year," Kumokums said. "Each can be six moons long."

"But there are thirteen moons in the year," Porcupine argued. "What are you going to do with the odd one?"

"We can cut it up," Kumokums decided, "and use one half in summer and one in winter, for moving."

Everybody agreed that that was a good plan, and they would go along with it. It was summer then and the middle of the Moon When the Loon Sings, so they all packed and moved to Yainax.

Kumokums and the animals lived very happily for many years, moving back and forth between their winter and summer villages. But they were so happy and well fed and contented that too many babies were beginning to be born. At last Porcupine took matters into his own hands, and went to talk to Kumokums about it.

"Kumokums," he said, "there are too many people around here. Our old people are dying off, and still there's too many people. We all know that when people die, they go to a land beyond, and if they have been good they are happy. Well, everybody in this village is well fed and contented, so they have been good. Why not let them go to the Land of the Dead, and they can be happy there?"

Kumokums sat and thought it over for a long time. Then he said, "I believe you are right. People should leave this earth forever when they die. The chief of the Land of the Dead is a good man, and they will be happy in his village."

"I'm glad you see it that way," said Porcupine, and waddled off.

Five days later, Kumokums came home from fishing up Sprague River, and he heard a sound of crying in his house. He threw down his catch, and rushed to the door in the roof of his house. He climbed down the pole ladder through the smoke hole. His daughter was lying on the ground and his wives were standing around, wringing their hands and crying.

"What has happened? What is the matter with her?" Kumokums cried. He loved his daughter very dearly.

"She has left us," his wives cried. "She has gone to the Land of the Dead."

"No! She can't do that!" Kumokums exclaimed, and he stroked his daughter's head, and called her name. "Come back to me," Kumokums begged. "Stay with us here in our villages."

Kumokums sent his wife through the village to bring in the most powerful medicine men. They sang and prayed over the girl's body, but no one could bring her back.

Finally, Porcupine came waddling backward down the pole ladder through the smoke hole.

"Kumokums," he said, "this is the way you said it should be. You were the one who set death in the world for everybody. Now you must suffer for it like everyone else."

"Is there no way to bring her back?" Kumokums pleaded.

"There is a way," said Porcupine, and Bear, who is as wise as Porcupine, nodded his head. "There is a way, but it is hard and it is dangerous. You yourself must go to the Land of the Dead, and ask its chief, who is your friend, to give you your daughter back."

"No matter how hard or how dangerous it is, I am willing to do it," Kumokums assured them. He lay down on the opposite side of the house, and sent his spirit out of his body, away and away to the Land of the Dead.

"What do you want and whom do you come for?" the chief asked. He was a skeleton, and all the people in his village were skeletons, too.

"I have come to take my daughter home," Kumokums answered. "I love her dearly, and I want her with me, but I do not see her here."

"She is here," replied the chief of the Land of the Dead. "I, too, love her. I have taken her into my own house to be my own daughter." He turned his head and called, "Come out, daughter," and a slim young girl's skeleton came out of the hole in the roof. "There she is," said the chief of the Land of the Dead. "Do you think you would know her now, or want her in your village the way she is?"

"However she is, she is my daughter and I want her," Kumokums said.

"You are a brave man," observed the chief of the Land of the Dead. "Nobody else who has ever come here has been able to say that. If I give her to you, and she returns to the Land of the Living, it will not be easy. You must do exactly what I tell you."

"I will do whatever you say," Kumokums vowed.

"Then listen to me carefully," said the chief of the Land of the Dead. "Take your daughter by the hand and lead her behind you. Walk as straight as you can to your own place. Four times you may press her hand, and it will be warmer and rounder. When you reach your own village, she will be herself again. But whatever you do, do—not —look—back. If you do, your daughter will return to me."

"I will do as you say," Kumokums promised.

Kumokums held out his hand behind his back, and felt his daughter's finger bones take hold of it. Together they set out for their own village. Kumokums led the way. Once he stopped and pressed his daughter's hand. There was some flesh on it, and Kumokums' heart began to feel lighter than it had since his daughter died.

Four times Kumokums stopped and pressed his daughter's hand, and each time it was warmer and firmer and more alive in his own. Their own village was ahead of them. They were coming out of the Land of the Dead and into the Land of the Living. They were so close Kumokums decided they were safe now. He looked back at his daughter. A pile of bones lay on the ground for a moment, and then was gone. Kumokums opened his eyes in his own house.

"I told you it was hard and dangerous," Porcupine reminded him. "Now there will always be death in the world."

SHAMAN'S SONG*

What do I remove from my mouth?
The disease I remove from my mouth.

What do I take out?
The disease I take out.

What do I suck out?
The disease I suck out.

What do I blow about?
The disease I blow about.

As a head only, I roll around.

I stand on the rim of my nest.

I am enveloped in flames.

What am I? what am I?

*From A.L. Kroeber, *Handbook of the Indians of California,* p. 321.

I, the song, I walk here.

I the dog stray.

In the north wind I stray.

An arrowpoint I am about to shoot.

A bad song I am.

The earth I sing of.

Northwest Coast

THE ORIGIN OF DEATH*

ONCE there lived two people who were related as younger brothers. They two lived together. Both had wives and each of their children were males. On one morning the child of one of these men became sick. It was not sick very long and died there and then. His heart felt very sore when his child died. Finally he dug a grave for it. For one whole day he did not eat but watched his child after it died. After four days he went, he came to see his cousin. "What is thy opinion, my cousin, concerning that boy of mine who died; suppose he should come back here in five days?" Thus he spoke. "No, my cousin. Thou shalt just keep on eating until thou wilt become well again." Thus he told him. And that other man said nothing to him. He was only thinking in his mind thus: "I will surely get even with thee again."

Then it was not very long afterward when the child of the second man became sick. It was not ailing very long when it died there and then. His heart was very sore when his boy died. So he said that he wanted his boy should come back to him. Then he went there. "My cousin, it will be very good if our two children should come back to us after five days." Thus he said to his neighbor: "Not so, my cousin. Thou shalt only eat and thou wilt feel well again." Thus he said to him: "I wanted very much that our dual children should come back to us, but thou didst not want it thus. People will habitually die but will never come back, because thou didst not want it thus at first. Thou didst tell me before, 'It is well if

*From Leo J. Frachtenberg, *Alsea Texts and Myths*, p. 117.

148

they do not come back.' " Thus he was thinking in his mind. And then he felt very good when he kept on telling him thus. People would have habitually come back after five days if he had said so at first. It would be very good if anybody who dies would always come back after five days.

Only now thus it ends. Thus the story was told in the beginning.

CHINOOK

THE CROW STORY*

THERE were the Crow and her five children. At the end of their house lived her cousin the Raven. They were hungry, and one day she went to look for food on the beach. She sang. She found a poggy [porgie], kicked it and went on. She repeated her song. Soon she found a flounder. Again she sang her song. Then she found a seal; she kicked it and went on. Again she sang her song. Then she found a sturgeon. She went around it twice, then she left it and kicked it. She went on and repeated her song. Then she found a sealion; three times she went around it. She kicked it and left it. She repeated her song. She went a long distance and found a whale. Four times she went around it, then she kicked it and kicked it again. She broke her leg. "Oh, my leg," she cried. She went up to the woods, pulled out some grass and tied it on to her leg. She went on and after a little while she found a salmon. "Oh! my salmon," she said. She was very glad and danced. She put it into her mat and went home. When she had almost arrived at her house she saw a woman. When she came nearer she recognized her. "Behold! the eagle," she said. The latter said: "What do you carry there?" "Oh," she replied, "a salmon." "I wish to buy it; I will give you my coat." "Plenty of coats are lying about in my house." "I will give you my blanket." "What shall I do with your blanket? I have many blankets." "I will give you my hat." "What shall I do with your hat? Maybe it is full of lice." "I will give you my hands." "What shall I do with your hands? I have hands as well." "Pull out that bunch of grass." The eagle went and pulled out the bunch of grass, which gave way at once. Then she said,

*From Franz Boas, *Chinook Tales*, pp. 125-126.

"Now you try to pull it out." The Crow went and tried to pull it out. It did not give way. "I will give you my eyes; you will be able to see a long distance." "What shall I do with your eyes? I have eyes as well." The eagle said: "Louse me." She did so and found a plate full of lice. [After she had finished the eagle said:] "Now I will louse you." She loused the Crow, who became sleepy and finally fell asleep. Then the eagle took the salmon and put a bunch of grass in her mat. She carried it to the top of a spruce tree. When the Crow awoke she saw the eagle sitting on top [of the spruce tree] eating her salmon. Then [she was so much grieved that she fell down at once. She asked the eagle]: "Please give me the gills." The Crow lay on her back and the eagle threw down the gills and the roe. The Crow went home angry. She arrived there. Her children were in the house. She came to her children. She roasted the salmon roe. [She asked] her eldest daughter: "Go and get some water." [She replied:] "The next younger one is there." She asked another one of her daughters: "Go and get some water." [She replied:] "The next younger one is there." She asked four of them. Now her youngest daughter brought her some water. When the salmon roe was nearly done she washed her face. [She asked her daughters:] "Is my face white now?" "No, it is still black." She washed it again and asked her children once more: "Is my face white?" "No, it is still black." Then the raven jumped up and took what she was roasting. He took it away and ate it all. Then the Crow cried again and the raven lay down. He was ashamed of himself. In the evening he fell sick and sang his conjurer's song: "O, my brass pin hit my eye and it got blind, qoāqoaxqoä', qoāqoaxqoä', qoāqoaxqoä'!"

After a while they went and asked the crabs and their young ones to come. The raven heated stones and when they were hot he shut the door. Then a crab thought: "He is cooking for us." But they threw all of them on the stones, old and young. They were steamed. When they were done he said to the Crow and her children: "Come eat!" Now she was glad, and she ate, together with her children.

The importance of salmon, the concern with status, the emphasis on trade rather than sharing are clearly delineated in this tale. The ordering of personal relationships through status and the tensions that derive from this ordering are quite marked.

MYTH OF THE SOUTHWEST WIND*

There were five Southwest winds. The people were poor all the year round. Their canoes and their houses were broken. The houses were blown down. Then Blue-jay said: "What do you think? We will sing to bring the sky down." He continued to say so for five years. Then their chief said: "Quick! call the people." All the people were called. Then they sang, sang, and sang, but the sky did not move. They all sang, but the sky did not move. Last of all the Snow-bird (?) sang. Then the sky began to tilt. [Finally] it tilted so [that it touched] the earth. Then it was fastened to the earth and all the people went up. They arrived in the sky. Blue-jay said: "Skate, you had better go home. You are too wide. They will hit you and you will be killed. Quick! go home." The Skate said: "Shoot at me; afterward I will shoot at you." The Skate stood up. Blue-jay took his bow and shot at him. But the Skate turned sideways and Blue-jay missed him. Then he told Blue-jay: "Now I shall shoot at you." Blue-jay stood up. The Skate said: "Raise your foot before your body; if I should hit your body, you would die." Blue-jay held up his foot. Then the Skate shot him right in the middle of his foot. He fell down crying. Now the people had arrived in the sky. It was cold. When it got dark, they said to the Beaver: "Quick! go and fetch the fire." The Beaver went up to the town. Then he swam about in the water. [Soon] he was seen, and one person said: "A Beaver is swimming about." Then a man ran down to the water, struck the Beaver, and killed him at once. He hauled him to the house, and said: "What shall we do with that Beaver?" "We sill singe him." They placed him over the fire and the sparks caught in his fur. Then he arose and ran outside. He swam away from the shore, carrying the fire. [Soon] he arrived at [the place where] his relatives [were staying] and brought them the fire. The people made a fire. Then they said to the Skunk: "Go and examine the house, and try to find a hole where we can enter in the night." The Skunk went and laughed, running about under the houses. Then an old man said: "Behold! there is a Skunk. Never before has a Skunk been here, and now we hear it. Search for it. Kill it." They looked for the Skunk. Then it ran home [because] it became afraid. They told Robin: "Quick! go and look at the house. See if there is a hole where we can enter at night." Robin went and entered a small house. There were two old women. He warmed himself and remained there. Then

*From Franz Boas, *Kathlamet Texts*, pp. 67-71.

they said to the Mouse and to the Rat: "Quick! go and look for Robin." The Mouse and the Rat went. They entered the last house. Then they cut the bowstrings and the strings of the coats of the women. They did so in all the houses. They cut all the bowstrings. Then they went home. [They said:] "We cut all their bowstrings." Robin had disappeared, and they said: "Perhaps they have killed him." Then they attacked the town. After a while Robin went home. His belly was burnt red by the fire. Then these people were killed. They tried to span their bows, but they had no strings. The women intended to put on their coats and to run away, but the strings were cut. They stayed there and they were killed. The Eagle took the eldest Southwest wind by its head; the Owl took another one, the Golden Eagle a third one, the Turkey the fourth one, and the Chicken-hawk took the youngest one by its head. After a little while the four [elder ones] were killed. Then the youngest one escaped from the Chicken-hawk. The one which the Turkey [held] would have escaped, if they had not helped him. Only the youngest Southwest wind escaped from them. Then the people went home. Blue-jay went down first. His foot was sore. Then the people descended. The Skate was still above. Then [Blue-jay] cut the rope and the sky sprang back. Part of the people were still above. They became stars. [Therefore] all kinds of things are [in the sky]—the Woodpecker, the Fisher, the Skate, the Elk, and the Deer. Many things are there. Only the youngest Southwest wind is alive nowadays.

As if to emphasize the fact that such stories deal with mythic times, social relationships and rules that govern the relationships between people and people or people and animals are nowhere apparent. Casual deceit and unpredictability lend such stories a bizarre quality which, perhaps, is precisely the effect desired by the storyteller.

THE POTLATCH*

When a chief intends to give a potlatch, four, five, or six men are sent out in a canoe [to invite the guests]. One man who has a guardian spirit is sent among them. When they approach a town the man who has the guardian spirit sings. The people of that town hear him and say, "Oh, we are going to be invited." The messengers land and tell the

*From Franz Boas, *Kathlamet Texts*, pp. 268-269.

people to come. Then they go to the next town. After having visited all the towns they go home. Now the people make themselves ready. They wait for those who live farthest away. When they arrive they all go down the river together. Thus they do also when a chief on the upper part of the river has sent an invitation. They go up the river together. When they reach the town to which they were invited they put their canoes side by side and lay planks across. This is done with all their canoes. Now they dance, and those who have guardian spirits sing. The people dance on the planks. Their faces are painted red, their hair is strewn with down. All the women wear their dentalia, their ear and hair ornaments, and their necklaces. They wear good blankets. Braves wear their head ornaments and their faces are blackened. Shamans carry their batons. They sing and finally land. Then they tell a woman, "You shall be our head dancer." She replies, "No; I do not dare to do it." One who knows how to dance well is made head dancer, a man or a woman. Now they enter the house dancing. When a woman [while dancing] bends her head, another one goes and raises it. Then she pays her for having made her head straight. When a person gets out of rhythm, he is taken to the side of the house and must sit down there. All those who have guardian spirits sing. When the people of one town have finished, those of another town enter dancing. When there are not many people of one town, those of two towns enter together. When the house is large, the people of three towns will enter together.

If the host has too little food, two youths are sent and told, "Go and ask my relatives to bring food." The youths go to a town and ask the [host's relatives] to bring food. They all come and bring food. They also dance on the canoes and land. They enter the house dancing. When they bring dry salmon, five men hold it in their mouths while they enter the house dancing. When they bring roots, five men carry them on their backs when they enter the house dancing. After the people have danced five days they receive presents. One man is asked [to stand near the host and] to name the people. First he names the chief of one town. When the host is liberal, he gives the man who calls out the names a blanket. Or he is given long dentalia. After one town is finished, another one receives presents. Again first the chief is called. When he drags his present he is called back. Men as well as women are thus given presents.

The people are forbidden to shoot with arrows during the potlatch. If a man should want to fight against the people of a town and shoot an arrow, then the people would fight and several would be killed.

The women receive each a fathom of short dentalia. Only men are given long dentalia. Common men receive short dentalia. If a chief has many dentalia, then every one receives two fathoms of short dentalia.

HAIDA

THE MAN WHO MARRIED A KILLER-WHALE WOMAN*

A man and his wife were abandoned at the town of Sqa-i. After they had lived there together for a while, his wife began getting mussels at Stasqa'os. Every day she went there for mussels.

After a while he became suspicious of her. And one time, when she went after mussels, he followed her stealthily. When she got near the place where she was going to get mussels she went along singing. She beat upon her mat with her digging stick in lieu of a drum. When she got near the place where the mussels were a whale jumped ashore sideways just in front of her. Then she went to it, and she lay with it. And the whale went off blowing. He saw it.

Then he knew, and he went away. Then he began to sharpen a mussel-shell at some place where she could not see him. It became sharp, and one day, when it was low tide, he sent his wife to get spruce roots for him.

Then he made clothing for himself like his wife's, took the basket, and wore the mat as a blanket. Then he went along the beach of Stasqa'os. And, when he approached the place where his wife was in the habit of getting mussels, he used his mat as a drum. When he sang the same words, the black whale came ashore on its side in front of him. Then he went to it and cut off its penis. Then it got up quickly and went into the water making a noise. Its cries died away into the ocean.

Then he came home and built a fire. And he put stones into the fire. Then he sliced it up, and, when the stones were hot, he steamed it. After it was cooked his wife came home.

Then she asked her husband: "What things are you steaming?" "I found some things which had floated ashore. I am steaming them for you.

*From John R. Swanton, *Haida Texts and Myths*, pp. 286-287.

They are cooked. Take the covers off." Then they took the covers off. Before they had even put them into the tray she took the piece off of the top and ate it.

After she had taken one bite he said to her: "Is your husband's penis sweet?" She dropped it at once. Immediately she turned toward the door. Right where she sat she shook. Even the ground shook.

And, when his wife started off, he tried to hold her. He could not. Then she went out, and he went out after her. And, after he had followed her closely for a while, she went up in the bed of a creek at the end of Stasqa'os. All that time he kept looking at her. And, when she got up toward the mountain, she again recalled her husband's words.

Now she sat on top of the mountain, and she again remembered what her husband had said. And, while sitting there, she became ashamed. Then she played in the earth with the tip of her finger. She made a hole with her finger far into the island. She did not feel how she did it. When she stood up she picked up some dirt and threw it into it. "All future people will do this way to you."

Then she went away and came to the west coast. And she went out on one side of Elderberry point. Then she jumped into the water in front of her. He did not know that he had married a female killer whale that had been born of a woman. Then she settled herself down before him. She became a reef. It is called "Woman." When people get off from a canoe upon it, it shakes with them, they say.

And there she again recalled her husband's words, and she went away from there also. Where she again settled down on the west coast as a reef, they also call it "Woman."

Fantastic man-animal relationships indicate that this story is myth, although the suspicion that envelops the marriage relationship and the right of a husband to exact revenge represent social realities. An insight into the self-image of the Haida is afforded by the Shaman's suggestions that supernatural beings cannot bear anything dirty—like humans—upon them.

SLAUGHTER-LOVER*

A chief in a certain town was married. Then he asked a good-looking woman in a neighboring town in marriage. After a while he married her.

*From John R. Swanton, *Haida Texts and Myths*, pp. 348-351.

On her account he rejected the one he had first married, and she sat around in the corner of the house weeping.

Then the uncles and the brothers of the one he had just married came to him, and he gave them food. They were unable to consume the cranberries and berries of all kinds which he gave them to eat. During the same time, his brothers-in-law gave him much property.

Once, when they went to bed, the one he disliked was weeping in the corner for her dead child with pitch on her face. And in the night she went to one of the chief's brothers-in-law of medium age who had paint on his face and feathers on his head. Then the woman rubbed herself against the paint upon his face, and she rubbed herself upon his hair. Then she went to where she had been lying.

Next morning the woman's nose and face had paint upon them, and her face had feathers upon it. And the man's face also had spots of pitch upon it. Then the chief took to his bed [with grief]. She did this because she wanted to see whether he had really rejected her. Then his brothers-in-law went away.

Some time after that he sent out to call his brothers-in-law, and his brothers-in-law came to him. Then he gave them food. And they went to bed. All slept. Then he put water on the fire, and he spilled it on them. And their bodies lay there motionless. Then he dragged the dead bodies of his wife's brothers and uncles to the bases of the trees. And he again refused to have her.

Now her mother (the mother of his second wife) was saved and cried about. She wept continually, holding her arms toward the sky. Then the chief went to the town and killed all the old people in it. And her mother went inland, made a house out of old cedar bark at a certain mountain, and wept there. All that time she held her hands toward the sky.

By and by her thigh swelled up. Before ten nights had passed it burst, and a child came out. Then she washed him. And not a long time afterward he wept for a bow. Then she broke off a hemlock branch and made one for him. Then he went out and brought in a wren. He skinned it and dried the skin.

The next time he went out he killed and brought in a song sparrow that went whistling along. And he also skinned that. He went out after that and brought in a robin, and he ate its meat. There was nothing [else] to eat.

After he had been bringing them in in this way for a while, one day he killed a black bear. After he had killed all kinds of animals, he killed a grizzly bear. That he also brought in to his mother.

By and by he asked his mother: "Mother, why do you live here all alone?" Then she said to her son: "My son, they destroyed your uncles. Your sister was married. Then your uncles went to her. There they were destroyed. They also came after us. I escaped from them. Therefore I am very careful where I go. I am afraid to look at the town."

Then he asked his mother: "Where is the town?" And she said to him: "It lies over there." And he said: "Mother, to-morrow, I am going to see it." "Don't, my child, they will kill you also." "Yet I will see it."

And next day he went down to see his sister. With his copper bow he went down to help her. He had concealed it outside from his mother, they say, and, when he went out, he threw away that she made for him just outside and took his own.

Now he went to the town. And he sat behind it and thought of his sister. He had something round his neck. It was made of copper. Then his sister came to him and he asked her questions. He asked her how he treated her. And she told him that he treated her badly.

The he pulled off what he had round his neck and gave it to his sister. "Tell him you found this for him. And, when it begins to burn a little, run out from him with it and come to me again."

Then the woman went in and said: "Here is something I found for you." When he took it, fire flashed out from it, and she ran out from him. Then her brother handed her his bow: "Say the same thing to him and run out from him." Then she went in and she gave him the copper bow. And at once she ran out. And behind her there was a great noise of burning inside of the house. The whole town burned the way (i.e., as rapidly as) a grouse flies away. Not even one was saved out of it. He did it on account of his uncles.

Then he went with his sister to where his uncles had had their town. And he asked his sister: "Where do my uncles' bones lie?" And she said: "They lie behind the burned town." Then they went there and put their bones together. And, after he had spit medicine upon them four times, they sat up. Then his uncles settled in the empty houses.

Then he went to get his mother. Now his mother was already an old woman. And he spit medicine over her, and she became young. Then he settled his mother down in the town. And he spit medicine upon the old people they had killed, and they also became young.

And he went out in the evening and came in next morning, and he told his mother he had killed a whale. And, when they went down to see it, a whale lay there. Then the town people cut it up. And the next evening he went out and came in in the morning. And he pulled some strings of halibut in in front of the town.

One day he called the people. At that time he gave them all kinds of food. The things in the trays were not consumed. Then they went away. Those he restored to youth were married. Then he said: "I will give you ten whales to eat." And, after they had returned home and the next morning had come, ten whales were floating in front of the town.

And after that he looked about in the neighboring towns for a wife. In the evening he went out. He came in very early. All that time he concealed the things with which he was born. Only his sister knew about them. By and by he prepared to ask the chief's daughter in a neighboring town in marriage. Presently he was accepted and all the town people went with him to get her. And she came in with him.

Then his uncles gave him the town. And he frequently gave them food. When he sent to call them in he told them to go out aimlessly and get things for him. It was as if things flowed in through the doorway, and he fed them.

After some time had passed he went to his father-in-law. Then all his uncles again went with him. But instead of receiving him kindly they used supernatural powers against him. Before anything they tried against him came to him, it was gone. By and by his father-in-law pulled him against a cloak he wore which was covered with needles. Then the needles dropped from it, and he threw it into the corner.

Then he said: "Did you lie to me formerly?" And he began to give his son-in-law something to eat. And, after he had got through feeding him, he arose very early next morning, and, when he went to the fire, something near him made a thundering noise. Now he sent his uncles home. And he remained behind. After he had received food there a while he asked his father-in-law to take him over. Then he took him over, and his father-in-law [returned without] going into the house. Then he said: "I am giving you ten whales." And the morning after they got back ten whales floated in front of the town.

And he again feasted the people. By and by one of his uncles came in to him, saying he was not in good circumstances. And he said to his uncle: "Live over there. You will be well off over there." And, after he had given his uncle food, he told his uncle he had better go. "Go. You will cease being poorly off. When I have food brought to you, invite your elder brothers." He went at once. Food came in of itself after him. Then he called the people for it.

And then his wife became pregnant. And her thigh was swollen, as that of his mother had been. Out of it came a woman. Within ten nights she started to walk. She was he himself born again.

And before he went away he stole a look at his father-in-law. Then he prepared to leave [him]. "I will go to renew my town, which has become old." And one evening he started. He was gone for good.

And he came to his town. His town was old, and he spit medicine upon it. It was as it had been before. Then his wife went back to her father's town.

And one of his uncles who was in the town went out one evening. Something took him up. Then he took their wives also to the town. That was the Moon who was helping them, because she raised her hands and wept. Then he took all of his uncles up and let them become his servants. There he took good care of them.

THE REJECTED LOVER*

At Q!adō' a certain person fell in love with a woman. She then refused to have him, but she told him to pull out his hair, and then she would fall in love with him. He went again to talk to her. She then told him to pull out his eyebrows and his eyelashes; she would then fall in love with him. After that he went again to speak with her. That time she told him to pull out his mustache and the hair on his body. Only then [she said] would she fall in love with him. After that he again went to her. Then she absolutely refused him.

He ceased going abroad among the people. When he needed anything he always went out at night. He began to work inside. He whittled. After he had done this for a while he had filled two boxes. And, when a moonlight night came, he went out.

He then shot the sky. He picked up another arrow and shot it into the notch of the first. He did the same thing again and again. After he had shot away his two boxfuls it hung a bow's length from the ground, and he laid the bow upon them. He at once went up upon it.

After mounting for some time he came to a town. That was the Moon's town, they say. After he had gone about the town for a while someone said to him out of a big house: "Your grandfather invites you in." And

*From John R. Swanton, *Haida Texts and Myths*, pp. 354–355.

he entered. He (the Moon) then had him sit at his right hand in the rear of the house.

After he had sat for a while looking at him, as he sat near him, he had a box brought to him. He saw that all of his hair was gone. At that time he saw only one box. After he had pulled them apart five times he took a small comb out of the inmost one.

He then had water brought and began to make his face look as it ought to look. Each time he wet his hands he rubbed them upon his eyes. When he had made him good looking he began to comb his hair. He ran the comb down along half of his head, and when it had passed below he took it off. And after he had done this to him three times he stopped. After that he also made his eyebrows with the comb, and his eyelashes, and he also brought out his mustache.

When he first came in he said to him: "Grandson, news had come that you were going to come up to let me set you to rights. I will make you quite proper."

He straightway made him good-looking. He finished him. He was there many nights. Then he gave the chief directions: "When the one that you loved, who made you pull out your hair, comes with the others to look at you do not turn your face toward her. Turn your back to her."

He then went down again upon the arrows. Now he sat erect in his father's house, and all the town of Q!adō' came in to look at him. Then the one with whom he had been in love looked in at him, and he turned his back upon her. By and by, fascinated by the sight of him, she died.

THE STORY OF ONE WHO SAW AN EAGLE TOWN*

He began gambling. After he had lost for some time he lost all of his property. Then he began to bid the property of his clansmen. When he had lost a great deal of that as well he was ashamed to enter the house.

By and by he went to the end of the town. It occurred to him to go into the woods. Then he did so. Then he thought of climbing a mountain. At once he went thither. Before him eagles wheeled about upon the mountain. Presently he came to a big town.

He saw eagles sitting upon something like a pole in front of the town. They were looking into the sea for something. Then he began to live with

*From John R. Swanton, *Haida Texts and Myths*, p. 281.

them. With the feather on the very tip of his wing one of them wiped something common out of his eyes. And in the evening they said they were going fishing. Then they killed a whale. Every evening they killed one whale.

By and by he started out fishing with a net. Then they told him not to put the whole net into the sea. And, when he fished with them, he let out two meshes. When he got something in it that time, it carried it away. He did not worry about it. Sometime after this he descended to his home. Then he again began gambling. At that time he won. At once he paid all his debts.

Although the vision quest was not formalized among West Coast Indians as it was in the Plains, both the power of such visions and the importance of the eagle as a symbol of power are apparent here. Like most gambling people the Haida exhibited great faith in luck—but luck was not a lady, as we sometimes personify her, but an eagle.

KWAKIUTL

CRADLE SONG*

When I am a man, then I shall be a hunter, O father!
    Ya ha ha ha.
When I am a man, then I shall be a harpooner, O father!
    Ya ha ha ha.
When I am a man, then I shall be a canoebuilder, O father!
    Ya ha ha ha.
When I am a man, then I shall be a carpenter, O father!
    Ya ha ha ha.
When I am a man, then I shall be an artisan, O father!
    Ya ha ha ha.
That we may not be in want, O father!
    Ya ha ha ha.

*From Franz Boas, "Stylistic Aspects of Primitive Literature," pp. 328-329.

THE CLAM AND THE OLACHEN*

"Am I only good being roasted?" said the Clam, "for there are many ways that are good."

"What are your good ways?" said the Olachen. . . .

"Is it not a good way when I am put side by side on the fire," said, on his part, the Clam to the Olachen.

"Is that the whole number of your good ways as you are a clam?" said, on his part, the Olachen to him.

"Is it not a good way when I am put in a row, when I am held by tongs, when it is as though I prettily open my mouth in the house?" said the Clam. "Is that the number of ways that you are good?" said the Clam to the Olachen.

". . . Is it not a good way for me when I am being picked out? I am dried on the ground so that my body gets dry. I am taken and I am roasted in tongs. I stand nèxt to the fire and one is taken and the fire is lighted. . . . I am turned over and over and I am taken and put on an old mat and I lie prettily on the floor. That is my good way, you Clam, as I am an Olachen."

Something antic about this conversation must strike a reminiscent chord in any reader familiar with *Alice in Wonderland,* one of the few tales in English in which shellfish are personified.

COAST SALISH

STAR HUSBAND**

TWO girls were once sleeping out. One said to the other, "See that great star up there in the sky? I wish I could have that star." The other said, "See that tiny star way off there? You can scarcely see it. I wish I could have that one."

That night, the girls found men sleeping with them—men lying along-

*From Franz Boas, *Kwakiutl Tales.*
**From *Folk Tales of the Coast Salish, Memoirs of the American Folk-Lore Society,* Volume 27, (1934), pp. 95-96.

side of them. The girl who had wished for the big star, had an ugly old man sleeping with her. He was so old that his eyes were red and the skin beneath them drawn down. The girl who had wished for the tiny star, found a nice young man sleeping with her.

Girls should not wish for anything like this—anything far away. It is uncalled for; bad luck may come to them. They should be careful what they say and what they do; they will have a long life if they do not wish for anything far off.

THE MAN WHO WAS ABANDONED*

PEOPLE living in a long town were suffering from famine. A certain man stayed with his uncle, who had two wives. The people were very hungry. This man was always sleeping, for he was lazy. When their food was all gone, they started away from the lazy man to camp, but his uncle's wife threw some dried fish into a hole beside the house post for him, while she was walking around back of the fire. Then she said to him, "I throw a piece of dried fish into the post hole for you." He would put a small piece of this into his mouth. When he took it out, he would go to sleep. He always had his head covered.

Suddenly something said to him, "I am come to help you." When he looked there was nothing there. At once he fell asleep. Hunger was overcoming him. At once he prepared himself for it. What was speaking to him was a small thing running around him. Its teeth were long. Then he took it away. He put it among his rags, and fell asleep again. Then he dreamed that it said to him, "Put me into the water." When it was getting light he did so. He went down into the water with it. He kept throwing it up and down in his hands. Saying, "You came to help me," he threw it into the water. Where he threw it in [the water] smoked. And when it was getting dark he covered his head. When day was beginning

*From John R. Swanton, *Tlingit Myths and Texts*, pp. 262-266.

to dawn he heard the cry of the raven below him. A halibut had drifted ashore there, and the thing that was helping him was at its heart.

Quickly he built a house. He built a big one. In the morning he went down to the beach with his helper and let it go. Toward daylight he again heard the raven's call at the beach, and he ran down. Then five seals were floating below him, one behind another. His helper hung around the neck of the fifth, and he took it off. One could not see about inside of his house on account of the drippings. His uncles who had left him, however, were suffering from famine.

Suddenly some mountain sheep came out above him. He let it go among them. Then all fell down. The inside of his house could not be seen on account of the great abundance of food.

Now when his uncle thought that he had died he sent someone thither to burn his body. His slaves that he told to go after him came thither, and he called the slaves into the house. They came up. He gave them things to eat, and they remained with him one night. One of these slaves had a child. Then he said to them, "Do not take away anything." The little slave, however, threw a piece inside of something. "Tell your household that you burned me up." He left those directions with them.

When they reached home that night the baby began to cry: "Little fat, Little fat," the slave's child began to cry out. There was a great famine in the town whither the people had moved. Some among them had died. Then the chief thought about the way the slave's baby was crying. He kept crying louder: "Little fat, Little fat," he cried. His mother said, "He is crying for the inside of a clam." But the slave had a piece of fat on her side for her baby. She sat up with it. Its mouth was greasy all over. At once she confessed to him. She said to her master, "He is there. The things that he has are many."

Then all started thither. Indeed it was a great quantity of things that he had. The wife of his uncle who had hated him tried to make herself look pretty, but when she wiped her face something got inside of the rag and she cut her face. But the one who had thrown something into the post hole for him, he thought kindly toward. Then the people moved to him. He willed, however, that the food should not fill his uncle or his uncle's wife. Just where they lay, his uncle and his uncle's wife were dead. So he married the other wife that helped him. The food his helper obtained for him, however, he sold for slaves. The people came to him to buy everything. Afterward he fixed a little box for the thing that had helped him. No one ever saw it because it was kept out of sight.

One day a whale came along, moving up and down, and he let his helper go at it. In the morning the big whale floated up below on the beach. When all were busy with the whale he forgot his helper. It was hanging to the last piece. When they took up the whale he forgot it. And because he forgot it all of the people were destroyed. This is why people say to a lazy man even now: "You will be like the man that was abandoned." All the things that had been killed came to life. Some ran into the water and some into the woods. The people were completely destroyed.

Interpersonal anxiety and tension, as well as the importance of work, are characteristic of much of Tlingit culture. Here, embodied in myth, are nightmarish events the impact of which is heightened by the matter-of-fact presentation.

THE SHAMAN WHO WENT INTO THE FIRE, AND THE HERON'S SON*

A little boy's friends were all gone. His uncle was a great hunter, and the little boy was always going around far up in the woods with bow and arrows. He was growing bigger. He also went out with his uncle. His uncle went about everywhere to kill things. He always brought plenty of game down from the mountains.

One time he again went hunting. At that time the inside of the house was full of the sides of mountain sheep, on racks. His uncle's wife hated her husband's little nephew very much. When she went outside for a moment, he broke off a little piece of fat from the sides of mountain sheep hanging on the rack, to put inside of his cheek. Although there was so much he broke off only so much. Then his uncle's wife looked all around. The end piece was not there. "Is it you that has done this?" she said to her husband's little nephew. He cried and said, "No." Then she put her hand inside of his cheek. "Why don't you go up on the mountain?" [she said.] She scratched the inside of his cheek. Blood ran out of his mouth. While crying he pulled his uncle's box toward him. He took his uncle's whetstone out of it. Meanwhile his uncle was far away.

Then he started off into the woods, carrying the whetstone, and came out to a creek. He came out on a sandy bank, pounded (or scooped)

*From John R. Swanton, *Tlingit Myths and Texts*, pp. 267-279.

it out like a salmon, and made a nest beside the water. He stayed upon it overnight. His dream was like this. He was told, "Let it swim down into the water." It was his spirit that told him to do this.

When his uncle came down he missed him. He asked his wife, "Where is my nephew?" She answered. "He went up that way with his bow and arrows."

When [the boy] got up farther he made another nest. This man was named "For-little-slave." He made eight nests. Now his spirit helper began to come to him on the last. At that time he took his whetstone down into the creek, and it swam up in it. Then he lost his senses and went right up against the cliff. He stayed up there against the cliff. Everything came to hear him there—sea gulls, eagles, etc. When his spirits left him they would always be destroyed—the eagles, sea gulls, all of them.

Now, his uncle hunted for him. After he had been out for eight days he discovered the nest his nephew had made by the creek. He saw all the nests his nephew had camped in. His uncle looked into the creek. The salmon was swimming there, and he camped under the nest. Afterward he listened. In the morning he heard the beating made by shamans' sticks. He heard it just in the middle of the cliff. Then he came up underneath it. Before he thought that [his nephew] had seen him, his nephew spoke to him: "You came under me the wrong way, uncle." The uncle pitied his nephew very much. "Come up by this corner," said his nephew. Ever afterward he was named, "For-little-slave." Then his uncle asked him, "What caused you to do this?" He did not say that his uncle's wife had scratched the inside of his cheek. Instead he said to his uncle: "Cave spirits told me to come here." This was a big cave, bigger than a house.

Then his spirits came to him while his uncle was with him. They went inside, and his uncle beat time for him. Then he told his uncle to remember this: "When the spirit Nixâ' runs into the fire with me, do not let me burn up. While I am getting small throw me into a basket." That was the way he did with him. It ran into the fire with him, and he threw him into the basket. Then he always came to life inside of the basket. He became a big man again.

That same evening he sent out his uncle to call, "This way those that can sing." Then the cliff could hardly be seen for the mountain sheep that came down to look into the cave. When they were seated there, he whirled about his bow and arrows and all the mountain sheep were destroyed. The inside of the cave was full of them. Now, he said to his uncle: "Take off the hides." He was singing for great Nixâ'. When the spirit came out of him he reminded his uncle, "When it runs into the fire with me, don't forget to take me out and put me into the basket."

After all of the sheep's sides were covered up he sent him for his wife. He came up with his wife into the cave. Then he said to his uncle: "Take the half-basket in which we cook. Mash up the inside fat for your wife." His spirits took out the woman's bottom part from her. For this reason the woman never got full eating the mountain-sheep fat. She could not taste the fat. He put her in this condition because she had scratched the inside of his cheek.

By and by he said to his uncle: "Make your mind courageous when Nixâ' comes in." In the evening he told his uncle to go out and call. The cliffs could hardly be seen. Grizzly bears came in front of the house to the door of the cave. They extended far up in lines. Then his uncle started the song for the spirit. They kept coming inside. Suddenly a grizzly bear came in. It was as if eagle down were tied around its ears. At that [the uncle's] wife became scared and broke in two. He did this to her because she had scratched on the inside of his cheek on account of the fat. His spirit also ran into the fire with him. While his uncle stood in fear of the grizzly bear, For-little-slave burned up in the fire.

At that the cave creaked, and every animal ran into its skin. The things they were drying did so. They did so because the shaman had burned up. So the shaman and his uncle also were finally burned up.

Now people were disappearing from the town they had left. There were two wood roads. When anybody went out on one of these roads he never came back, and a person who went out on the other also, never came back. When one went away by canoe, he, too, was never seen again. He did not come home. In a single year there was no one left in that town except two, a woman and her daughter. After she had thought over their condition, this woman took her daughter away. She said, "Who will marry my daughter?" A heron that was walking upon the shore ice spoke to them, "How am I?" "What can you do?" said the woman. "I can stand upon the ice when it comes up." "Come home with us," said the woman. So the heron married [the girl], and she became pregnant. She brought forth. She bore a son. It began to grow large. The heron said to his wife, "What is the matter with your friends?" and she answered, "When they went after wood they never came back."

After the child had become large he kept taking it to the beach. He would bathe it amid the ice. Then the little boy began shooting with arrows. He always took his bow and arrows around. When he killed anything his father would say of the little boy, "My little son is just like me." By and by he said to his wife, "I am going away." After that the little boy began to go into the water. He crawled up, when he was almost killed by it.

Once he started off with his bow and arrows. When he was walking along the beach [he saw] a hīn-tayi'ei swimming in a little pond of sea water. He took it up. It cut his hands with its sharp sides. He reared it in the little pond. As he was going along with his bow and arrows he would feed it.

One time he said to his mother, "I am going after firewood." "But your uncles never came down," [she said]. In the morning he jumped quickly out on the floor. He took a stone ax and ran up in one of the roads. In it there was a finger sticking up, which said to him, "This way with your finger." He took hold of it and pulled up the being which was there. He threw it down on a stone. In the place from which he took it bones were left where it had been killing. Then he cut off its head with his stone ax. He took it down to his mother. He threw it into the house to her and to his grandmother, and they cut the face all up. They burned its face in the fire along with urine. They treated it just as they felt like doing. By and by the boy went up to the hīn-tayī'ei he was raising. Before it got longer than himself he shot it in the head. He took off its skin. Then he put [the skin] on a stump. How sharp were its edges!

When he got home again he jumped quickly out on the floor in the morning. He took his stone ax along in the next road. When he got far up he saw a head sticking up in the road. He said, "Up with your eyes, Kucaqē'!tk." The head was bent far backward. After he had moved its head backward he cut it off. The place where he took up this head was all full of bones. He threw that also down into the house. They rubbed its face with dung. They did to it as they felt toward it. After that he kept taking his bow and arrows up. He brought all kinds of things into the house for his mothers (i.e., his mother and grandmother). The son of the heron who came to help the woman was doing this. By and by he asked his mother, "In which direction did my uncles go who went out by sea and never came home?" She said to him, "They would go this way, little son." He went in that direction with his bow and arrows, and came out above the hole of a devilfish. As he was sitting there ready for action he looked right down into it. Then he went back for the hin-tayii'ei coat he had hidden. When he returned he threw a stone down upon the devilfish. He put on the hin-tayii′ei coat in order to jump into the midst of the devilfish's arms. Then he went right into them very quickly. He moved backward and forward inside of the devilfish's arms, and cut them all up into fine pieces with his side. By and by he cut its color sac in the midst of its arms, and afterward he swam out of the hole. He was floating outside, and he came ashore and took off his coat. Then he put it on the stump, and came again to his mother. The large tentacles floated up below them. He had cut them up into small pieces. It was that which had destroyed the people.

Again he took his bow and arrows. He came across a rat hole. The rat's tail was hanging out. He came directly home and, early in the morning before the raven called, he set out for it. He took his hīn-tayī′ei shirt. When he got back he started to put [the shirt] on after he had sharpened its edges. After he had gotten into it he went up to the [rat] hole. Then he threw a stone down upon it, making it give forth a peeping sound, as if the mountain were cracking in two. He swam round a stone, waiting for it to swim out. When it swam out it ran its nose against him. It swam past him. It wanted to drop its tail down on him. Then he floated edge up, and it tried to drop its tail down upon him. When it dropped its tail down upon him it was cut up into small pieces. Then it swam up to his side, crying on account of what he had done. He cut it all up. Afterward he swam ashore. He put his skin back on the stump. In the morning its head floated in front of them. They cut it up.

After two days he pulled down his canoe. Going along for a while, he came up to the beach in front of a woman sitting in a house. She had only one eye. "Come up, my nephew. I have stale salmon heads, my nephew," she said to him. This person in front of whom he had come was the real one who had destroyed the canoes. Those were human heads that she spoke of as stale heads. He did not eat them. He saw what they were. "I have also fish eggs," [she said]. Those were human eyes, and he did not eat of them. He emptied them by the fire. The woman's husband, however, was away hunting for human beings. Lastly she got human ribs, and when he would not eat those she became angry about it. She threw a shell at him with which she used to kill human beings, but missed him, for he jumped away quickly. Then he took it up. He hit her with it in return, and the cannibal wife broke in two. After he had killed her he pulled her over on the fire. When he blew upon her ashes, however, they became mosquitoes. This is why mosquitoes eat people. After he had killed her he went away and met the cannibal man.

When he met him he killed him. He cut off his head and took it to his mother's home. There they cut his face all up. They burned his face with dung.

In olden times when a person finished a story he said, "It's up to you."

ORIGIN OF A LOW-CASTE NAME*

There was a certain village in the north from which the people were fond of going hunting. By and by three men went out, and finally came to the rocks among which they always hunted. After they reached the rocks they saw a little boy. Then they took him aboard, thinking it was strange that he should be there. When they spoke to him he did not reply. After that they came home. They kept him as their friend. Whenever they gave him something to eat he ate nothing. Only after everyone had gone to bed did he eat. Whatever thing he touched would spill on him. He was whimsical and they could do nothing with him. He was also lazy. When he was asked to chop wood he broke all of their stone axes. The axes were then valuable. Then the people who had kept him were very sorry. When he played with the children he hurt them badly. Afterward the people who kept him would have to pay for the injuries. If he made something with a knife he would break it. Right after a skin shirt had been put upon him it was in rags. If shoes were put on his feet they were soon in pieces. He drank a great deal of water. He was a great eater. He was a dirty little fellow. He was a crybaby. If they gave him anything to take to another place he lost it. So he made a great deal of trouble for the people.

Then they said of him, "He is really a man of the rocks." All the town people agreed to take him back to the place where he had been found. After he had been brought in it was very rainy. Then the people who had saved him got into their canoe and carried him back. They put him on the very same rock from which they had taken him. Then they went back. They reached home. The world was now calm. The rain also had ceased. Then the town people were all talking about it. They said to one another,

*From John R. Swanton, *Tlingit Myths and Texts,* pp. 369-371.

"What could it have been?" and no one knew. Finally the town people said, "Don't you see it was a rock-man's son?"

A double-edged tale, this brief account sets up standards for proper behavior in children, and also attributes such characteristics as laziness, dirtiness, and greed to the bearers of the low-caste name "rock-man."

TSIMSHIAN

THE STONE AND THE ELDERBERRY BUSH*

A little before the Stone gave birth to her child, the Elderberry Bush gave birth to her children. For that reason the Indians do not live many years. Because the Elderberry Bush gave birth to her children first, man dies quickly. If the Stone had first given birth to her children, this would not be so. Thus say the Indians. That is the story of the Elderberry Bush's children. The Indians are much troubled because the Stone did not give birth to her children first, for this is the reason that men die quickly.

THE WOLVES AND THE DEER**

The Wolves had a feast on a prairie at the mouth of Skeena river. They invited the chiefs of the Deer to the feast. The Deer who had been called came. Then they sat down on the prairie face to face with the Wolves. The Wolves said to the Deer, "You on the opposite side, begin to laugh." But the Deer did not agree. They said, "You shall laugh first." The Wolves replied, "Now we will laugh. Ha, ha, ha, ha, ha! Now you must laugh, you on the other side." Then the Deer laughed: "M, m, m, m, m! Now you laugh again, Wolves." Then the Wolves laughed again: "Ha, ha, ha, ha, ha!" Now the Deer were afraid when they saw the large teeth of the Wolves. The Wolves said, "Now, you on the other side, you shall laugh again. Don't keep your mouths closed when you are laughing. Nobody laughs like that. You must open your mouths as far as possible when you are laughing. Now do so. Try as hard as you can. Don't be afraid to open your mouths." Thus spoke the Wolves. "Now laugh." Then the Deer laughed again: "Ha, ha, ha, ha, ha!" They opened their

*From Franz Boas, *Tsimshian Texts,* p. 72.
**From Franz Boas, *Tsimshian Texts,* pp. 83-85.

mouths wide. They had no teeth. When the Wolves saw that they had no teeth they attacked them, and they bit them all over. Then they devoured the Deer. Only a few of the Deer succeeded in escaping. For this reason the Deer are afraid of the Wolves.

THE CHIEF WHO BEWITCHED HIS SON*

It is said that there was a son of a chief who had a friend who was also a prince. The chief was jealous of this prince, and he made up his mind to bewitch him. The chief told his son to invite his friend and to ask him to sleep in his house.

One day the chief's son invited his friend in, and they lay down. The prince lay on the outside and the chief's son on the inside of the bed. The chief's son fell asleep, but the prince could not sleep, because he was afraid the chief might bewitch him. He rose and changed places with the chief's son. He lay down on the inside and put the chief's son on the outside. When the chief heard that they were asleep, he rose and slowly walked to the bed on which the prince and his son were sleeping. The prince was much afraid when he heard the chief coming, but he pretended to sleep. The chief felt about with his hands until he found the place where the prince had lain down in the evening. Then he wiped out the mouth of his own son (thinking him to be the prince). Then the chief lay down again.

In the morning the prince rose and went out. After a short time the chief's son got sick. Then the chief knew at once that he had made a mistake. For four days the boy was sick. Then he died. Now the chief was much troubled. He cried because his son was dead, saying, "I have destroyed him myself! I have destroyed him myself!"

The fear of witchcraft and restrictions against its use are found among numerous Indian tribes.

*From Franz Boas, *Tsimshian Texts,* pp. 218-220.

YUROK

A SHAMAN'S ACQUISITION OF POWERS*

I BEGAN with a dream. At that time I was already married at Sregon. In the dream I was on Bald Hills. There I met a Chilula man who fed me deer meat which was black with blood. I did not know the man, but he was a short-nosed person. I had this dream in autumn, after we had gathered acorns.

In the morning I was ill. A doctor was called in to treat me and diagnosed my case. Then I went to the sweathouse to dance for ten nights. This whole time I did not eat. Once I danced until I became unconscious. They carried me into the living house. When I revived I climbed up the framework of poles for drying fish, escaped through the smoke hole, ran to another sweathouse, and began to dance there.

On the tenth day, while I was dancing, I obtained control of my first "pain." It came out of my mouth looking like a salmon liver, and as I held it in my hands blood dripped from it to the ground. This is what I had seen in my dream on Bald Hills. I then thought that it was merely venison. It was when I ate the venison that the pain entered my body.

On the eleventh day I began to eat again, but only a little.

All that winter I went daily high up on the ridge to gather sweathouse wood and each night I spent in the sweathouse. All this time I drank no water. Sometimes I walked along the river, put pebbles into my mouth and spat them out. Then I said to myself: "When I am a doctor I shall suck and the pains will come into my mouth as cool as these stones. I shall be paid for that." When day broke I would face the door of the sweat house and say: "A long dentalium is looking in at me." When I went up to gather wood, I kept saying: "The dentalium has gone before me; I see its tracks." When I had filled my basket with the wood, I said: "That large dentalium, the one I am carrying, is very heavy." When I swept the platform before the sweathouse clean with a branch, I said: "I see dentalia. I see dentalia. I am sweeping them to both sides of me." So whatever I did I spoke of money constantly.

Curing ceremonies among numerous Northwest groups involved sucking a presumed foreign (and dangerous) object from the mouth of the sick victim. Shamans —or those who would become Shamans—subjected themselves to more stressful experiences: fasting, extreme and abrupt temperature changes, which resulted in the visions from which they obtained their powers.

*From Robert F. Heizer and M.A. Whipple, *The California Indians*, p. 451.

Section II

After the White Man Came

Southeast

CHEROKEE

YOU WHISKY-MAKERS, THINK OF THE CHILDREN*

You whisky-makers, think of the young people!
Their parents cry over them; they weep for them.

CHORUS: How sad it is if one has a taste for whisky
For it takes many from the earth.

You whisky-makers, think of the children!
Their parents cry over them; they weep for them.

TSEG'SGIN' FOILS HIS CAPTORS**

There was once a king who had a daughter. All of the young men were trying to amuse her because if one of them could make her laugh, he was to have her for a wife.

The men had performed for a long time when Tseg'sgin' came riding up upon a bull. Tseg'sgin' was sitting backward upon the bull. He [the bull] ran in front of the woman, and the bull was bellowing as he ran. The woman laughed.

"Now she laughed at me!" they all said to each other as they squabbled. They were told to keep silent, and the woman was asked at whom she laughed. She said that the man who came by upon the bull made her laugh.

*From Jack F. and Anna G. Kilpatrick, *The Shadow of Sequoyah*, p. 82.
**From Jack F. and Anna G. Kilpatrick, *Friends of Thunder*, pp. 111-112.

177

They [the young men] all became angry at the man who had made her laugh, and they said, "Let's take him prisoner!" So they caught him, and they said, "Let's get a sack and throw him into the deep water." They put him into a sack, tied it, and took him down to the water to throw him into it.

While they were getting ready to put him into the water, someone herding sheep came by. He saw Tseg'sgin' and said, "Why are you in this condition?"

"They're going to take me to the big city where one can choose anything that he wants, but I don't want to go."

The sheepherder said, "I'll go." So the sheepherder untied the bag and let Tseg'sgin' out.

After a while his [Tseg'sgin' 's] captors returned. Tseg'sgin' had already driven the flock of sheep away. When his captors returned, they located the deep water. They took him [the sheepherder that they thought was Tseg'sgin'] to it.

"I'm not the one!"

"Yes, you are! Tseg'sgin', we had you in here!" So they threw him [the sheepherder] into the water.

Later on they saw him [Tseg'sgin'] herding the flock of sheep. "Look at him that we threw into the water!" they said.

"One could choose anything he wanted. He could even get two women, or the town itself. But I chose herding sheep!" he said.

That's all.

This is an Indian version of a popular European folktale.

FIRST CONTACT WITH WHITES*

At the creation an ulûñsû′ti was given to the white man, and a piece of silver to the Indian. But the white man despised the stone and threw it away, while the Indian did the same with the silver. In going about the white man afterward found the silver piece and put it into his pocket and has prized it ever since. The Indian, in like manner, found the ulûñsû′ti where the white man had thrown it. He picked it up and has

*From James Mooney, *Myths of the Cherokees*, p. 350.

kept it since as his talisman, as money is the talismanic power of the white man.

ON THE CHEROKEE ALPHABET*

When Sequoya, the inventor of the Cherokee alphabet, was trying to introduce it among his people, about 1822, some of them opposed it upon the ground that Indians had no business with reading. They said that when the Indian and the white man were created, the Indian, being the elder, was given a book, while the white man received a bow and arrows. Each was instructed to take good care of his gift and make the best use of it, but the Indian was so neglectful of his book that the white man soon stole it from him, leaving the bow in its place, so that books and reading now belong of right to the white man, while the Indian ought to be satisfied to hunt for a living.—*Cherokee Advocate,* October 26, 1844.

ON BLACK AND WHITE**

The Negro made the first locomotive for a toy and put it on a wooden track and was having great fun with it when a white man came along, watched until he saw how to run it, and then killed the Negro and took the locomotive for himself.

TO DESTROY LIFE***

Listen! Now I have come to step over your soul
You are of the Wolf clan.
Your name is A'yu'nini.
Your spittle I have put at rest under the earth.
I have come to cover you over with the black rock.
I have come to cover you over with the black cloth.
I have come to cover you over with the black slabs, never
      to reappear.

*From James Mooney, *Myths of the Cherokees,* p. 350.
**From James Mooney, *Myths of the Cherokees,* p. 351.
***From James Mooney, *The Sacred Formulas of the Cherokees*, p. 391.

Toward the black coffin of the upland in the Darkening Land
    your paths shall stretch out.
So shall it be for you.
The clay of the upland has come to cover you.
Instantly the black clay has lodged there where it is at
    rest at the black houses in the Darkening Land.
With the black coffin and with the black slabs I have come
    to cover you.
Now your soul has faded away.
It has become blue
When darkness comes your spirit shall grow less and dwindle
    away, never to reappear
Listen!

SEMINOLE

WE ARE GOING WITH GEORGE WASHINGTON*

We are going with George Washington
Which boat do we get in?

THEY ARE TAKING US BEYOND MIAMI*

They are taking us beyond Miami
They are taking us beyond the Caloosa River
They are taking us to the end of our tribe
They are taking us to Palm Beach, coming back beside
    Okeechobee lake.
They are taking us to an old town in the west.

*From Frances Densmore, *Seminole Music,* p. 202.

SHAWNEE

FATHER, LISTEN TO YOUR CHILDREN!*

FATHER, listen to your children! You have them now all before you.

The war before this, our British father gave the hatchet to his red children, when our old chiefs were alive. They are now dead. In the war, our father was thrown on his back by the Americans, and our father took them by the hand without our knowledge; and we are afraid that our father will do so again this time.

Summer before last, when I came forward with my red brethren, and was ready to take up the hatchet in favor of our British father, we were told not to be in a hurry that he had not yet determined to fight the Americans.

Listen! When war was declared, our father stood up and gave us the tomahawk and told us that he was then ready to strike the Americans; that he wanted our assistance; and that he would certainly get our lands back, which the Americans had taken from us.

Listen! You told us, at that time, to bring forward our families to this place; and we did so; and you promised to take care of them, and they should want for nothing, while the men would go out and fight the enemy; that we need not trouble ourselves about the enemy's garrisons; that we knew nothing about them, and that our father would attend to that part of the business. You also told your red children that you would take good care of your garrison here which made our hearts glad.

Listen! When we were last at the Rapids it is true we gave you little assistance. It is hard to fight people who live like groundhogs.

Father, Listen. Our fleet has gone out. We know they have fought. We have heard the great guns but we know nothing of what has happened to our father with that arm. Our ships have gone one way and we are much astonished to see our father tying up everything and preparing to run away the other, without letting his red children know what his intentions are. You always told us to remain here and take care of our lands. It made our hearts glad to hear that was your wish. Our great father, the king, is the head, and you represent him. You always told us that you would never draw your foot off British ground; but now, father,

*From Tecumseh, "Father, Listen to Your Children" in *History of the Choctaw, Chicasaw and Natchez Indians*.

we see you are drawing back and we are sorry to see our father doing so without seeing the enemy. We must compare our father's conduct to a fat dog, that carries its tail upon its back but when afrighted it drops it between its legs and runs off.

Father, Listen! The Americans have not yet defeated us by land. Neither are we sure that they have done so by water. We therefore wish to remain here and fight our enemy, should they make their appearance. If they defeat us, we will then retreat with our father.

At the battle of the Rapids, last war, the Americans certainly defeated us, and when we retreated to our father's fort at that place the gates were shut against us. We were afraid that it would now be the case; but instead of that we now see our British father preparing to march out of his garrison.

Father! You have got the arms and ammunition which our great father sent for his red children. If you have an idea of going away, give them to us and you may go and welcome for us. Our lives are in the hands of the Great Spirit. We are determined to defend our lands, and if it be his will, we wish to leave our bones upon them.

TECUMSEH

Northeast

DELAWARE

I AM THE MASTER OF LIFE*

I am the Master of Life, whom you wish to see and with whom you wish to speak. Listen to what I shall tell you for yourself and for all the Indians. The land on which you are, I have made for you, not for others. Wherefore do you suffer the whites to dwell upon your lands? Can you not do without them? I know that those whom you call the children of your Great Father (the King of France) supply your wants; but were you not wicked as you are you would not need them. You might live as you did before you knew them. Before those whom you call your brothers (the French) had arrived, did not your bow and arrow maintain you? You needed neither gun, powder, nor any other object. The flesh of animals was your food; their skins your raiment. But when I saw you inclined to evil, I removed the animals into the depths of the forest that you might depend on your brothers for your necessaries, for your clothing. Again become good and do my will and I will send animals for your sustenance. I do not, however, forbid suffering among you your Father's children. I love them; they know me; they pray to me. I supply their own wants and give them that which they bring to you. Not so with those who are come to trouble your possessions (the English). Give them away; wage war against them; I love them not; they know me not; they are my enemies; they are your brother; enemies. Send them back to the lands I have made for them. Let them remain there.

*From James Mooney, *The Ghost-Dance Religion and the Sioux Outbreak of 1890*, pp. 664-665.

183

(The Master of Life then gave him a prayer carved in Indian hiero-glyphics upon a wooden stick, which he was told to deliver to his chief on returning to earth.)

Learn it by heart and teach it to all the Indians and children. It must be repeated morning and evening. Do all that I have told thee and announce it to all the Indians as coming from the Master of Life. Let them drink but one draught or two at most, in one day. Let them have but one wife and discontinue running after other people's wives and daughters. Let them not fight one another. Let them not sing the medicine song for in singing the medicine song they speak to the evil spirit. Drive from your lands those dogs in red clothing; they are only an injury to you. When you want anything apply to me as your brothers do, and I will give to both. Do not sell to your brother that which I have placed on the earth as food. In short, become good and you shall want nothing. When you meet one another, bow and give one another the hand of the heart. Above all, I command thee to repeat morning and evening the prayer which I have given thee.

In 1762 a prophet appeared among the Delawares who preached a union of all the red tribes and a return to the old Indian life.

YOU PUT A WAR HATCHET INTO MY HANDS*

Father! Some time ago you put a war hatchet into my hands, saying, "Take this weapon and try it on the heads of my enemies, the Long Knives, and let me know afterwards if it was sharp and good."

Father! At the time you gave me this weapon, I had neither cause nor wish to go to war against a foe who had done me no injury. But you say you are my father—and call me your child—and in obedience to you I received the hatchet. I knew that if I did not obey you, you would withhold from me the necessaries of life, which I could procure nowhere but here.

Father! You may perhaps think me a fool, for risking my life at your bidding—and that in a cause in which I have no prospect of gaining anything. For it is your cause, and not mine—you have raised a quarrel

*From Charles E. Hamilton, *Cry of the Thunderbird*, pp. 143-144.

among yourselves—and you ought to fight it out. It is *your* concern to fight the Long Knives. You should not compel your children, the Indians, to expose themselves to danger for your sake.

Father! Many lives have already been lost on *your account*. The tribes have suffered, and been weakened. Children have lost parents and brothers. Wives have lost husbands. It is not known how many more may perish before *your war* will be at an end.

Father! I have said, you may perhaps think me a fool, for thus thoughtlessly rushing on your enemy! Do not believe this, Father: Think not that I want sense to convince me, that although you now pretend to keep up a perpetual enmity to the Long Knives, you may, before long, conclude a peace with them.

Father! You say you love your children, the Indians. This you have often told them; and indeed it is your interest to say so to them; that you may have them at your service.

But, Father! Who of us can believe that you can love a people a different color from your own; better than those who have a white skin, like yourselves?

Father! Pay attention to what I am going to say. While you, Father, are setting me on your enemy, much in the same manner as a hunter sets his dog on the game; and while I am in the act of rushing on that enemy of yours, with the bloody destructive weapon you gave me, I may, perchance, happen to look back at the place from whence you started me, and what shall I see? Perhaps, I may see my father shaking hands with the Long Knives; yes, with those very people he now calls his enemies, I may *then* see him laugh at my folly for having obeyed his orders; and yet I am now risking my life at his command! Father! Keep what I have said in remembrance.

Now, Father! Here is what has been done with the hatchet you gave me [handing the commandant the stick with the scalps on it]. I have done with the hatchet what you ordered me to do, and found it sharp. Nevertheless, I did not do all that I might have done. No, I did not. My heart failed within me. I felt compassion for your enemy. Innocence had no part in your quarrels; therefore I distinguished—I spared. I took some live flesh [prisoners], which, while I was bringing to you, I spied one of your large canoes, on which I put it for you. In a few days you will receive this flesh, and find that the skin is of the same color with your own.

Father! I hope you will not destroy what I have saved. You, Father, have the means of preserving that which would perish with us from want.

The warrior is poor, and his cabin is always empty; but your house, Father, is always full.

CHIEF HOPOCAN

During the Revolutionary War, some Indians joined the English forces fighting against the Americans. Among those who joined the English were the Delaware. The speech made here by Chief Hopocan expresses the distrust and disillusionment with which the Indians greeted the English, as well as their somewhat ambivalent feelings toward battling the Americans.

MOHEGAN

MOHEGAN PETITION TO THE CONNECTICUT STATE ASSEMBLY*

TO the Most Honorable Assembly of the State of Connecticut at Hartford, May 14, 1789.

Your Good old Steady Friends and Brethren the Mohegan Tribe of Indians Sendeth Greeting:

We beg Leave to lay our Concerns and Burdens at Your Excellencies Feet. The Times are Exceedingly Alter'd, Yea the Times have turn'd everything Upside down, or rather we have Chang'd the good Times, Chiefly by the help of the White People, For in Times past our Fore-Fathers lived in Peace, Love and great harmony, and had everything in Great plenty. When they Wanted meat they would just run into the Bush a little ways with their Weapons and would Soon bring home good venison, Racoon, Bear and Fowl. If they Choose to have Fish, they Wo'd only go to the River or along the Sea Shore and they wou'd presently fill their Cannous With Veriety of Fish, Both Scaled and shell Fish, and they had abundance of Nuts, Wild Fruit, Ground Nuts and Ground Beans, and they planted but little corn and Beans and they kept no Cattle or Horses for they needed none—And they had no Contention about their

*Quoted in Wissler 1966:318-320; original in the Connecticut State Library.

lands, it lay in Common to them all, and they had but one large dish and they Cou'd all eat together in Peace and Love—But alas, it is not so now, all our Fishing, Hunting and Fowling is entirely gone, And we have now begun to Work on our Land, keep Cattle, Horses and Hogs And we Build Houses and fence in Lots, And now we plainly See that one Dish and one Fire will not do any longer for us—Some few there are Stronger than others and they will keep off the poor, weake, the halt and the Blind, And Will take the Dish to themselves. Yea, they will rather Call White People and Molattoes to eat With them out of our Dish, and poor Widows and Orphans Must be pushed one side and there they Must Set a Craying, Starving and die.

And so We are now Come to our Good Brethren of the Assembly With Hearts full of Sorrow and Grief for Immediate help—And therefore our most humble and Earnest Request and Petition is That our Dish of Suck-uttush may be equally divided amongst us, that every one may have his own little dish by himself, that he may eat Quietly and do With his Dish as he pleases, and let every one have his own Fire.

Your Excellencies Compliance and Assistance at This Time will make our poor hearts very Glad and thankful.

This is the most humble Request and Petition of Your True Friend & Brethren Mohegan Indians,

By the Hands of our Brothers
Harry x Quaduaquid, his mark
Robert Ashpo

CAPTAIN KIDD AND THE PIRATES*

In the days of Captain Kidd he and other buccaneers used to come up the Thames River in their boats and lie to during the periods of pursuit. Up there among the Indians they could pass the time pleasantly, and also find secluded regions wherein to bury their booty. So the Mohegans have some tales of these visits from the pirates which have furnished the motive for many nightly excursions to dreamt-of spots where treasure is thought to

*From Frank G. Speck, *Native Tribes and Dialects of Connecticut*, p. 276.

exist. Until this day futile attempts are made to lay hands on some of the gold that is said to be buried along the river shores.

One time two Mohegans, having dreamed of a certain spot where Kidd's money was buried, went down to the river with spades. They began their trench, and soon had the good fortune to disclose the top of a great iron box with a ring in it. Their surprise was so great that one of them said, "Here it is!" At that moment a tremendous black dog appeared at the rim of the pit and growled. At the same moment the chest vanished. The men were so terrified that they never tried to find the place again.

THUNDER FROM THE CLEAR SKY*

Now, there was a time when an Indian man was a preacher here. He was Samuel Ashbow. He was a good man, but his wife was not a very good woman, being fond of "a'nkapi" (rum). For many years she was thus, and it made poor Ashbow very unhappy.

Then there came a certain time when something was going to happen; when something was going to happen from the sky. The Indians were helping a white man build a mill over on Stony Brook, and Ashbow used to go and help too. One time he took his wife along with him. Ashbow was a good man, but his wife had a bottle of "a'nkapi" hidden in her dress. She began to drink, and gave some to the other men. Ashbow only watched her a while, but soon got angry, and taking the bottle from her, threw it on a rock. It broke and the rum spilled on the earth. The wife became furious, and a few moments later, while Ashbow was stooping over a stone, she picked up a piece of rock and struck him on the forehead. He fell down with the blood streaming from him. Then there was a sharp clap of thunder from above, and all looked up, only to see a clear sky with a patch of cloud overhead only as large as a hand. It was a sign to Ashbow's wife, and from that time she never drank rum, neither did the other men who heard the thunder. Ashbow got well.

*From Frank G. Speck, *Native Tribes and Dialects of Connecticut*, pp. 277-278.

ONONDAGA

ON THE IROQUOIS LEAGUE*

Woe! Woe!
Hearken ye!
We are diminished!
Woe! Woe!
The cleared land has become a thicket.

Woe! Woe!
The clear places are deserted.
Woe!
They are in their graves—
They who established it—
Woe!
The great League
Yet they declared
It should endure—
The great League.
Woe!
Their work has grown old
Woe!
Thus we are become miserable.

*From Horatio Hale, *The Iroquois Book of Rites*, p. 153.

WAMPONOAG

THE UNFINISHED BRIDGE*

BECAUSE Moshop was a kindly person who greatly wished peace and contentment, not only for himself but for his family, he was unhappy when some of his people suggested he build a bridge to the mainland. A bridge, they argued, would allow them to visit other tribes for trading and would permit some of their friends as well as relatives to visit Capawack. There also would be more opportunity and adventure for the younger braves who were growing restless within the confines of Capawack.

The possibility of a bridge became the main topic discussed around the camp fires. By some it was thought to be good but there were others who voiced loud disagreement. Soon there was anger boiling up between friends. Neighbors refused to speak to neighbors. Even the children took it up and began a game of tossing stones out into the water to see who could be Moshop, with the rock that would fall farthest from shore in the direction of the mainland.

At last Moshop decided something must be done. A delegation had come to him, urging him to build a bridge of rocks across the expanse of water between Aquinnah and Cuttyhunk. From Cuttyhunk it would be an easy trail along the small islands to the mainland. Then there would be a way to the outside lands for those who wished to travel far from Capawack, but the bridge also would provide a safe means of return across the dangerous tidal waters.

When Moshop finally made it known he would build the bridge, there were those who continued to oppose the plan. They predicted Capawack would be overrun with people from the mainland and that these visitors might, in time, become an undesirable majority.

While all this was being discussed, a very old woman, bent with her years and said to have wisdom from unnamed sources, asked to be heard.

Her proposal was to have Moshop agree to work on the bridge only from sunset to cockcrow. Her listeners were not impressed. How, they asked, could this help matters? By the light of the full moon, Moshop easily could complete the bridge in that time. The old woman insisted and

*From Dorothy Scoville, *Indian Legends of Martha's Vineyard*, p. 8-9.

to please her, because they respected her years, they approached Moshop with the plan. Moshop, seeing this as a way to keep peace between the two factions, readily agreed.

Long before sunset, on the night of the full moon, the village people assembled along the top of Aquinnah's cliffs to watch Moshop build the bridge that was to link them with the mainland.

As the sun dipped into the sea, Moshop began his labor. From along shores of Aquinnah as far as Menemsha and Kuppi-egen Moshop collected rocks in his leather petunk or apron which he wore around his immense waist. One by one he tossed the big stones into the water between the cliffs of Aquinnah and the shores of Cuttyhunk.

He was wading out into the deeper water with another large rock in his arms, when suddenly he was seen to drop the boulder, yell loudly and kick one bare foot in the air. Attached to his great toe was a giant crab which flew through the air to drop with a splash and lie like a small island toward the southwest of Aquinnah. Later this island was known as Noman's Land, for Chief Tequenomans, an Indian owner.

Muttering in discomfort and anger, Moshop hobbled ashore to sit on the beach rubbing his great toe. At this moment, those watching on the shore heard the loud crowing of a cock, which was the agreed signal for Moshop to end his work. Amazed, the villagers saw the old woman who had set the time limit, standing on the cliff with her pet rooster. In one hand she held a lighted torch which she passed in front of his eyes. Thinking dawn had come, the rooster crowed loudly.

The bridge was unfinished but the bargain was binding, according to Moshop's decree. Those who opposed the bridge danced and laughed, while the others retired in disgruntled silence.

Moshop rose without speaking, reached out into the water and caught an unwary whale by the tail. With a swift swing of his arm, he killed the whale against one of the big rocks he had tossed from the shore. Then he told his people to prepare a feast and to forget their differences in sharing the food which Manitou, the Great Spirit, had provided.

Tales of the giant Moshop are quite common among many of the East Coast Indians. This particular tale suggests that commerce and traffic linked the inhabitants of off-shore islands with their mainland brethren. The ambivalence towards these trade networks which brought threat as well as riches is clearly evident in this tale. Anthropologists believe that these trade networks developed, at least in part, as the result of contact with European traders who stimulated the search for valuable trade objects and thus increased the contacts among Indians throughout the east coast.

SENECA

BROTHER, THE GREAT SPIRIT HAS MADE US ALL*

FRIEND and Brother! It was the will of the Great Spirit that we should meet together this day. He orders all things, and he has given us a fine day for our council. He has taken his garment from before the sun and has caused the bright orb to shine with brightness upon us. Our eyes are opened so that we see clearly. Our ears are unstopped so that we have been able to distinctly hear the words which you have spoken. For all these favors we thank the Great Spirit and him only.

Brother! This council fire was kindled by you. It was at your request that we came together at this time. We have listened with attention to what you have said. You have requested us to speak our minds freely. This gives us great joy, for we now consider that we stand upright before you, and can speak what we think. All have heard your voice and all speak to you as one man. Our minds are agreed.

Brother! You say that you want an answer to your talk before you leave this place. It is right that you should have one, as you are a great distance from home, and we do not wish to detain you. But we will first look back a little, and tell you what our fathers have told us, and what we have heard from the white people.

Brother! Listen to what we say. There was a time when our forefathers owned this great island (meaning the continent of North America—a common belief among the Indians). Their seats extended from the rising to the setting of the sun. The Great Spirit had made it for the use of Indians. He had created the buffalo, the deer, and other animals for food. He made the bear and the deer, and their skins served us for clothing. He had scattered them over the country, and had taught us how to take them. He had caused the earth to produce corn for bread. All this he had done for his red children because he loved them. If we had any disputes about hunting grounds, they were generally settled without the shedding of much blood. But an evil day came upon us. Your forefathers crossed the great waters and landed on this island. Their numbers were small. They found friends and not enemies. They told us they had fled from their own country for fear of wicked men, and had come here to enjoy their religion. They asked for a small seat. We took pity on them, granted

*From W. C. Vanderwerth, *Indian Oratory*, pp. 44-47.

their request and they sat down amongst us. We gave them corn and meat. They gave us poison (spiritous liquor) in return. The white people had now found our country. Tidings were carried back and more came amongst us. Yet we did not fear them. We took them to be friends. They called us brothers. We believed them and gave them a large seat. At length their numbers had greatly increased. They wanted more land. They wanted our country. Our eyes were opened, and our minds became uneasy. Wars took place. Indians were hired to fight against Indians, and many of our people were destroyed. They also brought strong liquors among us. It was strong and powerful and has slain thousands.

Brother! Our seats were once large, and yours were very small. You have now become a great people, and we have scarcely a place left to spread our blankets. You have got our country, but you are not satisfied. You want to force your religion upon us.

Brother! Continue to listen. You say that you are sent to instruct us how to worship the Great Spirit agreeably to his mind; and if we do not take hold of the religion which you white people teach we shall be unhappy hereafter. You say that you are right, and we are lost. How do you know this to be true? We understand that your religion is written in a book. If it was intended for us as well as for you, why has not the Great Spirit given it to us; and not only to us, but why did he not give to our forefathers the knowledge of that book, with the means of understanding it rightly? We only know what you tell us about it. How shall we know when to believe, being so often deceived by the white people?

Brother! You say there is but one way to worship and serve the Great Spirit. If there is but one religion, why do you white people differ so much about it? Why not all agree, as you can all read the book?

Brother! We do not understand these things. We are told that your religion was given to your forefathers and has been handed down, father to son. We also have a religion which was given to our forefathers, and has been handed down to us, their children. We worship that way. It teaches us to be thankful for all the favors we received, to love each other, and to be united. We never quarrel about religion.

Brother! The Great Spirit has made us all. But he has made a great difference between his white and red children. He has given us a different complexion and different customs. To you he has given the arts; to these he has not opened our eyes. We know these things to be true. Since he has made so great a difference between us in other things, why may not we conclude that he has given us a different religion, according to our understanding? The Great Spirit does right. He knows what is best for his children. We are satisfied.

Brother! We do not wish to destroy your religion, or to take it from you. We only want to enjoy our own.

Brother! You say you have not come to get our land or our money, but to enlighten our minds. I will now tell you that I have been at your meetings and saw you collecting money from the meeting. I cannot tell what this money was intended for, but suppose it was for your minister; and if we should conform to your way of thinking, perhaps you may want some from us.

Brother! We are told that you have been preaching to the white people in this place. These people are our neighbors. We are acquainted with them. We will wait a little while, and see what effect your preaching has upon them. If we find it does them good and makes them honest and less disposed to cheat Indians, we will then consider again what you have said.

Brother! You have now heard our answer to your talk, and this is all we have to say at present. As we are going to part, we will come and take you by the hand, and hope the Great Spirit will protect you on your journey, and return you safe to your friends.

RED JACKET

WYANDOT

THE WARNING OF THE BEES*

ONE summer day, whilst a party of children of nature were sitting around under shady trees on a bank of the stream, one of the very old men suddenly exclaimed, "Hun-haw!" [an expression of regret]. "Look here!" said he pointing toward a strange-looking insect that was buzzing around some wild flowers near them, "the white man," he continued, "is not very far off and this strange thing you see flying around here was brought over to this country by the white man from the other side of the 'big waters,' and who, before very long, will come and take the

*From Peter D. Clarke, *Origin and Traditional History of the Wyandotts,* p. 6.

whole country from the red man. Like the white man this strange thing represents the rapidly increasing and ever busy tribe it belongs to.'' The insect that attracted their attention was the honeybee. ''Thus you see,'' resumed the Wyandott, ''that what has been foretold by our fathers is now coming to pass.'' Presently the bee came buzzing around them, then darted into the forest.

Prairies

CADDO

SEE! THE EAGLE COMES*

See! the eagle comes,
See! the eagle comes;
Now at last we see him—look! look! the eagle comes,
Now at last we see him—look! look! the eagle comes;
Now we see him with the people,
Now we see him with the people.

Among the Caddo, the eagle was considered a sacred bird, which could be killed only by a medicine man who knew the proper formula. This song, part of the ghost dance ritual, refers to the return of the eagle feathers which were believed to have great power.

EXHORTATION**

Come on, Caddo, we are all going up,
Come on, Caddo, we are all going up
To the great village—He'e'ye'!
To the great village—He'e'ye'!
With our Father above
With our Father above when he dwells on high—He'e'ye!
Where our Mother dwells—He'e'ye!
Where our Mother dwells—He'e'ye!

---

*From James Mooney, *The Ghost-Dance Religion and the Sioux Outbreak of 1890*, p. 1100.
**From James Mooney, *The Ghost-Dance Religion and the Sioux Outbreak of 1890*, p. 1102.

Like most of the ghost dance songs, the verse pattern for the exhortation above is extremely stereotyped. Generally, the songs consisted of a few lines, each of which was repeated once. According to James Mooney, the number of such songs was endless since they were made up by individuals participating in the dance. During each dance, a trance subject produced a song which embodied his experience in the spirit world. Such a song was sung until it was superseded by other songs made up in the same way. A single dance could result in twenty or thirty new songs. While Christian imagery and ideas are apparent in many of the songs, the form itself may have been adopted from one used in gambling hand-games popular with the Indians.

Fox

EXCERPT FROM AUTOBIOGRAPHY OF A FOX WOMAN*

I was sixteen years old when we were making mats in the summer. In the winter we were making sacks and yarn belts (and) we were sewing appliqué ribbon work and bead work. Behold, it was true that I was constantly asked (to make) something, (and) I would be paid. "That is why," I would be told, "I continuously told you to learn to know how to make things. After these mats are completed, and any one is given them, soon he (she) (will) give something in return. And also in regard to these sacks, when (anyone) is given them, he (she) gives something in return, no doubt. That is why one is willing to make things, because they are benefited by what is made," I was told. Lo, surely when I began to realize it, what I had been told was true.

Now when I was more than seventeen, while living outside somewhere, after two days, late at night while I was still sleeping (someone) said to me, "Wake up." (The person) was holding a match, and lit it. Lo, it was a man when I looked at him. I was as frightened as possible. I trembled as I was frightened. When I ordered him away, (my voice) did not (sound) natural when I spoke. I was barely able to speak to him. And from then on, now and then men tried to come to me. I always had been instructed what was proper. When it was known (what kind of a person) I (was), they began to try to court me. . . .

I was nineteen years old. Then I made up my mind to begin talking with the one I was permitted. I did not like him very well. I thought more of the other one. Always I would think, "Would that I might talk

*From Truman Michelson, *The Autobiography of a Fox Woman,* pp. 309-313.

(with him).'' I really couldn't stop talking with him. I worried about him. And I again went around with the one I was permitted, when I went anywhere. Later on I became acquainted with him. But I always thought more of the other one, the one they hated on my account.

Soon the one I was permitted began to try to have me accompany him to his home. He always asked me to go with him whenever I saw him. Then I said to him, ''I am very much afraid of your parents.'' ''Well, I will go with you to your home,'' he said to me, ''we do not speak a different language, so it is not right for us to be afraid of each other. As for me, I am not afraid of your parents. For I have done nothing evil to you. As long as we have been talking together, I have been quiet with you. You know it too. I intend that we shall live quietly with each other. I always think, 'Oh that she were willing.' You are the only one with whom I wish to live. I shall treat you very nicely. Whatever you tell me, I shall do. And I shall always work. And I shall not hate your parents. I am not fooling you. What I say to you this day, I shall surely do,'' he said to me. Soon I consented. At night we departed. When it was daylight, I was (rather) ashamed to go where we lived with him. The next day when he was seen, he surely was treated very nicely, for I had taken for a husband the one they had wished me to. . . .

MENOMINI

FIRST MEETING OF THE MENOMINI AND THE WHITES*

WHEN the Menomini lived on the shore of the sea, they one day were looking out across the water and observed some large vessels, which were near to them and wonderful to behold. Suddenly there was a terrific explosion, as of thunder, which startled the people greatly.

When the vessels approached the shore, men with light-colored skin landed. Most of them had hair on their faces, and they carried on their shoulders heavy sticks ornamented with shining metal. As the strangers

*From Walter James Hoffman, *The Menomini Indians*, pp. 214-216.

came toward the Indians the latter believed the leader to be a great ma'nido, with his companions.

It is customary, when offering tobacco to a ma'nido, to throw it into the fire, that the fumes may ascend to him and that he may be inclined to grant their request; but as this light-skin ma'nido came in person the chief took some tobacco and rubbed it on his forehead. The strangers appeared desirous of making friends with the Indians, and all sat on the ground and smoked. Then some of the strangers brought from the vessel some parcels which contained a liquid, of which they drank, finally offering some to the Menomini. The Indians, however, were afraid to drink such a pungent liquor indiscriminately, fearing it would kill them; therefore four useless old men were selected to drink the liquor, and thus to be experimented on, that it might be found whether the liquid would kill them or not.

The men drank the liquid, and, although they had previously been very silent and gloomy, they now began to talk and to grow amused. Their speech flowed more and more freely, while the remainder of the Indians said, "See, now it is beginning to take effect!" Presently the four old men arose, and while walking about seemed very dizzy, when the Indians said, "See, now they are surely dying!" Presently the men dropped down and became unconscious; then the Indians said to one another, "Now they are dead; see what we escaped by not drinking the liquid!" There were sullen looks directed toward the strangers, and murmurings of destroying them for the supposed treachery were heard.

Before things came to a dangerous pass, however, the four old men got up, rubbed their eyes, and approached their kindred, saying, "The liquor is good, and we have felt very happy; you must try it too." Notwithstanding the rest of the tribe were afraid to drink it then, they recalled the strangers, who were about to return to their boats.

The chief of the strangers next gave the Indians some flour, but they did not know what to do with it. The white chief then showed the Indians some biscuits, and told them how they were baked. When that was over, one of the white men presented to an Indian a gun, after firing it to show how far away anything could be killed. The Indian was afraid to shoot it, fearing the gun would knock him over, but the stranger showed the Indian how to hold it and to point it at a mark; then pulling the trigger it made a terrific noise, but did not harm the Indian at all, as he had expected. Some of the Indians then accepted guns from the white strangers.

Next the white chief brought out some kettles and showed the Indians how to boil water in them. But the kettles were too large and too heavy to carry about, so the Indians asked that they be given small ones—cups as large as a clenched fist, for they believed they would grow to be large ones by and by.

The Indians received some small cups, as they desired, when the strangers took their departure. But the cups never grew to the kettles.

OMAHA

MEETING WITH THE WHITE MEN*

ONE day the people discovered white objects on the waters, and they knew not what to make of them. The white objects floated toward the shores. The people were frightened. They abandoned their canoes, ran to the woods, climbed the trees, and watched. The white objects reached the shore, and men were seen getting out of them. The Indians watched the strange men, but did not speak or go near them. For several days they watched; then the strangers entered into the white objects and floated off. They left, however, a man—a leader, the Indians thought. He was in a starving condition. Seeing this, the Indians approached him, extending toward him a stalk of maize having ears on it, and bade him eat and live. He did eat, and expressed his gratitude by signs. The Indians kept this man, treating him kindly, until his companions returned. Thus the white people became acquainted with the Omaha by means of one whom the latter had befriended. In return the white people gave the Indians implements of iron. It was in this way that we gained iron among us.

*From Alice C. Fletcher and Francis La Flesche, *The Omaha Tribe*, p. 81.

O YE WHO PRAY TO GOD, HELP HIM*

The man who is now on his way to the East is the only one who has obeyed God's words. He has not wished to transgress the commandments of God: it is good. When God made us in this country, He did not say, "You shall regard yourselves in the way of others." God did not say this to any race of people, whether they were Indians or white people, such as you are. Only that which God made is good. And you who have an abundance of possessions are, as it were, just like Him; therefore please listen to the words of no one except the man who has gone hence to you. He has gone to you to rectify several matters for us who are suffering. God made us in this country, and though we have continued in it, we have not succeeded at anything. Because we have not succeeded at anything you have made trouble for us Indians! The President desires us to go in the way in which there are usually very bad things. Therefore this man, who has really seen us, has gone to you to rectify several matters for us. O ye very strong men, O ye who pray to God, help him!

Big Elk

Recorded in 1879, this statement was one of many sent to government representatives in Washington by Indians suffering from hunger and disease as a result of the depredations of the white men upon their land. Betrayed by the government-appointed Indian agents, these men had small hope of aid from Washington and were bitterly disappointed with the attitude of the President, whom one of them referred to as "Slayer of the Indians." Nevertheless, they continued to plead for understanding and to hope that the white man might treat them like human beings. Their faith in Christian charity, as it turned out, was sadly misplaced.

Osage

DRY IS MY TONGUE**

Dry is my tongue from marching,
O my elder brother, O my elder brother.
Dry is my tongue from marching,
And, lo, death draws near to me.

*From James Owen Dorsey, *Omaha and Ponka Letters,* p. 31.
**From Francis La Flesche, *The War Ceremony and Peace Ceremony of the Osage Indians.*

Dry is my tongue from marching,
O my elder brother, O my elder brother.
Dry is my tongue from marching.

OSAGES HAVE TALKED LIKE BLACKBIRDS IN THE SPRING*

There have been many words. Wichitas have sent many words from their tongues; they have said little. Osages have talked like blackbirds in the spring; nothing has come from their hearts. When Osages talk this way, Wichitas believe they are talkers like blackbird. I have listened long time to this talk of blackbirds, and I said when my people talk like blackbirds, Wichitas think they are women. I want to say a few words, then Wichitas can go to their lodges and mourn for their chief. I want Wichitas to know this thing. I want them to know that Osages are great warriors. Today they have talked like women, but they are warriors. They have those things which Wah'Kon-Tah gave to men, so that he could tell them from women. They know how to die in battle. I want Wichitas to know this thing. We will give ponies to Wichitas for this chief, then they can go home to their lodges. I have spoken.

PA-I''M-NO-PA-SHE (GOVERNOR JOE)

The speech was delivered by an Osage chief whose name meant "Not Afraid of Longhairs." The occasion was the killing of a Wichita chief by two Osage braves. The Wichitas were ready to go on the warpath when an Indian agent arranged for a meeting between the two groups. The initial debate reached no conclusion; then Governor Joe rose and spoke, resolving the problem by offering restitution, in the form of ponies, for the dead chief. The warfare that erupted more and more frequently among the Indians was exacerbated by the presence of whites who gradually forced the various tribes into closer physical proximity to each other, and whose acquisition of Indian lands served to increase the opportunity for intertribal conflict.

*From John Joseph Mathews, *Wah'Kon Tah—The Osage and the White Man's Road,* p. 241.

WINNEBAGO

JOHN RAVE'S ACCOUNT OF THE PEYOTE CULT
AND OF HIS CONVERSION*

DURING 1893-94 I was in Oklahoma with peyote eaters.

In the middle of the night we were to eat peyote. We ate it and I also did. It was the middle of the night when I got frightened, for a live thing seemed to have entered me. "Why did I do it?" I thought to myself. I should not have done it, for right at the beginning I have harmed myself. Indeed, I should not have done it. I am sure it will injure me. The best thing will be for me to vomit it up. Well, now, I will try it. After a few attempts I gave up. I thought to myself, "Well, now you have done it. You have been going around trying everything and now you have done something that has harmed you. What is it? It seems to be alive and moving around in my stomach. If only some of my own people were here! That would have been better. Now no one will know what has happened to me. I have killed myself."

Just then the object was about to come out. It seemed almost out and I put out my hand to feel it, but then it went back again. "O, my, I should never have done it from the beginning. Never again will I do it. I am surely going to die."

As we continued it became day and we laughed. Before that I had been unable to laugh.

The following night we were to eat peyote again. I thought to myself, "Last night it almost harmed me." "Well, let us do it again," they said. "All right, I'll do it." So there we ate seven peyote apiece.

Suddenly I saw a big snake. I was very much frightened. Then another one came crawling over me. "My God! where are these coming from?" There at my back there seemed to be something. So I looked around and I saw a snake about to swallow me entirely. It had legs and arms and a long tail. The end of this tail was like a spear. "O, my God! I am surely going to die now," I thought. Then I looked again in another direction and I saw a man with horns and long claws and with a spear in his hand. He jumped for me and I threw myself on the ground. He missed me. Then I looked back and this time he started back, but it seemed to me that he was directing his spear at me. Again I threw myself on the ground and

*From Paul Radin, *The Winnebago Tribe*, pp. 389-394.

he missed me. There seemed to be no possible escape for me. Then suddenly it occurred to me, "Perhaps it is this peyote that is doing this thing to me?" "Help me, O medicine, help me! It is you who are doing this and you are holy! It is not these frightful visions that are causing this. I should have known that you were doing it. Help me!" Then my suffering stopped. "As long as the earth shall last, that long will I make use of you, O medicine!"

This had lasted a night and a day. For a whole night I had not slept at all.

Then we breakfasted. Then I said, when we were through, "Let us eat peyote again to-night." That evening I ate eight peyote.

In the middle of the night I saw God. To God living up above, our Father, I prayed. "Have mercy upon me! Give me knowledge that I may not say and do evil things. To you, O God, I am trying to pray. Do thou, O Son of God, help me, too. This religion, let me know. Help me, O medicine, grandfather, help me! Let me know this religion!" Thus I spoke and sat very quiet. And then I beheld the morning star and it was good to look upon. The light was good to look upon. I had been frightened during the night but now I was happy. Now as the light appeared, it seemed to me that nothing would be invisible to me. I seemed to see everything clearly. Then I thought of my home and as I looked around, there I saw the house in which I lived far away among the Winnebago, quite close to me. There at the window I saw my children playing. Then I saw a man going to my house carrying a jug of whisky. Then he gave them something to drink and the one that had brought the whisky got drunk and bothered my people. Finally he ran away. "So, that is what they are doing," I thought to myself. Then I beheld my wife come and stand outside of the door, wearing a red blanket. She was thinking of going to the flagpole and was wondering which road she should take. "If I take this road I am likely to meet some people, but if I take the other road, I am not likely to meet anyone."

Indeed, it is good. They are all well—my brother, my sister, my father, my mother. I felt very good indeed. O medicine, grandfather, most assuredly you are holy! All that is connected with you, that I would like to know and that I would like to understand. Help me! I give myself up to you entirely!

For three days and three nights I had been eating medicine, and for three days and three nights I had not slept. Throughout all the years that I had lived on earth, I now realized that I had never known anything holy.

Now, for the first time, I knew it. Would that some of the Winnebagoes might also know it! . . .

Whoever has any bad thoughts, if he will eat this peyote he will abandon all his bad habits. It is a cure for everything bad.

To-day the Indians say that only God is holy. One of the Winnebagoes has told me, "Really, the life that I led was a very bad one. Never again will I do it. This medicine is good and I will always use it." John Harrison and Squeaking-Wings were prominent members of the medicine dance; they thought much of themselves as did all the members of the medicine dance. They knew everything connected with this medicine dance. Both of them were gamblers and were rich because they had won very much in gambling. Their parents had acquired great possessions by giving medicines to the people. They were rich and they believed that they had a right to be selfish with their possessions. Then they ate peyote and ever since that time they have been followers of this medicine. They were really very ill and now they have been cured of it. Now if there are any men that might be taken as examples of the peyote, it is these three. Even if a man were blind and only heard about them he would realize that if any medicine were good, it is this medicine. It is a cure for all evil. Before, I had thought that I knew something but I really knew nothing. It is only now that I have real knowledge. In my former life I was like one blind and deaf. My heart ached when I thought of what I had been doing. Never again will I do it. This medicine alone is holy and has made me good and has rid me of all evil. The one whom they call God has given me this. That I know positively. Let them all come here; men and women; let them bring with them all that they desire; let them bring with them their diseases. If they come here they will get well. This is all true; it is all true. Bring whatever desires you possess along with you and then come and eat or drink this medicine. This is life, the only life. Then you will learn something about yourself, so come. Even if you are not told anything about yourself, nevertheless you will learn something of yourself. Come with your disease, for this medicine will cure it. Whatever you have, come and eat this medicine and you will have true knowledge once and for all. Learn of this medicine yourself through actual experience. . . .

It is now 23 years since I first ate peyote, and I am still doing it (1912). Before that my heart was filled with murderous thoughts. I wanted to kill my brother and sister. It seemed to me that my heart would not feel good until I killed one of them. All my thoughts were fixed on the warpath. This is all I thought of. Now I know that it was because the evil spirit possessed me that I felt that way. I was suffering from a disease. I even desired to kill myself; I did not care to live. That feeling, too, was caused by this evil spirit living within me. Then I ate this medicine and everything changed. The brother and sister I wanted to kill before I became attached to and I wanted them to live. The medicine had accomplished this.

John Rave, a Winnebago who introduced peyote, gave this account of the Peyote cult to anthropologist Paul Radin. According to Radin, the performance of the cult ritual began with the eating of peyote and the reading of speeches from the Bible. As the effects of the peyote grew stronger, the participants engaged in ritual chant and confessions. The contrast between the message of the ghost dance and that of the peyote ritual is quite sharp. The former represented an attempt to restore to the Indian his former sense of power and his pride in his ancient ways; the latter, on the contrary, seemed designed to facilitate his acceptance of Christian teachings.

I GET DELIRIUM TREMENS AND SEE STRANGE THINGS*

During the cranberry-picking season, I drank all the time and after that again "chased payments." I continued drinking. Finally all the payments had been made and I went to Black River Falls. I was entirely without money. I was supposed to go back to Wittenberg but I did not have the fare. I went back to the Indians and stayed all night. In the morning I was sick. I was shaking from head to foot. When I tried to drink coffee I would spill it. When I lay down I would see big snakes. I would cry out and get up and then when I was about to go to sleep again I would think that someone had called me. Then I would raise my cover and look around, but there would be nothing. When the wind blew hard (I seemed) to hear singing. These (imaginary) people would spit very loudly. I heard them and I could not sleep. Just as soon as I closed my eyes, I would begin to see things. I saw things that were happening in a distant country.

I saw ghosts on horseback drunk. Five or six of them were on one horse and they were singing. I recognized them for they were people who had died long ago. I heard the words of their song as they sang,

"I, even I, must die sometime, so of what value is anything,
    I think."

*From Paul Radin, *Crashing Thunder: Autobiography of a Winnebago Indian*, p. 40-41.

Thus they would sing and it made a good song. I myself learned it and later on it became a drinking song. . . .

The experience of the Winnebago while drinking and the experience of the Indian involved either in the ghost dance ritual or in a peyote ceremony are strangely similar. The visions of snakes, ghosts, revered animals, are common to both. The remaking of the experience into a song is common to all three experiences. But the faith and hope evident in the communally mediated experience of ghost dance and peyote ritual have here given way to hopelessness. The drinking song, too, attempts a resolution—found only in personal resignation to one's fate.

WHAT THE SHAWNEE PROPHET TOLD THE WINNEBAGO*

Now this is what the Winnebago heard from the Shawnee prophet; this is what he said, it is said, by those who heard him:

"Let the people give up the customs they are now observing and I will give them new ones." This is what he said.

Some of the Winnebago did this and threw away their war bundles. But he had meant their bad customs. Some also threw away their good medicines. At last they decided to go over to where he was. A man named Smoke-Walker led a number of young men over. "We will walk as the thunderbirds do," said the leader. Then a great and holy man called Dog-Head said that he also was going along. He was then an old man. The leader said, "You had better not come along for we are going to walk as the thunderbirds do, and for that reason I wish only young men." But Dog-Head said, "I am going along nevertheless, and whenever you wish to walk like the thunderbirds and walk above the earth, then I can turn back. I will go along."

There were eleven who went along. When they got to the place where the Shawnee prophet was staying they found all the other tribes (represented) there except the Winnebago.

Then the prophet said, "It is good, my younger brothers." He called the Winnebago younger brothers. "There are many tribes here, but I wanted to see you here especially. It is good you have come. I want to talk to you, but it is impossible (because I cannot speak your language)." Now the old man who had come along against the wishes of the chief could speak any Indian language, so the leader said to Dog-Head, "Older brother, you used to speak almost any language; can you still do it?" Then Dog-Head said, "My younger brother, I can understand

*From Paul Radin, *The Winnebago Tribe,* pp. 69-74.

what he is saying, but I don't know whether I could talk the language myself. I may or may not be able to speak it (enough to make myself understood). I don't know." Then the leader said, "It is good, older brother. Try to talk to him, and whatever you do will be better than nothing." Then Dog-Head said to the Shawnee prophet, "I can understand what you are saying, but I am afraid to talk to you because I don't know whether I could make myself clear to you." The prophet thanked him and said, "It is good. I want to talk to you Winnebago."

Then they had a long conversation and this is what he said, "Younger brothers, we are not doing the right thing and that is why we are not getting along very well in life."

At that time they (the other tribes) were having their night dances, so the Winnebago moved over to them. There they heard the prophet speak. He said that he had been sent by the Creator because the Indians were wandering away from their old customs. For that reason the Creator had sent him to tell them of it. He at first forgot all about it, for the devil misrepresented things to him and he believed him. The devil had told him that he would go to heaven and that he could not be killed. He had told him that he had given him a holy belt. He was a bad person. Whenever he got angry he would throw his belt down on the ground and it would change into a yellow rattlesnake and rattle. When he did this the rest of the people were afraid of him. He was very mean when drunk. They were afraid of him, not only on account of his belt, which he could turn into a yellow rattlesnake, but also because of the fact that he was very strong. If, when he was drunk, a number of people jumped on him, afterwards he would find out about it and hit them. If they would resist he would kill them.

It was utterly impossible for him to be killed. He was unkind to the women. They would go with him not because they liked him but because they were afraid of him. It was a dangerous thing to say anything about him. Whenever he wished to drink he would take some person's valuables and buy drink with it. These are the things he did. The Creator had sent him on a mission to the earth, but the devil had misled him. . . .

Now, it is four generations since the Shawnee prophet prophesied, and from that time there have been many prophets among us, as he is said to have told the people. Many have prophesied, but none have told anything that seemed reasonable. The Shawnee prophet was good, but those who have come after him have prophesied so that people might praise them, or just for the sake of talking.

It is said that the Shawnee prophet said that there would come a time when a woman would prophesy and that she should be immediately killed. The end of the world would be near then. Then he is said to have said that a little boy would prophesy and that one was to give ear to what he said.

The Peyote people claim that their ceremony is the fulfillment of this prophecy and that is true. The Shawnee prophet had said that there would be springs of water in front of the people's lodges and it is so at the present time, for the water is at our very doors. His prophecy was correct and he told the truth. Then he said that trees would travel and this is happening to-day, for trees are loaded into trains and are carried all around the country. He told the truth and he knew what was going to happen. He said that one day we would be able to write our own language and we are doing that to-day, for we have a Bible in Winnebago and we are able to write to one another in our own language. All these things he was able to foretell four generations ago.

A Winnebago by the name of Noise-Thunder had also prophesied that we would be able to write our own language. One thing that he said, however, was not correct. He said that the bad thing that has come upon us will make us forget our own ways. He meant that we should not take up with the white man's ways. "Don't do it, for if you do, we will all die." Now, he was mistaken in that. "The Creator has given two plates and they are getting empty. He gave the men a plate for them to fill and the women a plate for them to fill. The women's plate is empty." He meant that the Creator had made men to hunt and the women to dig the soil and raise vegetables, and that the latter were not doing it. That is what he meant by saying that their plates were empty. Noise-Thunder insisted that this was the white man's fault; he thought that we were being weakened by the white man's food. Quite a number of people believed him. "The birds eat what was provided for them to eat, game and vegetables, and the whites eat what was provided for them. Why should we not eat what was provided for us?" He was right, but then the Creator also created the food that the whites are eating. We are now getting accustomed to it and are getting stronger on this food.

The Winnebago were decreasing in number, so the Creator gave them a medicine which would enable them to get accustomed to the white man's food; that, also, they might know the Creator and that he is the true bread and food. This they found out by using this medicine. They are going into it deeper and deeper all the time, they who had been lost, and this has all been accomplished by the medicine (the peyote).

Plains

I GAVE THEM FRUITS*

My children, I when at first I liked the whites
My children, I when at first I liked the whites
I gave them fruits.
I gave them fruits.

  Father have pity on me
Father have pity on me
I am crying for thirst
I am crying for thirst
All is gone—I have nothing to eat.

  Typical of the ghost dance songs—among which the Arapaho songs are the most numerous—is this highly repetitive, almost hypnotic chant.

*From James Mooney, *The Ghost-Dance Religion and the Sioux Outbreak of 1890*, p. 961.

ASSINIBOINE

THE SPIRIT WORLD*

IN the lodge where my grandfather lay ill with the disease, two other members of the family were dead and their bodies were left where they died. Many families fled to other parts of the country.

Grandfather was so near death that the surroundings did not matter a great deal. He said, "I was very ill, but I noticed that a person looked in and perhaps thought the three of us were dead. He secured the doorway, piled objects against it, and closed up the smoke hole.

"Some time after that, I seemed to fall asleep, and the next thing I knew, I was outside, walking toward where the sun rises. I traveled along a narrow path that seemed to be on an upgrade. After going in that direction for some time, I came to where a man sat with his back to me. When he turned around, I recognized him as a person who had died some time before.

"The man said: 'Perhaps you want to know where your folks live. I will tell you. There is a large encampment over that hill, and the lodge painted blue belongs to your parents.' When I entered the lodge, I saw my father and mother there. My father was busy with some wood he was shaving. My mother, too, was busy at some task.

"With a smile, I said to them: 'I had no trouble to find your lodge.' My mother did not seem to hear me, but my father looked up and stared at me without any sign that he recognized me. I became uneasy, and hesitated to take my usual place in their lodge. After a time I went out and looked around for someone to whom I could talk. I recognized several persons and attempted to talk to them, but each time I was not answered.

"I finally retraced my steps and knew I was on the right path, because I came back to the place where the man sat. He spoke: 'You did not stay long, my friend; perhaps someone has come to take you back.' I do not remember if I made any answer.

"I hurried back along the trail and arrived at our lodge. The entrance was barred and I said to myself: 'How can I go in through the smoke hole, the poles are too close together there.' Then a voice awakened me; it was my sister's. She said: 'My brother, you are alive, your eyes are

*From James Larpenter Long, *The Assiniboines: From the Accounts of the Old Ones Told to First Boy,* pp. 168-170.

open.' She told me how they decided to flee to some other part, as did the others, and she had said to them: 'For the last time I want to see the body of my brother.'

"That was how she found me, and through her help I recovered."

The coming of the white man brought many diseases to the Indians. This account of a journey to the spirit world commemorates a smallpox epidemic that decimated the Assiniboine during the nineteenth century.

THE ONES WHO PADDLE A CANOE*

Many, many winters ago, when our people traveled on foot and used dog travois to carry their belongings, and the weapons consisted of bows, arrows, and stone clubs, it was told that a medicine man had a vision, in which a Being appeared.

This legend was recounted by Dry Bone, from Sintaluta, Saskatchewan, Canada, as told to him by Braids in Middle, of the Fort Belknap Reservation:

The Supreme One said to him, "Select four strong young warriors among your people, for you will lead them on a journey across the big water that extends away from your land. When you have gathered your young men together, make sacrifices and I will tell you more about my plan."

The medicine man invited many likely warriors to his lodge and told them of his vision.

"Talk it over among yourselves," he told them. "I will leave the selection to you men. Whoever the four may be, they will make a name for themselves."

It was no easy task to form a crew of that kind. Many excuses were made by parents, relatives, and sweethearts, for this was a journey so different from a war party. A journey across so large a body of water where no man ever had gone before did not appeal to them. But finally there appeared four braves who said they were the chosen four.

The journey was not started at once, but preparations for it were made with much excitement. The tribe considered the adventure a dangerous one, for it was believed that the party would never return.

*From James Larpenter Long, *The Assiniboines: From the Accounts of the Old Ones Told to First Boy*, pp. 1173-1176.

The leader finally received instructions from the Being, to the effect that round hide boats should be made for each man and that each boat should be loaded with two kinds of pemmican. One kind was to consist of pounded chokecherries and pounded dried buffalo meat mixed with buffalo marrow fat. The other was to be of pounded dried buffalo meat with chunks of hard tallow. Good bows and many arrows, together with the necessary clothing, were to be part of the equipment. The final instruction was for the medicine man to make eagle feathers, dyed in many colors, into a large bundle.

When all preparations were completed, the medicine man and the four braves paddled away with farewells from their people on the shore. Some of the people sang the death song while others sang songs of encouragement and praise.

This water was dotted with many islands, and no one could see to the other shore. The trip across that vast sea took many days. Each evening the party tied up at one of the islands for the night. Occasionally, when the sign of a storm approached, the leader took one of the colored feathers and dropped it into the water as an offering. Later, when a sea monster appeared near them, a feather offering was immediately made to it. In that way the journey proceeded smoothly. At the islands, feathered and small game were taken with their bows and arrows.

After many days, a long black cloud was noted on the horizon and on approaching closer, it turned out to be land. When the party arrived ashore, they saw other human beings, but their faces were covered with hair like their heads.

The Assiniboines were afraid of them, but by signs and gestures conversation was carried on. The party was given food and told to rest from their journey.

The travelers had come to the land of the white race, it was explained to them.

During the night the medicine man had a visit from the Being, who said, "You have arrived at the end of your journey. These people that you see will not harm you but they will help you and your people to live better. It is because their weapons are much better than your bows and arrows. Such will be given to you and you will be taught how to use them. Other things to use and to wear will also be made known to you."

Next day the white men called the Indians together and showed them a gun. They were taught how to load and to fire it. At first the report frightened them and the recoil knocked them down, but finally they were able to master it and use it as their teachers did. That took many days, and many more days were needed to learn other things that were used by the white people.

A large boat with many sails was loaded with guns, ammunitions, food, clothing, utensils, tools, and trinkets. When all was ready, the Indians were told to go on board and direct the way to their land.

After many days, the boat arrived at the shore from which the party had started, but no one was in sight. The people had fled into the woods at the sight of the large boat, it was believed.

The medicine man and his four young men went ashore and called to their people. No one appeared for a long time. Then finally a spokesman came forward and looked them over. When he was satisfied that they were the party that had left on a journey many moons ago, he said, "Speak up, my friends, tell me that you are alive and that it is not your spirits who have returned. Explain the meaning of the large boat with wings. Has the Being brought you back?"

"It is I and my four young men," said the medicine man. "We have brought our people good words; we have brought friends who will teach us many new things. Go back, call our people together in council so our friends will meet them."

So a crier was sent who called the people together. A council was held that welcomed the brave travelers and the white men they had brought with them.

And so, that was the way the Assiniboines, known as "The Ones Who Paddle a Canoe," met the whites for the first time.

While contact between whites and Indians was eventually detrimental to the Indians, initially the Indians received the whites and their goods quite readily. This account views the white men as friends and benefactors, a position they were to betray soon afterwards.

THE RIVALS*

Two young men were camping together. They both desired a young girl in the camp. One of them said, "I want to go to her first." The other refused, but finally consented to let him go first. The man went in, but afterwards refused to let his comrade enter. The man outside got angry, seized a bull-dog flies' nest and approached the lodge. He threw the nest at the lovers' genitals. The flies bit the lovers, so that both jumped up and down with pain. The girl cried continually, and the other inmates of the lodge were also bitten, while the man outside held the door, so that no one could escape. At last, he released his hold, and fled. The girl could not walk at all, but had to be carried. Her lover also could hardly move. His rival waited for him. "What's the matter, why don't you walk?" The injured man did not answer. Again he asked him. Then both raised their guns and killed each other.

THE TWO HUNTERS*

Two men were traveling together. They were starving, so that they could hardly walk. Only one of them had a gun, and he had but a single cartridge. They caught sight of a buffalo. "I'll shoot." "No, I'll shoot first." The man with the gun crawled along, followed by his companion. Just as the man in front was pulling the trigger, his comrade thrust his moistened finger into the shooter's anus. The shot went wide of the mark, and the man in the rear laughed aloud. The other man would have shot him, but he had no more cartridges.

Commentators on Indian life have often remarked upon the high incidence of violence that characterizes male relationships. Such violence seems to have been rare before the erosion of the Indian way of life and the destruction of Indian values by the white culture. The two brief tales "The Rivals" and "The Two Hunters" suggest both the breakdown of cooperative values and the futility (as well as the black humor) of life.

*From Robert H. Lowie, *The Assiniboine*, pp. 225, 229.

OLD MAN AND THE GREAT SPIRIT*

THERE was once a Great Spirit who was good. He made a man and a woman. Then Old Man came along. No one made Old Man; he always existed. The Great Spirit said to him, "Old Man, have you any power?" "Yes," said Old Man, "I am very strong." "Well," said the Great Spirit, "suppose you make some mountains." So Old Man set to work and made the Sweet-Grass Hills. To do this he took a piece of Chief Mountain. He brought Chief Mountain up to its present location, shaped it up, and named it. The other mountains were called blood colts. "Well," said the Great Spirit, "you are strong."

"Now," said Old Man, "there are four of us—the man and woman, you and I." The Great Spirit said, "All right."

The Great Spirit said, "I will make a big cross for you to carry." Old Man said, "No, you make another man so that he can carry it." The Great Spirit made another man. Old Man carried the cross a while, but soon got tired and wanted to go. The Great Spirit told him that he could go, but he should go out among the people and the animals, and teach them how to live, etc.

Now the other man got tired of carrying the cross. He was a white man. The Great Spirit sent him off as a traveller. So he wandered on alone. The man and woman who had been created wandered off down towards Mexico, where they tried to build a mountain in order to get to the sky to be with their children; but the people got mixed up until they came to have many different languages.

---

*From C. Wissler and D.C. Duvall, *Mythology of the Blackfoot Indians*, pp. 23-24.

CHEYENNE

WE ARE LIVING HUMBLY ON THIS EARTH*

We are living humbly on this earth,
We are living humbly on this earth
We are living humbly on this earth
We are living humbly on this earth
We are living humbly on this earth,

    Our heavenly Father, we want everlasting life
      through Jesus Christ.

We are living humbly on this earth.

WHEN I DIE*

When I die I will be at the door of heaven and
Jesus will take me in.

  Two songs of the Native American Church, these mix Indian qualities of repetition
with Christian invocations.

THE SHARPENED LEG**

    There was a man whose leg was pointed, so that by running and jump-
ing against trees he could stick in them. By saying *naiwatoutawa*, he
brought himself back to the ground. On a hot day he would stick himself
against a tree for greater shade and coolness. However, he could not do
this trick more than four times. Once while he was doing this, Vihuk
(White-man) came to him, crying, and said: "Brother, sharpen my leg!"
The man replied: "That is not very hard. I can sharpen your leg."
White-man stood on a large log, and the other, with an axe, sharpened
his leg, telling him to hold still bravely. The pain caused the tears to

*From Frances Densmore, "Two Songs of the Native American Church," pp. 81, 82.
**From A. L. Kroeber, *Cheyenne Tales*, p. 169.

come from his eyes. When the man had sharpened his leg, he told him to do the trick only four times a day, and to keep count in order not to exceed this number. White-man went down toward the river, singing. Near the bank was a large tree; toward this he ran, then jumped and stuck in it. Then he called himself back to the ground. Again he jumped, this time against another tree; but now he counted one, thinking in this way to get the better of the other man. The third time, he counted two. The fourth time, birds and animals stood by, and he was proud to show his ability, and jumped high, and pushed his leg in up to the knee. Then coyotes, wolves, and other animals came to see him; some of them asked how he came to know the trick, and begged him to teach it to them, so they could stick to trees at night. He was still prouder now, and for the fifth time he ran and jumped as high as he could, and half his thigh entered the tree. Then he counted four. Then he called to get to the ground again. But he stuck. He called out all day; he tried to send the animals to the man who had taught him. He was fast in the tree for many days, until he starved to death.

"Sharpened leg" tales come in many varieties. This particular version pokes fun at the white man who is duped into destroying himself. A series of such stories told to A. L. Kroeber were similar to this one. In each case the white man fails to heed a warning and suffers as a result. It seems clear that the white man was used as a figure of fun, described as a fool, and proposed as a model of nonhuman behavior —inheriting this role from Coyote before him.

A WHITE MAN BECOMES A BUFFALO*

It was spring, and the grass was green along the riverside, and all over the land. A buffalo bull was having a fine time eating the fresh grass, while a white man near by had a hard time to make his living. Day after day he watched the bull and wished to be a buffalo. So one day he approached him and stood near him, and cried, thinking that if he were a buffalo he would enjoy himself all his life, and all winter he would have a good robe on him, and he would not have to pay for his clothing and food. The buffalo looked at him and said to him: "What can I do for you?" But the man continued to cry, and answered that he wanted to be a buffalo. The bull told him not to be afraid, and to stand at a little distance away. Then he charged at the man four times, and the man was not afraid of

*From A. L. Kroeber, *Cheyenne Tales*, p. 170.

him, because he wished to become a buffalo. At the fourth charge the man turned into a buffalo, and then the bull taught him how to live. But at once the white man thought he could make money by teaching his friends to become buffalo. But a white man, whom he approached, ran away from him in fear.

In another version White-man is hunted after he has become a buffalo. He tries to tell the hunters that he is a man, but cannot, and is shot.

THE CROW*

The crow—*Ehe'eye'!*
The crow—*Ehe'eye'!*
I saw him when he flew down,
I saw him when he flew down.
To the earth, to the earth.
He has renewed our life,
He has renewed our life.
He has taken pity on us,
He has taken pity on us.

The crow is the most important symbol of the ghost dance. Here he is considered the lord of the new spirit world which was supposed to revitalize Indian life and traditions.

CROW

THE CHARACTER OF THE WHITE MAN**

WHITE men with their spotted-buffalo [cattle] were on the plains about us. Their houses were near the water-holes, and their villages on the rivers. We made up our minds to be friendly with them, in spite of all the changes they were bringing. But we found this difficult, because the white men too often promised to do one thing and then, when they acted at all, did another.

*From James Mooney, *The Ghost-Dance Religion and the Sioux Outbreak of 1890*, p. 1035.
**From Charles Everett Hamilton, *Cry of the Thunderbird*, pp. 213-214.

They spoke very loudly when they said their laws were made for everybody; but we soon learned that although they expected us to keep them, they thought nothing of breaking them themselves. They told us not to drink whisky, yet they made it themselves and traded it to us for furs and robes until both were nearly gone. Their Wise Ones said we might have their religion, but when we tried to understand it we found that there were too many kinds of religion among white men for us to understand, and that scarcely any two white men agreed which was the right one to learn. This bothered us a good deal until we saw that the white man did not take his religion any more seriously than he did his laws, and that he kept both of them just behind him, like Helpers, to use when they might do him good in his dealings with strangers. These were not our ways. We kept the laws we made and lived our religion. We have never been able to understand the white man, who fools nobody but himself.

CHIEF PLENTY-COUPS

KIOWA

THE SPIRIT ARMY IS APPROACHING*

The spirit army is approaching,
The spirit army is approaching,
The whole world is moving onward,
The whole world is moving onward.
See! Everybody is standing watching,
See! Everybody is standing watching.
Let us all pray,
Let us all pray.

Another song from the ghost dance which affirms the strength of the new movement by asserting that the spirits are arriving as an army. Not apparent in this translation is an Indian terminal expression which implies, as well, that the approach of the spirit army is a matter of common faith or belief rather than personal knowledge.

*From James Mooney, *The Ghost-Dance Religion and the Sioux Outbreak of 1890*, p. 1082.

THE WHITE CHIEF IS A FOOL:
DEFIANT SPEECH OF DOHASAN*

THE white chief is a fool. He is a coward. His heart is small—not larger than a pebble stone. His men are not strong—too few to contend against my warriors. They are women. There are three chiefs—the white chief, the Spanish chief, and myself. The Spanish chief and myself are men. We do bad toward each other sometimes, stealing horses and taking scalps, but we do not get mad and act the fool. The white chief is a child, and like a child gets mad quick. When my young men, to keep their women and children from starving, take from the white man passing through our country, killing and driving away our buffalo, a cup of sugar or coffee, the white chief is angry and threatens to send his soldiers. I have looked for them a long time, but they have not come. He is a coward. His heart is a woman's. I have spoken. Tell the great chief what I have said.

Eloquent—and often contemptuous—rhetoric was greatly admired by Indians. Here a white man is measured against Indian values and found wanting.

WHAT'S HE TO ME**

Ah, I never, never can forget
The playful word you spoke long since
This man who seeks to marry me
He with his sore-backed ponies,
    What's he to me!

Songs made by women while men were on the warpath are found among the Plains people. Called "wind songs" because they are songs of loneliness, like the prairie, these songs celebrated female fidelity.

*From James Mooney, *Calendar History of the Kiowa Indians*, p. 176.
**From Natalie Curtis, *The Indians' Book*, p. 229.

Sioux

SONG CONCERNING A MESSAGE FROM WASHINGTON*

The great grandfather (The President)
has said
    so they report
"Dakotas
    be citizens,"
he said
    so they report
but
    it will be impossible for me
the Dakota ways
Them
    I love
    I said
    therefore
    I have helped (to keep up the old ways)

WAR SONG**

Soldiers,
You fled.

Even the eagle dies.

LAST SONG OF SITTING BULL*

A warrior I have been
Now
It is all over
A hard time

I have

---

*From Frances Densmore, *Teton Sioux Music*, p. 517.
**From Frances Densmore, *Teton Sioux Music*, pp. 314, 459.

Because warfare was so much a part of Plains culture, much of their oral literature consists of war songs as well as songs celebrating courage, individualism, and the fidelity of women whose husbands were away at war. Sitting Bull, an important Sioux leader, was famous as a medicine man and for his ability in creating and singing songs.

THE SACRED TREE IS DEAD*

I did not know then how much was ended. When I look back now from this high hill of my old age, I can still see the butchered women and children lying heaped and scattered all along the crooked gulch as plain as when I saw them with eyes still young. And I can see that something else died there in the bloody mud, and was buried in the blizzard. A people's dream died there. It was a beautiful dream.

. . . the nation's hoop is broken and scattered. There is no center any longer, and the sacred tree is dead.

BLACK ELK

The ghost dance religion that swept across the Plains seems to have been thoroughly misunderstood by the whites, who rigorously suppressed its ceremonies. Although the original message of the prophet Wovoka was a message of peace, the Western Sioux appeared to have used the rites as an incitement against the whites. In nervous retaliation, a group of American forces wiped out, without provocation, two hundred men, women, and children in the massacre at Wounded Knee. The massacre marked the end of the ghost dance.

*From John G. Neihardt, ed., *Black Elk Speaks*, p. 276.

THE WHITE MEN HAVE SURROUNDED ME*

The white men have surrounded me and have left me nothing but an island. When we first had this land we were strong. Now our nation is melting away like snow on the hillsides where the sun is warm; while the white people grow like blades of grass when summer is coming. I do not want the white people to make any roads through our country.

RED CLOUD

As the white settlers moved westward, the Indians were often removed to remote, and in the eyes of the white men, worthless territories. But no matter how worthless the Indian land may have initially appeared, sooner or later the whites discovered a need for it. Some Indian land proved to contain valuable mineral resources; other land was a barrier to movement. Despite Indian sentiment against the establishment of roads or industry upon their lands, white law succeeded in most cases in encroaching on the reservations.

AN INDIAN ACCOUNT OF WOUNDED KNEE**

[From the Report of the Commissioner of Indian Affairs for 1891, volume 1, pages 179-181. Extracts from verbatim stenographic report of council held by delegations of Sioux with Commissioner of Indian Affairs, at Washington, February 11, 1891.]

TURNING HAWK, Pine Ridge (Mr Cook, interpreter). Mr Commissioner, my purpose to-day is to tell you what I know of the condition of affairs at the agency where I live. A certain falsehood came to our agency from the west which had the effect of a fire upon the Indians, and when this certain fire came upon our people those who had far-sightedness and could see into the matter made up their minds to stand up against it and fight it. The reason we took this hostile attitude to this fire was because we believed that you yourself would not be in favor of this particular mischief-making thing; but just as we expected, the people in

*From John G. Neihardt, ed., Black Elk Speaks, p. 289.
**From James Mooney, The Ghost-Dance Religion and the Sioux Outbreak of 1890, pp. 884-886.

authority did not like this thing and we were quietly told that we must give up or have nothing to do with this certain movement. Though this is the advice from our good friends in the east, there were, of course, many silly young men who were longing to become identified with the movement, although they knew that there was nothing absolutely bad, nor did they know there was anything absolutely good, in connection with the movement.

In the course of time we heard that the soldiers were moving toward the scene of trouble. After awhile some of the soldiers finally reached our place and we heard that a number of them also reached our friends at Rosebud. Of course, when a large body of soldiers is moving toward a certain direction they inspire a more or less amount of awe, and it is natural that the women and children who see this large moving mass are made afraid of it and be put in a condition to make them run away. At first we thought that Pine Ridge and Rosebud were the only two agencies where soldiers were sent, but finally we heard that the other agencies fared likewise. We heard and saw that about half our friends at Rosebud agency, from fear at seeing the soldiers, began the move of running away from their agency toward ours (Pine Ridge), and when they had gotten inside of our reservation they there learned that right ahead of them at our agency was another large crowd of soldiers, and while the soldiers were there, there was constantly a great deal of false rumor flying back and forth. The special rumor I have in mind is the threat that the soldiers had come there to disarm the Indians entirely and to take away all their horses from them. That was the oft-repeated story.

So constantly repeated was this story that our friends from Rosebud, instead of going to Pine Ridge, the place of their destination, veered off and went to some other direction toward the "Bad Lands." We did not know definitely how many, but understood there were 300 lodges of them, about 1,700 people. Eagle Pipe, Turning Bear, High Hawk, Short Bull, Lance, No Flesh, Pine Bird, Crow Dog, Two Strike, and White Horse were the leaders.

Well, the people after veering off in this way, many of them who believe in peace and order at our agency, were very anxious that some influence should be brought upon these people. In addition to our love of peace we remembered that many of these people were related to us by blood. So we sent out peace commissioners to the people who were thus running away from their agency.

I understood at the time that they were simply going away from fear because of so many soldiers. So constant was the word of these good men from Pine Ridge agency that finally they succeeded in getting away half of the party from Rosebud, from the place where they took refuge, and finally were brought to the agency at Pine Ridge. Young-Man-Afraid-of-his-Horses, Little Wound, Fast Thunder, Louis Shangreau, John Grass, Jack Red Cloud, and myself were some of these peacemakers.

The remnant of the party from Rosebud not taken to the agency finally reached the wilds of the Bad Lands. Seeing that we had succeeded so well, once more we sent to the same party in the Bad Lands and succeeded in bringing these very Indians out of the depths of the Bad Lands and were being brought toward the agency. When we were about a day's journey from our agency we heard that a certain party of Indians (Big Foot's band) from the Cheyenne River agency was coming toward Pine Ridge in flight.

CAPTAIN SWORD. Those who actually went off of the Cheyenne River agency probably number 303, and there were a few from the Standing Rock reserve with them, but as to their number I do not know. There were a number of Ogalallas, old men and several school boys, coming back with that very same party, and one of the very seriously wounded boys was a member of the Ogalalla boarding school at Pine Ridge agency. He was not on the warpath, but was simply returning home to his agency and to his school after a summer visit to relatives on the Cheyenne river.

TURNING HAWK. When we heard that these people were coming toward our agency we also heard this. These people were coming toward Pine Ridge agency, and when they were almost on the agency they were met by the soldiers and surrounded and finally taken to the Wounded Knee creek, and there at a given time their guns were demanded. When they had delivered them up, the men were separated from their families, from their tipis, and taken to a certain spot. When the guns were thus taken and the men thus separated, there was a crazy man, a young man of very bad influence and in fact a nobody, among that bunch of Indians fired his gun, and of course the firing of a gun must have been the breaking of a military rule of some sort, because immediately the soldiers returned fire and indiscriminate killing followed.

SPOTTED HORSE. This man shot an officer in the army; the first shot killed this officer. I was a voluntary scout at that encounter and I saw exactly what was done, and that was what I noticed; that the first shot killed an officer. As soon as this shot was fired the Indians immediately began drawing their knives, and they were exhorted from all sides to desist, but this was not obeyed. Consequently the firing began immediately on the part of the soldiers.

TURNING HAWK. All the men who were in a bunch were killed right there, and those who escaped that first fire got into the ravine, and as they went along up the ravine for a long distance they were pursued on both sides by the soldiers and shot down, as the dead bodies showed afterwards. The women were standing off at a different place from where the men were stationed, and when the firing began, those of the men who escaped the first onslaught went in one direction up the ravine, and then the women, who were bunched together at another place, went entirely in a different direction through an open field, and the women fared the same fate as the men who went up the deep ravine.

AMERICAN HORSE. The men were separated, as has already been said, from the women, and they were surrounded by the soldiers. Then came next the village of the Indians and that was entirely surrounded by the soldiers also. When the firing began, of course the people who were standing immediately around the young man who fired the first shot were killed right together, and then they turned their guns, Hotchkiss guns, etc., upon the women who were in the lodges standing there under a flag of truce, and of course as soon as they were fired upon they fled, the men fleeing in one direction and the women running in two different directions. So that there were three general directions in which they took flight.

There was a woman with an infant in her arms who was killed as she almost touched the flag of truce, and the women and children of course were strewn all along the circular village until they were dispatched. Right near the flag of truce a mother was shot down with her infant; the child not knowing that its mother was dead was still nursing, and that especially was a very sad sight. The women as they were fleeing with their babes were killed together, shot right through, and the women who were very heavy with child were also killed. All the Indians fled in these three directions, and after most all of them had been killed a cry was made that all those who were not killed or wounded should come forth and they would be safe. Little boys who were not wounded came out of their places of refuge, and as soon as they came in sight a number of soldiers surrounded them and butchered them there.

Of course we all feel very sad about this affair. I stood very loyal to the government all through those troublesome days, and believing so much in the government and being so loyal to it, my disappointment was very strong, and I have come to Washington with a very great blame on my heart. Of course it would have been all right if only the men were killed; we would feel almost grateful for it. But the fact of the killing of the women, and more especially the killing of the young boys and girls who are to go to make up the future strength of the Indian people, is the saddest part of the whole affair and we feel it very sorely.

I was not there at the time before the burial of the bodies, but I did go there with some of the police and the Indian doctor and a great many of the people, men from the agency, and we went through the battlefield and saw where the bodies were from the track of the blood.

TURNING HAWK. I had just reached the point where I said that the women were killed. We heard, besides the killing of the men, of the onslaught also made upon the women and children, and they were treated as roughly and indiscriminately as the men and boys were.

Of course this affair brought a great deal of distress upon all the people, but especially upon the minds of those who stood loyal to the government and who did all that they were able to do in the matter of bringing about peace. They especially have suffered much distress and are very much hurt at heart. These peacemakers continued on in their good work, but there were a great many fickle young men who were ready to be moved by the change in the events there, and consequently, in spite of the great fire that was brought upon all, they were ready to assume any hostile attitude. These young men got themselves in readiness and went in the direction of the scene of battle so they might be of service there. They got there and finally exchanged shots with the soldiers. This party of young men was made up from Rosebud, Ogalalla (Pine Ridge), and members of any other agencies that happened to be there at the time. While this was going on in the neighborhood of Wounded Knee—the Indians and soldiers exchanging shots—the agency, our home, was also fired into by the Indians. Matters went on in this strain until the evening came on, and then the Indians went off down by White Clay creek. When the agency was fired upon by the Indians from the hillside, of course the shots were returned by the Indian police who were guarding the agency buildings.

Although fighting seemed to have been in the air, yet those who believed in peace were still constant at their work. Young-Man-Afraid-of-his-Horses, who had been on a visit to some other agency in the north or northwest, returned, and immediately went out to the people living about White Clay creek, on the border of the Bad Lands, and brought his people out. He succeeded in obtaining the consent of the people to come out of their place of refuge and return to the agency. Thus the remaining portion of the Indians who started from Rosebud were brought back into the agency. Mr Commissioner, during the days of the great whirlwind out there, those good men tried to hold up a counteracting power, and that was "Peace." We have now come to realize that peace has prevailed and won the day. While we were engaged in bringing about peace our property was left behind, of course, and most of us have lost everything, even down to the matter of guns with which to kill ducks, rabbits, etc, shotguns, and guns of that order. When Young-Man-Afraid brought the people in and their guns were asked for, both men who were called hostile and men who stood loyal to the government delivered up their guns.

The massacre at Wounded Knee was the last major engagement between the U.S. army and Indians. The slaughter of women and children was a tragic outrage which has, today, become the symbol of Indian-white relationships and mutual mistrust.

YOU ARE LIKE DOGS IN THE HOT MOON*

You are like dogs in the hot moon when they go mad and snap and bite. We are only a little herd of buffalo left scattered. The great herds that once covered the prairies are no more.

The white men are like locusts when they fly so thick that the whole sky is like a snowstorm. You may kill one, two, ten; yes, as many as the leaves in the forest yonder, and their brothers will not miss them. Count your fingers all day long and white men with guns in their hands will come faster than you can count. You are fools, you die like rabbits when the hungry wolves hunt them in the hard moon.

I am no coward. I shall die with you.

CHIEF SHAKOPEE

The democratic relationship that obtained between the Indian chief and his braves is apparent in this statement by Chief Shakopee. His recognition of the futility of battling the whites and the foolishness of his braves is coupled with his determination, nonetheless, to fight and die with them.

*From Meridel LeSeuer, *North Star Country*, p. 88.

EVERYTHING OF EARTH WAS LOVED*

I know of no species of plant, bird, or animal that were exterminated until the coming of the white man. For some years after the buffalo disappeared there still remained huge herds of antelope, but the hunter's work was no sooner done in the destruction of the buffalo than his attention was attracted toward the deer. They are plentiful now only where protected. The white man considered natural animal life just as he did the natural man life upon this continent, as "pests." Plants which the Indian found beneficial were also "pests." There is no word in the Lakota [Dakota] vocabulary with the English meaning of this word.

There was a great difference in the attitude taken by the Indian and the Caucasian toward nature, and this difference made of one a conservationist and of the other a non-conservationist of life. The Indian, as well as all other creatures that were given birth and grew, were sustained by the common mother—earth. He was therefore kin to all living things and he gave to all creatures equal rights with himself. Everything of earth was loved and reverenced. The philosophy of the Caucasian was, "Things of the earth, earthy"—to be belittled and despised. Bestowing upon himself the position and title of a superior creature, others in the scheme were, in the natural order of things, of inferior position and title; and this attitude dominated his actions toward all things. The worth and right to live were his, thus he heartlessly destroyed. Forests were mowed down, the buffalo exterminated, the beaver driven to extinction and his wonderfully constructed dams dynamited, allowing flood waters to wreak further havoc, and the very birds of the air silenced. Great grassy plains that sweetened the air have been upturned; springs, streams, and lakes that lived no longer ago than my boyhood have dried, and a whole people harassed to degradation and death. The white man has come to be the symbol of extinction for all things natural to this continent. Between him and the animal there is no rapport and they have learned to flee from his approach, for they cannot live on the same ground.

Because the Indian was unable, and in some cases refused, to accept completely the white man's ways which were so contrary to his heritage and tradition, he earned for himself the reputation of being lazy. He preferred his tribal ways all the more on account of his disappointment with the white man whose deceit and weaknesses filled the Indian soul with distrust. He clung to his native customs and religion, which he could

*From Charles Everett Hamilton, *Cry of the Thunderbird*, p. 211.

scarcely change if he would; and so the Indian, who had lived the most active of lives and who had developed an unusually high physical perfection, was adjudged the most indolent of characters. And this reputation, false as it is, has become fixed in the mind of the public.

STANDING BEAR

I BRING YOU WORD FROM YOUR
FATHERS, THE GHOSTS*

My brothers, I bring to you the promise of a day in which there will be no white man to lay his hand on the bridle of the Indian's horse; when the red men of the prairie will rule the world and not be turned from the hunting grounds by any man. I bring you word from your fathers the ghosts, that they are now marching to join you, led by the Messiah who came once to live on earth with the white men, but was cast out and killed by them. I have seen the wonders of the spirit-land, and have talked with the ghosts. I traveled far and am sent back with a message to tell you to make ready for the coming of the Messiah and return of the ghosts in the spring.

In my teepee on the Cheyenne reservation I arose after the corn-planting, sixteen moons ago, and prepared for my journey. I had seen many things and had been told by a voice to go forth and meet the ghosts, for they were to return and inhabit the earth. I traveled far on the cars of the white men, until I came to the place where the railroad stopped. There I met two men, Indians, whom I had never seen before, but who greeted me as a brother and gave me meat and bread. They had three horses, and we rode without talking for four days, for I knew they were to be witnesses to what I should see. Two suns had we traveled, and had passed the last signs of the white man—for no white man had ever had the courage to travel so far—when we saw a strange and fierce-looking black man, dressed in skins. He was living alone, and had

*From James McLaughlin, *My Friend, the Indian*, p. 197-201.

medicine with which he could do what he wished. He would wave his hands and make great heaps of money; another motion, and we saw many spring wagons, already painted and ready to hitch horses to; yet another motion of the hands, and there sprung before us great herds of buffalo. The black man spoke and told us that he was the friend of the Indian; that we should remain with him and go no farther, and we might take what we wanted of the money, and spring wagons, and the buffalo. But our hearts were turned away from the black man, my brothers, and we left him and traveled for two days more.

On the evening of the fourth day, when we were weak and faint from our journey, we looked for a camping place, and were met by a man dressed like an Indian, but whose hair was long and glistening like the yellow money of the white man. His face was very beautiful to see, and when he spoke my heart was glad and I forgot my hunger and the toil I had gone through. And he said, "How, my children. You have done well to make this long journey to come to me. Leave your horses and follow me." And our hearts sang in our breasts and we were glad. He led the way up a great ladder of small clouds, and we followed him up through an opening in the sky. My brothers, the tongue of Kicking Bear is straight and he cannot tell all that he saw, for he is not an orator, but the forerunner and herald of the ghosts. He whom we followed took us to the Great Spirit and his wife, and we lay prostrate on the ground, but I saw that they were dressed as Indians. Then from an opening in the sky we were shown all the countries of the earth and the camping grounds of our fathers since the beginning; all were there, the teepees, and the ghosts of our fathers, and great herds of buffalo, and a country that smiled because it was rich and the white man was not there. Then he whom we had followed showed us his hands and feet, and there were wounds in them which had been made by the whites when he went to them and they crucified him. And he told us that he was going to come again on earth, and this time he would remain and live with the Indians, who were his chosen people.

Then we were seated on rich skins, of animals unknown to me, before the open door of the teepee of the Great Spirit, and told how to say the prayers and perform the dances I am now come to show my brothers. And the Great Spirit spoke to us saying:

> Take this message to my red children and tell it to them as
> I say it. I have neglected the Indians for many moons, but I
> will make them my people now if they obey me in this mes-

sage. The earth is getting old, and I will make it new for my chosen people, the Indians, who are to inhabit it, and among them will be all those of their ancestors who have died, their fathers, mothers, brothers, cousins and wives—all those who hear my voice and my words through the tongues of my children.

I will cover the earth with new soil to a depth of five times the height of a man, and under this new soil will be buried all the whites, and all the holes and the rotten places will be filled up. The new lands will be covered with sweet-grass and running water and trees, and herds of buffalo and ponies will stray over it, that my red children may eat and drink, hunt and rejoice. And the sea to the west I will fill up so that no ships may pass over it, and the other seas will I make impassable. And while I am making the new earth the Indians who have heard this message and who dance and pray and believe will be taken up in the air and suspended there, while the wave of new earth is passing; then set down among the ghosts of their ancestors, relatives and friends. Those of my children who doubt will be left in undesirable places, where they will be lost and wander around until they believe and learn the songs and the dance of the ghosts.

And while my children are dancing and making ready to join the ghosts, they shall have no fear of the white man, for I will take from the white man the secret of making gunpowder, and the powder they now have on hand will not burn when it is directed against the red people, my children, who know the songs and dances of the ghosts; but that powder which my children, the red men, have, will burn and kill when it is directed against the whites and used by those who believe. And if a red man die at the hands of the whites while he is dancing, his spirit will only go to the end of the earth and there join the ghosts of his father and return to his friends in the spring. Go then, my children, and tell these things to all the people and make all ready for the coming of the ghosts.

We were given food that was rich and sweet to taste, and as we sat there eating, there came up through the clouds a man, tall as a tree and thin like a snake, with great teeth sticking out of his mouth, his body covered with short hair, and we knew at once it was the Evil Spirit. And he said to the Great Spirit, "I want half the people of the earth." And the Great Spirit answered and said, "No, I cannot give you any; I love them all too much." The Evil Spirit asked again and was again refused, and asked the third time, and the Great Spirit told him that he could have the whites to do what he liked with, but that he would not let him have any Indians, as they were his chosen people for all future time. Then we were shown the dances and taught the songs that I am bringing to you, my brothers, and were led down the ladder of clouds by him who had taken us up. We found our horses and rode back to the railroad, the Messiah flying along in the air with us and teaching us the songs for the new dances. At the railroad he left us and told us to return to our people, and tell them, and all the people of the red nations, what we had seen; and he promised us that he would return to the clouds no more, but would remain at the end of the earth and lead the ghosts of our fathers to meet us when the next winter is passed.

KICKING BEAR

According to the notes printed with this statement, the speech was delivered in 1890 to a council of Sioux by Kicking Bear. Major James McLaughlin asked Short Bull, another Sioux, who had attended the council to repeat what Kicking Bear had said. Apparently he did so without hesitation, a prodigious memory feat which seemed to be commonplace among the Indians. While the oration is fantastic, it was reported to have held its audience spellbound and seems to represent the same willingness to believe that, in the form of the ghost dance, afforded one last hope of salvation to the despairing Indians.

THE TEACHINGS OF WOVOKA*

When you get home you have to make dance. You must dance four nights and one day time. You will take bath in the morning before you go to yours homes, for every body, and give you all the same as this. Jackson Wilson likes you all, he is glad to get good many things. His heart satting fully of gladness after you get home. I will give you a good cloud

*From James Mooney, *The Ghost-Dance Religion and the Sioux Outbreak of 1890*, p. 781.

and give you chance to make you feel good. I give you a good spirit, and give you all good paint. I want you people to come here again, want them in three months any tribe of you from there. There will be a good deal snow this year. Some time rains, in fall this year some rain, never give you any thing like that, grandfather said, when they were die never cry, no hurt any body, do any harm for it, not to fight. Be a good behave always. It will give a satisfaction in your life. This young man is a good father and mother. Do not tell the white people about this, Jesus is on the ground, he just like cloud. Every body is a live again. I don't know when he will be here, may be will be this fall or in spring. When it happen it may be this. There will be no sickness and return to young again. Do not refuse to work for white man or do not make any trouble with them until you leave them. When the earth shakes do not be afraid it will not hurt you. I want you to make dance for six weeks. Eat and wash good clean yourselves.

Southwest

THE FLOOD BEFORE THE EMERGENCE*

BEFORE the beginning of this world there were an old man and woman living. They were sitting on the earth. Dios came over and told them what was going to happen. He told them there was going to be rain for forty days and forty nights.

"Only four mountains will stand above the water. You must get on top of one of these mountains," Dios said. "Do this if you want to be saved."

These two old people told the others, but they wouldn't believe it.

Tsisnatcin was one of the four mountains mentioned; Tsabidzili was another, Becdilgai another; the other is not known, but there were four. All the people were warned to get on top of these mountains.

They were told, "When you get up there, do not look at the flood. If you do you may turn to a fish, frog, or duck." The old people were warned of this and told the others.

"Don't look up at the sky. You may turn to a bird," they were told.

They told all this to the people, but the people laughed at these two and called them great liars.

The time came. It started to rain. It rained and rained. The people wanted it to stop, but it continued to rain. The people ran for the mountains. Most of them were drowned. A few got to the mountain tops. They shut their eyes and kept them that way.

They were told, "When you get hungry, think of what you want and Dios will feed you."

*From Morris Opler, *Myths and Folklore of the Jicarilla Apache Indians*, pp. 111-113.

Some who didn't escape to the mountains but were in the water and didn't want to drown, said, "I want to turn to a fish," and they did. Some said they wanted to turn to frogs and other water beings.

The people stayed there eighty days. Whoever opened his eyes was missed by the others later.

After eighty days the people were sitting in a circle with their heads down.

"Open your eyes," Dios said. "Get down to earth again."

Only a few were left. There were only twenty-four people left.

Dios said, "Now you are each going into a mountain. Go into twenty-four mountains. New people are coming and then you can come out again. I am going to make another people."

This happened before the Apache came up from the underworld. These people went into the mountains. They were told that these new people were coming on top of the world from below and were going to be here 2,000 years. Now only sixty-five years are left. They were told that when these people, the Jicarilla Apache, were getting small in numbers, the earth would be destroyed again.

Dios told the survivors, "After those Apache come, when they grow few in numbers, there will be hard times. There will be starvation. Other people will come and these others will increase. But the world will be destroyed just the same."

Now there are many Mexicans and Americans, but just let them grow. They can't stop it, for it is the business of Dios.

When the flood was on the earth there were eight people who traveled with their eyes; they looked at the place where they wanted to go, and at once they were there. They traveled back and forth like this. The twenty-four survivors went into the mountains.

Then the Jicarilla Apache came from the underworld. They didn't know what had happened before this. The people came up and traveled all around the world. Then the people began to separate.

Dios told these eight people who could travel with their eyes, "Now you had better go back in the mountains."

These eight were separate from the twenty-four in the other mountains. These eight were among the Apache for a while. They told the Apache of what had happened before. That is why the Apache know this story. Four of the eight went to Wide Grass, a mountain. It is near Antonito, south of Antonito. Red Mountain was the other mountain. It is near the Rio Grande, south of Wide Grass Mountain. Four went in there.

Dios told them, "You must come back when the earth is destroyed again."

At the end of the world these people who travel with their eyes are going to come back and go to all directions and see what is happening in the east, south, west, and north. For the telephone and telegraph are not going to be here any more. They are all going to burn. Next time the earth will be destroyed by fire. All are going to be destroyed. Maybe another world will be made; I don't know.

At Taos where there used to be a lake there is now some soft ground. There have been two fires there. When four fires have occurred there, the earth is going to be destroyed. The first time there was a fire at that place the Pueblos went and dug a ditch to it and tried to put it out with water, but the water burned like oil. Finally they called upon an old Apache man and woman. The man's name was Bánàn; the woman's name I do not know. They don't say how these two put out the fire, but they did put it out.

The second time it burned I was alive. I saw it from a distance. An old Apache who just died a while back stopped the fire. It will burn twice more. The fourth time no one will be able to stop it. The fire is going to start there and burn all over the world.

That is all they say about this.

While traditions of a primordial flood seem to exist throughout the Southwest, researchers are not certain that they are derived from Christian Biblical accounts of the flood. Whether the tradition is indigenous or not, however, elements of Christian tradition have become intrinsic parts of the legend, as this story clearly indicates.

THE CREATION OF THE WHITE MAN*

One time Coyote was teasing Cyclone. Every day he went over there and teased him. Coyote could run fast and get away before Cyclone could catch him.

*From Morris Opler, *Myths and Folk Tales of the Jicarilla Apache Indians*, pp. 95-100.

Then one time Coyote went to see Child-of-the-Water. He said, "My partner, let us go and visit our friend, Cyclone."

He lied about his friendship. Coyote was that way. He always tried to test the power of another, to see whether others were really powerful or were just ordinary people.

So they went to see Cyclone at his home.

When they got near, Coyote ran to Cyclone and began to mock him again. "You can't do anything! You can't catch me!" he said.

So Cyclone started to run after Coyote. Coyote ran away and left Child-of-the-Water behind, for Child-of-the-Water could not run very fast.

Cyclone was breaking things to pieces, and Child-of-the-Water, who was in his path, was lifted up and broken into many pieces and scattered all over.

There were some people living at a spring. The woman went to get some water. She saw some blood spilled on the leaves, little drops of it. She looked at it. "Oh, that will make good soup!" she thought. She broke off the leaves and carried them home with water. She was going to make soup with this.

When she got home she put the leaves in the pot. She started to boil the soup. After a while she heard somebody crying. She looked around all over. The only place she didn't look was in the pot.

At last she came near the pot and listened. The noise seemed to come from there. It sounded like a baby crying in that pot.

She took the pot off the fire. There was a baby in there, and she picked it up. It was a little boy. She took care of that baby until it was a big boy. The woman did not know it, but this was Child-of-the-Water.

He grew up. He was nearly twenty years old now. But he was always rather weak and puny and shy.

Evil, sickness, and sorcerers couldn't bother him; they couldn't make him ill.

Hactcin asked the people, "Do you want a round house?"

"No," they answered, "we want a square house."

So the mud was reshaped and the kind of house they wanted was given to them. Then the bird made them a chimney for the house. The roof was first made round and the two people did not like it. The bird did not know how to change the roof to suit them. So they sent for the woodpecker.

Woodpecker was to be the carpenter for this dwelling. And they sent for Lightning too. Lightning came and split the spruce and piñon trees. It was at this time that these people, the first white people, received the gun from Lightning.

They all brought over the beams. Woodpecker started to construct the roof. To hold the beams he used spider's rope (spider web thread). Then the people wanted the chimney changed. Instead of having it round, they wanted it square with each corner pointing to one of the cardinal directions. Woodpecker fixed this also.

Now the house was finished and the couple was told to enter. They went in and looked around. But there were no windows.

So Hactcin said, "I think we should give this house windows just as the human body has windows to let in the light."

So Child-of-the-Water gave Hactcin rock crystal of four colors, black, blue, yellow, and glittering. The black one was pushed into the mud wall at the east side of the house, the blue one was placed in the south wall, the yellow one in the west wall, and the glittering one in the north wall.

Now all came into the house, and all thought it beautiful, for there was plenty of light in the house now.

The Hactcin turned to Woodpecker and said, "Now you must stay here and work for these people until all is finished. Whatever they wish to have, you are to make for them."

So the woodpeckers stayed on and worked as carpenters.

Now Hactcin sent for the turkey. To him Hactcin said, "Now make a garden for these people near the edge of the water." Water was already flowing there.

They called all the other animals too, for Hactcin had great power. All the animals and birds came around to have a conference with these people.

"Deer skins will be your clothing," Hactcin said to these people. And he told them, "You must take care of all these animals. These are all your animals and these are all your birds too. All this meat is your meat. And the garden will yield food for you. Here you are, and all this is given to you. Now I am going back."

So Hactcin and Child-of-the-Water and the birds and Lightning and the others all went back. Child-of-the-Water started, then, to return to his stepmother's home.

Thus Child-of-the-Water made the white people when he went to the east that time. Now he is up in the heavens, above the earth. He went up in a cloud after creating the white man. That is why the white men say they will go to Heaven when they die. Child-of-the-Water, who made them, is up there. He is living to the east with White-Shell Woman, his mother.

And the reason the white man cannot be hurt by sorcerers and can handle snakes and evil things like that without harm is that Child-of-the-Water created him after being blown to pieces by Cyclone. Child-of-the-Water was not killed even though he was blown to pieces by Cyclone. Where his blood fell there was life. He made the white man to be just like that, so that nothing could hurt him. That is why the white man says, "We do not die. We are going to Heaven." The white men are following in the path of Child-of-the-Water.

When Child-of-the-Water was returning to his stepmother's home, he made a path for the white people to take in coming to this country. That is why the white people were not afraid. They knew a path had been made for them across the ocean.

Once, at this time, Child-of-the-Water was walking to the east. He came to the ocean. He walked on the water. He found a fish there with blue eyes. He picked up a female fish of this kind and a male fish. He took them along with him to the other side of the ocean. He put the fishes on the ground.

Then Child-of-the-Water sent for White Hactcin. White Hactcin came.

Child-of-the-Water said, "Help me make people of these fish."

White Hactcin said to him, "You lie down."

Child-of-the-Water lay face downward and White Hactcin traced his outline on the earth.

"Get up now and stand to one side."

Then Hactcin took both fish and put them within the outline of the figure of Child-of-the-Water.

Hactcin said to Child-of-the-Water, "Now turn around and face the east." He had him walk to the east, then turn to the south without looking at the fish and walk there. He had him walk to the west and the north in the same manner. Next Hactcin told him to walk once more to the east. Then Hactcin said, "Now turn around and look."

When Child-of-the-Water turned he saw that someone was lying there where the outline of his body had been traced.

Then Hactcin said, "Now face to the south," and Child-of-the-Water did so.

"Now turn around again."

He looked and saw that it was a man stretching out his arms to his knees and attempting to rise.

Then Hactcin said, "Turn to the west," and Child-of-the-Water did so. "Now look."

He saw that the man was sitting up.

He went through the same procedure to the north and when he turned and looked this time, the man was sitting with his legs crossed under him.

Both White Hactcin and Child-of-the-Water came to the man and picked him up.

Hactcin said to Child-of-the-Water, "Make him get up," and Child-of-the-Water did so.

They motioned four times to make him walk. Child-of-the-Water led him for four steps, and then they turned around.

Hactcin said, "Talk, talk, talk, talk." The fourth time he said it, the man spoke.

"Laugh, laugh, laugh, laugh," Hactcin said. After the fourth time he was told to do it, the man laughed.

"Shout, shout, shout, shout," the man was told, and after the fourth time he did so.

Now he was fully formed.

Hactcin told the man to lie down this time. Child-of-the-Water traced his figure on the ground. The man was told to rise.

Again the Hactcin set out to give life to the figure. The man and Child-of-the-Water did exactly what Child-of-the-Water had done the first time. The man led and Child-of-the-Water stood behind him. White Hactcin gave this figure life and made it sit up and walk and talk and laugh just as had been done to the man. But the one that was made this time was a woman.

Child-of-the-Water asked Hactcin, "Where are these people to live?"

Hactcin said, "What home do you think will be best for them?"

They both thought it over. Hactcin sent for the swallow, and this bird came.

The bird went to the river. He brought back mud from the bottom. He put down the mud. Then he went away and brought back the wind. The wind blew into the mud and made it large and round.

Child-of-the-Water came back to his stepmother's home. He got inside a cloud. The cloud began to sail upward towards the heavens. This woman who had cared for him was the only one who saw this happen.

Before he started, Child-of-the-Water said to his stepmother, "I've made another creation of man. They will come here some day."

So he went up on the other side of the sky. That is where Child-of-the-Water is now. No one halted him. What he meant by the other creation of man was the creation of the white people.

His stepmother did not know what Child-of-the-Water meant when he spoke of another creation. Child-of-the-Water said to her, "You do not understand what I mean by a new creation of man, but some day you will see them. They will be different from you, but they will be good people. They will be shaped like your people."

Many years later she heard of people who came from the other side of the ocean. She remembered what Child-of-the-Water had told her. She was eager to see what these people looked like.

The chief of her group received a message that some people were coming from the other side of the ocean. They were called White-Eyed Travelers. The chief told the people, "They are coming. They will give us guns, they will give us cloth for clothes. They will give us different food too. These are the people that Child-of-the-Water is sending to us. Child-of-the-Water has not forgotten us, even though he didn't do much for us about killing the monsters. He is helping us in some other good way."

The other people did not know what the chief was talking about. Some of them began to joke. They said to each other, "When those people give you a gun, I'm going to take it away from you." Some said, "I'm going to hunt with the gun I shall take from you, so we will not have hard times any more."

Not very long after this they heard that these people had really come across the ocean.

These white people met these Indians and became friendly with them. They took out some money and showed that it had a head of the president on one side and an arrow on the other. "One face belongs to us and one to you," they said. "Take this money and we will give you all our property." They clasped hands and were at peace with each other.

The white man said, "I'm going to live on your territory, but I am going to divide my property with you always. If I fail to do this, you can chase me from your territory." And the white man signed a promise and gave it to the Indian.

The white man went back and returned with much property, guns and food, and gave it to the Indians. He gave them flour, sugar, coffee, baking powder, and cloth for clothes.

The Indians did not understand. Some did not know how the flour was to be used and some just dumped it out. But they recognized the salt and kept it and used it. The sugar they tasted and it was sweet, so they kept it and used it. But the baking powder they did not recognize, so they threw it away. Some tried to eat the baking powder just as it was and ate too much and killed themselves. Some put their hands right into the flour and ate it and made themselves sick. The coffee they thought was some kind of beans, so they cooked the coffee all day, and then for two days and a night trying to soften it. But the coffee beans never got done; they were as tough as ever. Some then ground the coffee beans on the metate, but they didn't taste good when cooked. The Indians didn't know how to use it. So they gave up and threw it all away.

After a while they took some coffee to the Mexicans and asked to be shown how to use it. The Indians called it "black water," and they call it that still. The Mexicans told them how to use it and said to them, "Put sugar in it and it is good." But some do not like it that way. After that some kept coffee, and some did not but gave it to the Mexicans. Some did not like the smell when it was ground and so didn't wish to have it.

Although the tale of the creation of the white man suggests friendship rather than animosity between Indian and white, the association of Child-of-the-Water, the lesser of the two culture heroes of the group, with the origin of the white man, suggests that the Indian both recognized the social distance between them, and also looked upon the white man as a being lesser than himself. Among the Mescalero and Chiricahua Apache, where Child-of-the-Water is the stronger of the two culture heroes, it is Killer-of-Enemies who is seen as the white man's benefactor.

Mescalero (Western) Apache

ORIGIN OF THE PEYOTE CEREMONY*

THEY say peyote eating all began with a Lipan Indian. Peyote had never been known before. This Lipan was about fifty years old when his people began to die out. There were ceremonial people among the Lipan, but they did no good. No kind of medicine was found that did any good.

This Lipan was far out on a raid for horses. He was thinking of how his people were dying from sickness and how no one had been able to help them. He was a good man, eager to help his people. He began to

*From Morris E. Opler, *Mescalero Apache Account of the Origin of Peyote Ceremony*, pp. 211-212.

look for something that would do them good. He prayed to anything that looked pretty and which he thought might help. He went from one kind of plant to another.

He happened to come to a place where many peyote plants were growing. The plants were bearing flowers and he stood in the midst of them. He said to the peyote flower, "What a pretty thing you are! There must be something to you, or you wouldn't be so beautiful. Whoever made you made you very plentiful and very beautiful." He prayed in the midst of these flowers. He said, "I'd like to see my people as thick as you are. I'd like to hear you speak if you can. You are the prettiest thing I have ever seen." He did all he could to get this plant to speak to him. Soon one of these beautiful flowers spoke to him.

It said, "Pull me. Pull as many of me as you can. Take us home. Make a tipi. Have the doors towards the east. Then eat me. Then give me to anyone who takes an interest in me and wants to eat me."

His people were dying day and night. He hurried home with his peyote. As soon as he got there he told the chief and all the people to come to his camp. He explained to the people what he had learned, how he had got it, what he was to do with it, and how it was to be used. He went ahead and did just as he had been told to do. He went into a tipi with the people and fed them all they wanted of it. He didn't have so much of it and thought the supply he had brought back would not be enough. But the supply didn't diminish. Though he gave peyote to many, the pile was as before. He fed all of them. This man had been told to take one big one home and to put it in the center and to pray to that one and talk to it. He did so and afterwards this was always done in peyote meetings.

Everyone was feeling good. The different kinds of sickness went away. That is where their belief in peyote started.

HOPI

THE TWO WAR GODS AND THE TWO MAIDENS*

A LONG time ago Pöokónghoya and his little brother Balöngahoya lived north of the village at the shrine of the Achámali. One day they heard

*From H.R. Voth, *The Traditions of the Hopi*, pp. 81-82.

that two beautiful maidens were watching some fields west of the village of Húckovi, of which the ruins may still be seen a few miles north-west of Oraibi. They concluded that they would go hunting and at the same time visit those two maidens. When they arrived there the maidens joyfully greeted them and they were joking and teasing each other. The maidens believed that the two brothers had come with the intention to marry them, and they said, in a half-jesting manner, to their suitors: "We will cut off an arm from each one of you, and if you do not die you may own us." The younger brother was at once willing, saying to his elder brother: "They are beautiful; let us not be afraid of having our arm cut off." The elder brother hesitated, saying that that would hurt. So the younger brother said, "I am willing," laid his right arm over the edge of the mealing trough at which the maidens had been working, and one of the maidens struck the arm with the upper mealing stone and cut it off, the arm dropping into the trough or bin. His elder brother hereupon laid his arm over the edge of the bin, which consisted of a thin, sharp slab, and the other maiden also cut his arm off with her mealing stone. Now the two brothers said: "If we recover, we shall come after you. Hand us our arms now." The maidens did so and the two brothers left, each one carrying his severed arm. Arriving at their home north of Oraibi, they told their grandmother what had happened. "There," she said, "you have been in something again and have done some mischief." "Yes," they said, "We met two beautiful maidens and liked them very much, and so we allowed them to cut off our arms." "Very well," she said, "I am going to set you right again." So she asked them to lay down north of the fireplace. She placed the two arms by their sides, covered them up, whereupon she commenced to sing a song. When she was through singing, she told them now to get up. They did so and found their arms healed.

The next day they proceeded to the house of the maidens, who were surprised to see them fully recovered. The older of the two sisters was the prettier one and Pöokónghoya wanted to choose that one. His younger brother protested, saying: "Yesterday you were not willing to have your arm cut off, as you were then afraid, and now you want to have the first choice. I had my arm cut off first and I am going to choose first," to which his elder brother finally consented. They slept with the maidens that night and then left them and returned to their home north of Oraibi.

THE POOKONGHOYAS AND THE CANNIBAL MONSTER*

A very long time ago a large monster, whom our forefathers called Shíta, lived somewhere in the west, and used to come to the village of Oraibi and wherever it would find children it would devour them. Often also grown people were eaten by the monster. The people became very much alarmed over the matter, and especially the village chief was very much worried over it. Finally he concluded to ask the Pöokónghoyas for assistance. These latter, namely Pöokónghoya and his younger brother Balöngahoya, lived north of and close to the village of Oraibi. When the village chief asked them to rid them of this monster they told him to make an arrow for each one of them. He did so, using for the shaft feathers, the wing feathers of the blue-bird. These arrows he brought to the little War Gods mentioned. They said to each other: "Now let us go and see whether such a monster exists and whether we can find it." So they first went to Oraibi and kept on the watch around the village. One time, when they were on the east side of the village at the edge of the mesa, they noticed something approaching from the west side. They at once went there and saw that it was the monster that they were to destroy. When the monster met the two brothers it said to them: "I eat you" (Shita). Both brothers objected. The monster at once swallowed the older one and then the other one. They found that it was not dark inside of the monster, in fact, they found themselves on a path which the younger brother, who had been swallowed last, followed, soon overtaking his older brother. The two brothers laughed and said to each other: "So this is the way we find it here. We are not going to die here." They found that the path on which they were going was the oesophagus of the monster, which led into its stomach. In the latter they found a great many people of different nationalities which the monster had devoured in different parts of the earth; in fact, they found the stomach to be a little world in itself, with grass, trees, rock, etc.

Before the two brothers had left their home on their expedition to kill the monster, if possible, their grandmother had told them that in case the monster should swallow them too, to try to find its heart; if they could shoot into the heart the monster would die. So they concluded that they would now go in search of the heart of the monster. They finally found the path which led out of the stomach, and after following that path quite a distance they saw way above them hanging something which

*From H.R. Voth, *The Traditions of the Hopi*, pp. 82-83.

they at once concluded must be the heart of the monster. Pöokónghoya at once shot an arrow at it, but failed to reach it, the arrow dropping back. Hereupon his younger brother tried it and his arrow pierced the heart, whereupon the older brother also shot his arrow into the heart. Then it became dark and the people noticed that the monster was dying. The two brothers called all the people together and said to them: "Now let us get out." They led them along the path to the mouth of the monster, but found that they could not get out because the teeth of the monster had set firmly in death. They tried in vain to open the mouth but finally discovered a passage leading up into the nose. Through this they then emerged.

It was found that a great many people assembled there north of the village. The village chief had cried out that a great many people had arrived north of the village and asked his people to assemble there too. They did so and many found their children and relatives that had been carried off by the monster, and were very glad to have them back again.

The two brothers then said to the others that they should now move on and try to find their own homes where they had come from, which they did, settling down temporarily at different places, which accounts for the many small ruins scattered throughout the country. The old people say that this monster was really a world or a country, as some call it, similar to the world that we are living in.

A constant theme of Hopi literature seems to be a quarrel between two brothers or between leaders of two clans resulting in the separation of the two and formation of a new clan. The fear of intratribal and intertribal rivalry seems to be played out and resolved in this legend.

THE EARLY SPANISH MISSIONS AT ORAIBI*
Told by Wikvaya (Oraibi)

A long time ago the Oraibi were living in their village. The Spaniards often made inroads upon them and warred against them. Finally they made peace with each other and the Spaniards requested that they be permitted to live in Oraibi. The Hopi consented, so they hunted a place

*From H.R. Voth, *The Traditions of the Hopi,* pp. 244-253.

where the Spaniards could build their house, and selected a place north of the village of Oraibi, where the ruins of the old Spanish buildings may still be seen. Here the Hopi assisted them in building their house. They got the stone for them and helped them to build their house, which the old people say was built in a spiral or snail-house shaped form, there being four spirals. In the center of the spiral-shaped construction was the house, or rather kiva, as the Hopi call it in their tales. Here, tradition says, the Spaniards withdrew, especially in winter when it was cold. Coming out of this kiva they had to go around four times through the long winding hallway which ended in the square house with four rooms. From this house the egress or ingress was made through doors, while from the place in the center the Hopi say they came out through the roof.

Soon another house, which tradition calls an "assembly house," was built north-east of this structure. This large house had a tower in which bells were suspended. When this assembly house was finished, the Spaniards called all the people from the village, and when they had assembled at their house, they told them that they should all go to the new, large assembly house, and when they had done so the Tūtáachi told them that he was going to wash their heads (baptize them). They asked him what that was, what that meant. He told them that that was something very good. So they consented and he poured a little water on the heads of those present. After this the Tūtáachi called another Tūtáachi from Basoi, who came with a number of others and brought clothing and shoes for the Hopi. The shoes were made of leather, the clothing of some gray woolen stuff. The things were brought on carts with heavy wooden wheels, but there was no iron on them.

It seemed that this Tūtáachi was to be the assistant of the one living in Oraibi, at least the new arrival remained in Oraibi. The Hopi then had to assemble in the assembly house on Sundays, where the Tūtáachis, or priests, spoke to them. Soon they asked the Hopi to work for them. The water in the springs around Oraibi not being good, they requested them to get drinking water for them from Mūenkape, which is far away. The Oraibi soon got tired of this and sometimes, instead of going to Mūenkape; they went to Tūhciva, a spring south of the mesa on which the sun shrine is situated, about three miles south-east of Oraibi. But the priests soon found out the deception, and were angry. They soon set the inhabitants of Oraibi to work at making cisterns, and the Hopi themselves were pleased with this, as they were now not requested to get water so often from the distance.

The Spaniards also soon brought cattle, and the Oraibi would occasionally buy calves from them for corn. Some of the cattle were very gentle and were used to drag logs to the village, which the Hopi had to get for the Spaniards from Kí'shiwuu, fifty or sixty miles north-east. The deep cuts and ruts in the rocks north-east of Oraibi where many logs were dragged up may still be seen to-day. Some also had to get logs from the San Francisco Mountains (near Flagstaff), but as parts of the road from there were very sandy, not so many were gotten from that place as from Kí'shiwuu.

Thus the Spaniards kept the Hopi at work in various ways, and they were not bad to them at first. For four years everything went along well, and it rained often too, so that there was water in the cisterns; but at the end of four years things began to change. The priests commenced to forbid the Hopi to have Katcina dances and to make báhos. They demanded of them to attend the meetings in the assembly house, and they did not let them concern themselves about the clouds and the rain, and that year (the fifth) it was very warm and very dry. The Hopi began to be very tired and did not plant much that year, so the chiefs called a council and they talked the matter over. "We are not getting along well," they said to each other, "we are not happy. It does not rain. Let us try it with báhos again. The Hopi have always had it that way, and known it that way, to make báhos for the clouds." So they again began to have ceremonies, each fraternity with its own altar, and they made báhos, but did not tell the priests about it. They deposited the prayer-offerings in the different directions, but it did not rain. So the chiefs and leaders were very much discouraged. Their "fathers," as they had to call the Spanish priests, demanded food from them, and yet they had very little to eat themselves, only some votáka (corn-meal mush).

So they decided to try the Katcinas again, and they arranged a Katcina dance, but one of the Hopi went and informed the padres that they were going to have a Katcina dance again; then they had the dance, and it rained some, but very little. The padres in the meanwhile continued to oppress the Hopi and made them work very hard, and demanded contributions of food, etc., from them. They would also disregard all the feelings of the Hopi as to their own (the Hopi's) religion. They would trample under foot the chastity of the Hopi women and maidens. So finally the Hopi became angry and began to discuss the advisability of getting rid of their oppressors. One time a number of the latter went away, east somewhere, to get some supplies, clothing, etc., it is said, so that the padre remained at the Mission alone. When the Hopi saw that the priest's assistants had left, they met in council in the Nashebe, the chief's kiva, and talked the matter over. Some were in favor of going and killing the padre, others objected, saying that certainly the Spaniards would then come and punish them. But finally the party that was in favor of getting rid of the oppressors prevailed, and they concluded that they would stand the oppression no longer, but get rid of the priest. The question then came up, Who should go and kill him? Nobody wanted to do it. Finally the Badger clan volunteered to go. "You are not brave," they said, "we shall go."

So they proceeded to the Mission and knocked at the door. The padre was asleep and after they had roused him up he refused to open the door at first, but when they continued to knock he opened the door, whereupon they rushed into the room, grabbed him, dragged him out of the house, threw him on the ground and then cut his throat, one holding his head. Hereupon they carried the corpse eastward down the mesa, where they threw it into a gulch and piled stones upon it. Hereupon they waited for some time to see whether anybody would come, or what would happen.

The killing of the padre in Oraibi was the signal for the other villages to get rid of the padres that lived at those mesas also. The Hopi then waited, expecting that Spaniards would come and avenge their brethren, but no one came, so they destroyed the houses of the Spaniards, divided their logs and timbers, and used them for their kivas. Some of the smaller bells are still owned by the Agave Fraternity. No one has ever come to punish the Hopi for killing the padres. The places where the latter had their large sheep corrals can still be seen, especially near the spring Nawáivöcö, and at a place about four miles south of Oraibi. From that time on the Hopi again had their dances and their sacred altar performances in their kivas.

Like their neighbors to the south, the Hopi had myths about the coming of the white man—their long-lost brother Pahana. While the Hopi were cordial to the Spaniards who first arrived, they waged a constant battle against them and against the imposition of Christianity. While outwardly adhering to the Christian faith, they practiced their own religions secretly, and revolted first at the Pueblo of Oraíbi, later at Awatovi. These revolts shook the foundation of the Hopi belief in peace and led, later, to intertribal schisms.

THE COMING OF THE HOPI FROM THE UNDERWORLD*

A long time ago the people were living below. There were a great

*From H.R. Voth, *The Traditions of the Hopi*, pp. 271-277.

many of them, but they were often quarreling with one another. Some of them were very much depraved. They abused the women and the maidens, and that led to very many contentions. So the chiefs, who were worried and angry over this, had a council and concluded that they would try to find another place to live. So they first sent out a bird named Mótsni, to find a place of exit from this world. He flew up high but was too weak and returned without having been successful. They then sent the Mocking-bird (Yáhpa). He was strong and flew up very high and found a place of exit. Returning, he reported this to the chiefs.

In the meanwhile the chiefs had caused a great flood. Many Bálölöokongwuus came out of the ground with the water, and a great portion of the people were destroyed. When the Mocking-bird had made his report to the chiefs the latter said: "All right, that is good. We are going away from here." They then announced through the crier that in four days they would leave, and that the women should prepare some food, and after they had eaten on the fourth day they would all assemble at the place right under the opening which the Mocking-bird had found. This was done.

The chiefs then planted a pine-tree (calávi), sang around it, and by their singing made it to grow very fast. It grew up to the opening which the Yáhpa had found, and when the chiefs tried and shook it, they found that it was fairly strong, but not strong enough for many people to climb up on, especially its branches, which were very thin. So they planted another kind of pine (löoqö), sang around it, and made it also to grow up fast. This tree and its branches was much stronger than the other, but while the first one had grown through the opening, this one did not reach it entirely, its uppermost branches and twigs spreading out sideways before they reached the opening. Hereupon they planted in the same manner a reed (bákavi), which proved to be strong, and also grew through the opening like the calávi. Finally they planted a sunflower (áhkawu), and as it was moist where they planted it, it also grew up very fast and to a great size, its leaves also being very large; but the sunflower did not reach the opening. Its very large disk protruded downward before it reached the opening. The sunflower was covered with little thorns all over. Now they were done with this.

Hereupon Spider Woman, Pöokónghoya, his brother Balöongawhoya, and the Mocking-bird that had found the opening, climbed up on the calávi in the order mentioned. After they had emerged through the opening, Pöokónghoya embraced the calávi, his brother the reed, both holding them firmly that they should not shake when the people were climbing up. The Mocking-bird sat close by and sang a great many songs, the songs that are still chanted at the Wūwūchim ceremony. Spider Woman was also sitting close by watching the proceedings. Now the people began to climb up, some on the calávi, others on the lööqö, still others on the ahkàvu and on the bákavi. As soon as they emerged, the Mocking-bird assigned them their places and gave them their languages. To one he would say: "You shall be a Hopi, and that language you shall speak." To another: "You shall be a Navaho, and you shall speak that language." And to a third: "You shall be an Apache," "a Mohave," "a Mexican," etc., including the White Man. The language spoken in the under-world had been that of the following Pueblo Indians: Kawáhykaka, Akokavi, Kátihcha, Kótiyti; these four branches of the Pueblo Indians speaking essentially the same language.

In the under-world the people had been very bad, there being many sorcerers and dangerous people, just like there are in the villages to-day who are putting diseases into the people. Of these Pópwaktu, one also found his way out with the others. The people kept coming out, and before they were all out the songs of the Mocking-bird were exhausted. "Hapi! pai shúlahti! Now! (my songs) are gone," and at once the people who were still on the ladders commenced returning to the under-world, but a very great many had already come out, an equally large number having remained in the under-world, but the Kik-mongwi from below was with the others that came out of the kiva. The people who had emerged remained around the sipapu, as the opening was, and has ever since been called.

At this time no sun existed and it was dark everywhere. The half-grown son of the Kik-mongwi took sick and died, so they buried him. His father was very angry. "Why has some Powáka come out with us?" he said. "We thought we were living alone and wanted to get away from those dangerous men. That is the reason why we have come out, and now one has come with us." Hereupon he called all the people together and said: "On whose account have I lost my child? I am going to make a ball of this fine corn-meal and throw it upward, and on whose head that ball alights, him I shall throw down again through the sipapu." Hereupon he threw the ball upward to a great height, the people all standing and watching. When it came down it fell upon the head of some one and was shattered. "Ishohi! so you are the one," the chief said to him. But as it happened this was the chief's nephew (his younger sister's son). "My nephew, so you are núkpana (dangerous); why have you come out with us? We did not want any bad ones here, and now you have come with us. I am going to throw you back again." So he grabbed him in order to throw him back. "Wait," he said, "wait! I am going to tell you something." "I am going to throw you back," the chief replied. "Wait," his nephew said again, "until I tell you something. You go there to the sipahpuni and you look down. There he is walking." "No, he is not," the chief replied, "I am not going to look down there, he is dead." But he went and looked down and there he saw his boy running around with other children, still showing the signs of the head washing which the Hopi practice upon the dead immediately after death. "Yes, it is true, it is true," the chief said, "truly there he is going about." "So do not throw me down there," his nephew said, "that is the way it will be. If any one dies he will go down there. Let me remain with you, I am going to tell you some more." Then the chief consented and let his nephew remain.

It was still dark, and as there was no sunshine it was also cold, and the people began to look for fire and for wood, but as it was so dark, they could find very little wood. They thus lived there a while without fire, but all at once they saw a light in the distance and the chief said: "Some one go there and see about it." When they had still been in the lower world they had occasionally heard footsteps of some one up above. So some one went in search of the light, but before he had reached it he became tired and returned. Another was sent and he got there. He found a field in which corn, watermelons, beans, etc., were planted. All around this field a fire was burning, which was kept up by wood, and by which the ground was kept warm so that the plants could grow. The messenger found a very handsome man there. He had four strands of turquoise around his neck and very large turquoise ear pendants. In his face he had two black lines running from the upper part of his nose to his cheeks, and made with specular iron. By his side was standing his friend (a mask) which looked very ugly, with large open eye-holes and a large mouth. So it was Skeleton (Másauwuu) whom they had heard walking about from the other world. "Who are you?" Skeleton asked the messenger. "Where do you come from?" "Yes," he replied, "we have come from below, and it is cold here. We are freezing and we have no fire." "You go and tell your people and then you all come here to me." So he returned and the people asked him: "Now, what have you found out? Have you found anybody?" "Yes," he said, "I have found somebody and he has a good crop there." Skeleton had fed the messenger with some of his good things which he had there. The people had not brought much food with them from below and so they had not very much left. The people were very glad for this invitation and went to the place where Skeleton lived. But when they saw the small field they thought: "Well, that will be gone in a very short time," but Skeleton always planted and the food was never gone. When they came there they gathered some wood and built a fire and then they warmed themselves and were happy. Skeleton gave them roasting ears, and watermelons, melons, squashes, etc., and they ate and refreshed themselves. Some of the plants were very small yet, others still larger, so that they always had food.

So the people remained there, made fields, and they always kept up a fire near the fields, which warmed the ground so that they could raise a crop. When the crop had matured they gathered it all in, and when they now had provisions they planned to start off again, but there was still no sun, and it was cold. So they talked about this, saying: "Now, it ought not remain this way." So the chiefs all met in council with Skeleton, and talked this matter over in order to see whether they could not make a sun as they had had it in the under-world, but they did not just know how to do it. So they finally took a piece of dressed buffalo hide (hākwávu), which they cut in a round shape, stretched it over a wooden ring, and then painted it with white dúma (kaoline). They then pulverized some black paint (tóho) with which they drew a picture of the moon around the edge of this disk, sprinkling the center of the disk with the same black color. They then attached a stick to this disk. Hereupon they stretched a large piece of white native cloth (möchápu) on the floor and placed this disk on it. All these objects they had brought with them from the under-world.

They then selected some one (the story does not say whom) and directed him to stand on this moon symbol. Hereupon the chiefs took the cloth by its corners, swung it back and forth, and then threw it upward, where it continued swiftly flying eastward into the sky. So the people sat and watched. All at once they noticed that it became light in the east. Something was burning there as they thought. The light became brighter and brighter, and something came up in the east. It rose higher and higher, and where the people were it became lighter and lighter. So now they could go about and they were happy. That turned out to be the moon, and though it was light, the light was only dim and the people, when working in the fields, would still occasionally cut off their plants because they could not see very distinctly, and it was still cold and the people were freezing, and they still had to keep the ground warm with fires. So the people were thinking about it. The chiefs again met in council, and said: "Ishohi! It is better already, it is light, but it is not quite good yet, it is still cold. Can we not make something better?" They concluded that perhaps the buffalo skin was not good, and that it was too cold, so they decided that this time they would take a piece of mōchápu. They again cut out a round piece, stretched it over a ring, but this time painted it with oxide of copper (cákwa). They painted eyes and a mouth on the disk, and decorated the forehead of what this was to resemble in yellow, red, and other colors. They put a ring of corn-husks around it, which were worked in a zigzag fashion. Around this they tied a táwahona, that is, a string of red horse-hair, finally thrusting a number of eagle-tail feathers into a corn-husk ring, fastened to the back of the disk. In fact, they prepared a sun symbol as it is still worn on the back of the flute players in the Flute ceremony. To the forehead of the face painted on the disk they tied an abalone shell. Finally the chief made nakwákwosis of the feathers of a small yellowish bird, called iráhoya, which resembles a fly-catcher, but has some red hair on top of the head.

Of these nakwákwosis the chief tied one to the point of each eagle-tail feather on the sun symbol. They then placed this symbol on the white cloth again, again asked some one to stand on it, and, as in the case of the moon, they swung the cloth with its contents into the air, where it kept twirling upward and upward towards the east. Soon they again saw a light rise in the east. It became brighter and brighter and warmer. That proved to be the sun, and it had not come up very high when the Hopi already felt its warmth. After the sun had been created and was rising day after day, the people were very happy, because it was now warm and very light, so that they could attend to their work very well. The children were running around and playing. They were now thinking of moving on. They had a great many provisions by this time, and so the chiefs again met in a council to talk the matter over. "Let us move away from here," the chiefs said; "let us go eastward and see where the sun rises, but let us not go all together. Let some take one route, others another, and others still further south, and then we shall see who arrives at the place where the sun rises first." So the people started. The White People took a southern route, the Hopi a more northern, and between them traveled what are now the Pueblo Indians of New Mexico. Often certain parties would remain at certain places, sometimes for several years. They would build houses and plant.

Soon they became estranged from each other, and would begin to attack and kill one another. The Castilians were especially bad, and made wars on other people. When starting, the chiefs had agreed that as soon as one of the parties should reach the place where the sun rises, many stars would fall from the sky, and when that would happen all the traveling parties should remain and settle down where they would be at that time. The White People having taken a southern route, were more gifted than the other people. When they had become very tired carrying their children and their burdens, one of the women bathed herself and took the scales that she had rubbed off from her body and made horses of these scales. These horses they used after that for traveling, so that they could proceed very much faster. In consequence of this they arrived at the place where the sun rises before any of the other parties arrived there. And immediately many stars fell from the sky. "Aha!" the people said who were still traveling: "Some one has already arrived." Hereupon they settled down where they were. It had also been agreed upon before the different parties started, that whenever those who did not reach the place where the sun rises should be molested by enemies, they should notify those who had arrived at the sunrise, and the latter would then come and help them.

ORIGIN MYTH*

A very long time ago there was nothing but water. In the east Hurúing Wuhti, the deity of all hard substances, lived in the ocean. Her house was a kiva like the kivas of the Hopi of to-day. To the ladder leading into the kiva were usually tied a skin of a gray fox and one of a yellow fox. Another Hurúing Wuhti lived in the ocean in the west in a similar kiva, but to her ladder was attached a turtle-shell rattle.

The Sun also existed at that time. Shortly before rising in the east the Sun would dress up in the skin of the gray fox, whereupon it would begin to dawn—the so-called white dawn of the Hopi. After a little while the Sun would lay off the gray skin and put on the yellow fox skin, whereupon the bright dawn of the morning—the so-called yellow dawn of the Hopi—would appear. The Sun would then rise, that is, emerge from an opening in the north end of the kiva in which Hurúing Wuhti lived. When arriving in the west again, the sun would first announce his arrival by fastening the rattle on the point of the ladder beam, whereupon he would enter the kiva, pass through an opening in the north end of the kiva, and continue his course eastward under the water and so on.

By and by these two deities caused some dry land to appear in the midst of the water, the waters receding eastward and westward. The Sun

*From H.R. Voth, *The Traditions of the Hopi*, pp. 1-5.

passing over this dry land constantly took notice of the fact, that no living being of any kind could be seen anywhere, and mentioned this fact to the two deities. So one time the Hurúing Wuhti of the west sent word through the Sun to the Hurúing Wuhti in the east to come over to her as she wanted to talk over this matter. The Hurúing Wuhti of the east complied with this request and proceeded to the west over a rainbow. After consulting each other on this point the two concluded that they would create a little bird; so the deity of the east made a wren of clay, and covered it up with a piece of native cloth (möchápu). Hereupon they sang a song over it, and after a little while the little bird showed signs of life. Uncovering it, a live bird came forth, saying: "Uma hínok pas nui kitá náwakna?" (why do you want me so quickly). "Yes," they said, "we want you to fly all over this dry place and see whether you can find anything living." They thought that as the Sun always passed over the middle of the earth, he might have failed to notice any living beings that might exist in the north or the south. So the little Wren flew all over the earth, but upon its return reported that no living being existed anywhere. Tradition says, however, that by this time Spider Woman (Kóhkang Wuhti) lived somewhere in the south-west at the edge of the water, also in a kiva, but this the little bird had failed to notice.

Hereupon the deity of the west proceeded to make very many birds of different kinds and form, placing them again under the same cover under which the Wren had been brought to life. They again sang a song over them. Presently the birds began to move under the cover. The goddess removed the cover and found under it all kinds of birds and fowls. "Why do you want us so quickly?" the latter asked. "Yes, we want you to inhabit this world." Hereupon the two deities taught every kind of bird the sound that it should make, and then the birds scattered out in all directions.

Hereupon the Hurúing Wuhti of the west made of clay all different kinds of animals, and they were brought to life in the same manner as the birds. They also asked the same question: "Why do you want us so quickly?" "We want you to inhabit this earth," was the reply given them, whereupon they were taught by their creators their different sounds or languages, after which they proceeded forth to inhabit the different parts of the earth. They now concluded that they would create man. The deity of the east made of clay first a woman and then a man, who were brought to life in exactly the same manner as the birds and animals before them. They asked the same question, and were told that they should live upon this earth and should understand everything. Hereupon the Hurúing

Wuhti of the east made two tablets of some hard substance, whether stone or clay tradition does not say, and drew upon them with the wooden stick certain characters, handing these tablets to the newly created man and woman, who looked at them, but did not know what they meant. So the deity of the east rubbed with the palms of her hands, first the palms of the woman and then the palms of the man, by which they were enlightened so that they understood the writing on the tablets. Hereupon the deities taught these two a language. After they had taught them the language, the goddess of the east took them out of the kiva and led them over a rainbow, to her home in the east. Here they stayed four days, after which Hurúing Wuhti told them to go now and select for themselves a place and live there. The two proceeded forth saying that they would travel around a while and wherever they would find a good field they would remain. Finding a nice place at last, they built a small, simple house, similar to the old houses of the Hopi. Soon the Hurúing Wuhti of the west began to think of the matter again, and said to herself: "This is not the way yet that it should be. We are not yet done," and communicated her thoughts to the Hurúing Wuhti of the east. By this time Spider Woman had heard about all this matter and she concluded to anticipate the others and also create some beings. So she also made a man and woman of clay, covered them up, sang over them, and brought to life her handiwork. But these two proved to be Spaniards. She taught them the Spanish language, also giving them similar tablets and imparting knowledge to them by rubbing their hands in the same manner as the woman of the East had done with the "White Men." Hereupon she created two burros, which she gave to the Spanish man and woman. The latter settled down close by. After this, Spider Woman continued to create people in the same manner as she had created the Spaniards, always a man and a woman, giving a different language to each pair. But all at once she found that she had forgotten to create a woman for a certain man, and that is the reason why now there are always some single men.

She continued the creating of people in the same manner, giving new languages as the pairs were formed. All at once she found that she had failed to create a man for a certain woman, in other words, it was found that there was one more woman than there were men. "Oh my!" she said, "How is this?" and then addressing the single woman she said: "There is a single man somewhere, who went away from here. You try to find him and if he accepts you, you live with him. If not, both of you will have to remain single. You do the best you can about that."

The two finally found each other, and the woman said, "Where shall we live?" The man answered: "Why here, anywhere. We shall remain together." So he went to work and built a house for them in which they lived. But it did not take very long before they commenced to quarrel with each other. "I want to live here alone," the woman said. "I can prepare food for myself." "Yes, but who will get the wood for you? Who will work the fields?" the man said. "We had better remain together." They made up with each other, but peace did not last. They soon quarreled again, separated for a while, came together again, separated again, and so on. Had these people not lived in that way, all the other Hopi would now live in peace, but others learned it from them, and that is the reason why there are so many contentions between the men and their wives. These were the kind of people that Spider Woman had created. The Hurúing Wuhti of the west heard about this and commenced to meditate upon it. Soon she called the goddess from the east to come over again, which the latter did. "I do not want to live here alone," the deity of the west said, "I also want some good people to live here." So she also created a number of other people, but always a man and a wife. They were created in the same manner as the deity of the east had created hers. They lived in the west. Only wherever the people that Spider Woman had created came in contact with these good people there was trouble. The people at that time led a nomadic life, living mostly on game. Wherever they found rabbits or antelope or deer they would kill the game and eat it. This led to a good many contentions among the people. Finally the Woman of the west said to her people: "You remain here; I am going to live, after this, in the midst of the ocean in the west. When you want anything from me, you pray to me there." Her people regretted this very much, but she left them. The Hurúing Wuhti of the east did exactly the same thing, and that is the reason why at the present day the places where these two live are never seen.

Those Hopi who now want something from them deposit their prayer offerings in the village. When they say their wishes and prayers they think of those two who live in the far distance, but of whom the Hopi believe that they still remember them.

The Spanish were angry at Hurúing Wuhti and two of them took their guns and proceeded to the abiding place of the deity. The Spaniards are very skillful and they found a way to get there. When they arrived at the house of Hurúing Wuhti the latter at once surmised what their intentions were. "You have come to kill me," she said; "don't do that; lay down your weapons and I shall show you something; I am not going to hurt you." They laid down their arms, whereupon she went to the rear end of the kiva and brought out a white lump like a stone and laid it before the two men, asking them to lift it up. One tried it, but could not lift it up, and what was worse, his hands adhered to the stone: The other man tried to assist him, but his hands also adhered to the stone, and thus they were both prisoners. Hereupon Hurúing Wuhti took the two guns and said: "These do not amount to anything," and then rubbed them between her hands to powder. She then said to them: "You people ought to live in peace with one another. You people of Spider Woman know many things, and the people whom we have made also know many, but different, things. You ought not to quarrel about these things, but learn from one another; if one has or knows a good thing he should exchange it with others for other good things that they know and have. If you will agree to this I shall release you." They said they did, and that they would no more try to kill the deity. Then the latter went to the rear end of the kiva where she disappeared through an opening in the floor, from where she exerted a secret influence upon the stone and thus released the two men. They departed, but Hurúing Wuhti did not fully trust them, thinking that they would return, but they never did.

KERES (ACOMA)

AUTOBIOGRAPHY OF AN ACOMA INDIAN*

THE church was there [at Acoma] when I first opened my eyes. A priest lived there all alone. Before that time there used to be judges and constables living there with the priest. Everybody had to go to church then. If a man or woman did not go, the judges or constables came and got him, or her, and took him to the church. They tied him to a post and whipped him, or her, until he said "yes." If a husband or a wife ran around with someone else, the wife or husband could tell the judges. They decided what to do. If they decided that the accused was guilty they took him to the Komanira [the house in which "council" meetings are held] and whipped him.

*From Leslie A. White, *New Material from Acoma*, pp. 301-360.

The people had to supply the priest and the judges and constables with food and wood. The Bickale [fiscales] had charge of that. Every family had to contribute. The unmarried girls and boys had to work in the church and the school and in the quarters of the priest, judges, and constables. They had a school in those days; they taught the children to read and write Spanish and they taught the Catholic religion. Whenever they had katsina dances at Acoma the priest and the constables had to stay in their rooms or leave the mesa.

But when I was a little boy only the priest lived at Acoma, alone. I don't know why the teachers and judges left. Someone told me that they had a quarrel with the Indians and the Indians were going to kill them. When I was a little boy the convento was in good shape and very pretty. We used to have Mass every morning and on Sunday, too.

In the house where I first opened my eyes lived my mother and father, my mother's mother and father, three brothers and two sisters of my mother, and my mother's mother's mother. One of my lanawe (mother's brother), the oldest, was married and lived at his wife's house. My mother's eldest sister was married; her husband lived there with us. I was the oldest among my brothers and sisters.

In those days there were no doors on the first floor of the houses. There were little isinglass (h'a.ck'a.nyi) windows. There was no air except, perhaps, through a little hole in the window. Whenever there was any hollering [specifically, announcements of the war chief or governor] in the streets, my mother would listen at this hole, or else look out. Indoors we spent most of our time on the ground floor in wintertime. In summer we lived on the second (or third) floor. We slept on sheep pelts [as many do today].

I used to play with a boy about my size who lived next door. He was not a relative. We used to hunt squirrels and birds with bow and arrow, both on top of the mesa and at the bottom.

My mother's mother (sapapa) and mother's father (sanana), he especially, used to tell me stories. I used to spend a lot of time with them.

We didn't have any wagons or kerosene lamps then. We had some two-wheeled carts with solid wooden wheels. For light we had a bowl with sheep fat in it and a wick. We never had any matches; we made fire with a fire drill (a.tyu tcó'mi). There were only a few guns in the peublo, mostly flint locks. Most hunters hunted with bow and arrows and clubs. Some people had a few Mexican dishes, but most of the families had only [Indian] pottery bowls. At that time no one did any farming in the Acomita valley. There were only a few houses at Acomita; they belonged to people who used to graze their sheep down there.

When I was very small my mother's father and mother went to Laguna to sell some pottery and buy some things. They brought back some wheat. That was the first time I ever saw it. Once in a while they got some coffee and sugar. Poor Mother! She was very fond of coffee. But we were very poor and never had much.

My father was a medicine man: he was the head of the Fire Society. These tcaianyi used to perform their ceremony twice a year. My mother and I used to go with them. Everybody had to wait on top of the k'a'atc [kiva; chamber where the society held its meeting] until the tcaianyi sang the song for us to come down. When they sang the song for us to come in, one medicine man would come up and remove the line of ashes with his flint. We were all eager to get in first in order to get the good seats. Women with small children went into a room on the west side of the curing chamber.

There used to be lots of medicine men, more than there are now. When we would come in, the tcaianyi would have their ya.Baic*ini* [wooden slat altar] up. The head man would be sitting in front of the sand painting by his two medicine-bowls. These bowls were made of gypsum (Spanish, yeso; Keresan, ba.´tyu) hollowed out; they had terraced sides, and pictures of snakes, clouds, lightning, etc., painted or carved on the sides. . . .

I used to get scared at these ceremonies. The tcaianyi used to tell us about witches, and how they went around killing people. When they would look through the ma.´caiyoyo [the quartz crystal that gives second sight] . . . to find the witches, they would yell and scare us. My mother and I and my sisters used to have to stay after the ceremony was all over, as my mother had to pack up my father's things and take them home. My father had three or five yaya (honani, corn-ear fetich); one was made for him at the time of initiation, the others he had received at the death of society members.

There were no American doctors anywhere near Acoma in those days. The tcaianyi (medicine men) were all we had. But there were lots of them: we had Hakanyi (Fire), Hictianyi (Flint), Kapina, and Sii (Ant) tcaianyi.

When I was 5 I was "whipped into katsina." They were very strict about the katsina in those days—not like it is now; everyone had to join and take part [i.e., in the masked dances]. I was pretty scared when they initiated me. I thought Tsitsinits (the katsina whipper) was real. They didn't show us the masks until 2 or 3 years afterward, when we got to be old enough to know about such things.

We didn't have any fights with the Navahos when I was a boy. When I was about 7 years old a bunch of Indians from Cochiti, Domingo, and other pueblos near there, about 40 of them, passed through Acoma on their way to California. They were going out there to work in sheep camps or do some other work so they could buy some horses and bring them back. They stopped at Acoma over night. After supper they went through the streets singing, "Californiya omi´aro.tsi, wiya heya," etc. It was a Comanche song saying, "California, I am going out there." One of the earliest of the "California, here I come" songs.

NAVAJO

SONG OF THE HORSE*

How joyous his neigh!
Lo, the Turquoise Horse of Johano-Ai
How joyous his neigh!
There on precious hides outspread standeth he;
How joyous his neigh!
There on tips of fair fresh flowers feedeth he;
How joyous his neigh!
There of mingled waters holy drinketh he;
How joyous his neigh!
There he spurneth dust of glittering grains;
How joyous his neigh!
There in mist of sacred pollen hidden, all hidden;

*From Natalie Curtis, The Indians' Book.

How joyous his neigh!
There his offspring may grow and thrive forevermore;
How joyous his neigh!

This ritual chant for the blessing and protection of the horses is part of a myth involving the sun god, Johano-Ai, who drives his horse and chariot across the sky. The influence of Old World thought is obvious here, but the joy and pleasure in the horse, which formed the basis of the tribal wealth, is quite uniquely Indian.

TEWA

THE THREE BEARS*

ONE woman and one man were living, they had three boys. The man would go and get wood and sell the wood in town. The three boys wanted to go where their father was getting wood, but their mother would not let them go. One boy was little, another a little bigger, another still bigger. They started to where their father was getting wood. The smallest boy got tired. The other boys said, "Younger brother, you stay here. We will go where father is getting wood, and we will come back here quickly." So the two boys went on to where their father was getting wood. He asked them if they had come by themselves. They said yes, they did not tell him that they had left their younger brother way back. When they did not come back their younger brother looked for a place to hide. Bear Woman lived there and two little bears. They had gone out to look for berries. They had lots of berries, their bowls were full. The little boy went in to their house, he found nobody. Their table was laid with their bowls of berries. The little boy ate from one bowl and then from another. Then he lay down in the bed of one of the little bears. At dinner time the bears came back. The little boy was asleep. The bears went up to the table. One said, "Who was eating in my bowl?" Another said, "Who was eating in my bowl? Just look at it!" They said, "Who came in here?" One little bear said, "Somebody is

*From Elsie Clews Parsons, *Tewa Tales*, pp. 132-133.

lying in my bed.'' They saw the little boy lying down. They woke him up. He sat up, he got scared and started to scratch his head. Bear Woman said to him, ''Don't be scared. Who brought you here?'' He said, ''I was looking for my father and I came here.'' — ''So!'' said she. ''Now you must stay and live with us.'' Meanwhile his mother was crying because her little boy was lost, and she scolded the other boys. . . . Bear Woman asked the little boy to eat. ''Eat!'' she said. He did not want to eat. Bear Woman talked nicely to him so he would not be afraid. She said to the two little bears, ''This is your younger brother.'' That night he stayed there, that little boy. The next day Bear Woman went out to get some more berries. She said to the little bears, ''You must stay here with your younger brother. Don't make him cry.'' So she left them. The little boy and the little bears played out-doors. While they were playing the little boy hid from the little bears, then he ran off to look for his house. In his house his father and mother were crying. The little boy could not find his house and he began to cry. A man heard him crying and went up to him and took him home. His mother was crying because they could not find him. They asked him where he had slept. He said, ''I went to the house of Bear Woman. They treated me well, and I slept there.'' His mother was frightened. ''When I came there, nobody was there. The table was set and I ate from the bowls. I lay down to sleep. The bears came in and woke me up. Bear Woman asked me to eat, she told the little bears I was their younger brother. Next day she went hunting berries and left me with my bear brothers. I was frightened and ran away from them.'' His mother was glad that Bear Woman had treated him well. So she said to her husband. ''Whenever you see a bear, do not kill it because Bear Woman was good to our child.'' That is the way it happened to the little boy.

The adoption of European literary forms by Indian storytellers offers great insight into the differences in attitudes and values between the two peoples. This version of ''Goldilocks and the Three Bears'' utilizes the European form to reaffirm the continuity of kinship between animals and men.

THERE IS NO INDIAN COULD DO THIS*

I have read the magazine printed by Washington in 1932. The history is true and exact, but the pictures to complete it are missing. I have drawn some of them. . . .

These drawings you will never see anywhere because no one could do them, it is too hard. They are afraid to die if they do them. I don't want any soul to know as long as I live that I have drawn these pictures. I want good satisfaction because they are valuable and worth it. They are most secret. No one can see them but Indians who believe.

I have no way of making a living, no farm. . . . If I had some way to get help in this world I would never have done this. . . .

The excerpt above is from a letter sent from Isleta Pueblo near Albuquerque, New Mexico, to Dr. Elsie Clews Parsons at the Bureau of American Ethnology in Washington. It was written by a man who called himself Felipe but whose real name, revealed only after his death, was Joseph Lent. From 1936 to 1941 Felipe worked to illustrate Dr. Parsons' monograph of Isleta life. He produced over 150 paintings. In constant fear for his life—fear based on his certain knowledge that what he was doing was forbidden by Pueblo law and tradition—Felipe nevertheless continued to write and paint. Although he cites a need for money as one consideration in his willingness to do this work, a profound esthetic impulse as well as great pride in his traditions is evident in both drawings and letters. Pueblo traditions—though they are, indeed, an amalgam of Indian and white cultures—remain strong today in good part because Pueblo residents have maintained tight boundaries against outside interference. It was clearly Felipe's intention not to betray his people but rather to explain and glorify them.

*From Elsie Clews Parsons, *Isleta Paintings*, p. 1.

Plateau

THE WHITE MAN*

A white man went along. He saw another white man on the branch of a tree. He was chopping off the limb close to the trunk. The white man was told: "You will fall." The white man said: "I shall not fall." He said no more. This one started. The other one was chopping along. He chopped it off. He fell down.

THE MOTHER-IN-LAW TABOO**

Long ago the people used to be ashamed of each other. Mother-in-law and son-in-law could not talk to each other. They could not look at their faces. When mother-in-law and son-in-law met, they were afraid of each other. Those who were not ashamed of the mother-in-law were known not to love her. Whoever was much ashamed of his mother-in-law was known to love her very much. The reason why he is ashamed is that then his mother-in-law will never get angry at him and never scold him. Whoever is not ashamed of his mother-in-law is known to be always angry at her, and never afraid to scold his mother-in-law. The people held it this way in olden times. Now they forget how their grandparents used to do, because they met white people. This is the way the mother-in-law and son-in-law did, and why they are not ashamed of each other any more.

*From Franz Boas, *Kutenai Tales,* p. 33
**From Franz Boas, *Kutenai Tales,* p. 279

MODOC

I AM THE VOICE OF MY PEOPLE*

I am but one man. I am the voice of my people. Whatever their hearts are, that I talk. I want no more war. I want to be a man. You deny me the right of a white man. My skin is red; my heart is a white man's heart; but I am a Modoc. I am not afraid to die. I will not fall on the rocks. When I die, my enemies will be under me. Your soldiers began on me when I was asleep on Lost River. They drove us to these rocks like a wounded deer. . . .

I have always told the white man heretofore to come and settle in my country; that it was his country and Captain Jack's country. That they could come and live here with me and that I was not mad with them. I have never received anything from anybody, only what I bought and paid for myself. I have always lived like a white man, and wanted to live so. I have always tried to live peaceably and never asked any man for anything. I have always lived on what I could kill and shoot with my gun and catch in my trap.

KINTPUASH (CAPTAIN JACK)

The poignant dilemma of an Indian who tried to befriend the white man and ended by murdering a white man in order to maintain his relationship to his own people is etched sharply in this statement. Captain Jack was a leader of the Modocs, but because of his friendship with the white men, he had trouble maintaining his leadership. Under great pressure from his people he killed General E. R. S. Canby, a member of a peace conference, and fled with his men. Outnumbered, he surrendered and was hanged on October 3, 1873.

*From Dee Brown, *Bury My Heart at Wounded Knee*, p. 213.

NEZ PERCE

MY YOUNG MEN SHALL NEVER WORK*

MY young men shall never work. Men who work cannot dream and wisdom comes in dreams.

You ask me to plow the ground. Shall I take a knife and tear my mother's breast? Then when I die she will not take me to her bosom to rest.

You ask me to dig for stone. Shall I dig under her skin for bones? Then when I die I cannot enter her body to be born again.

You ask me to cut grass and make hay and sell it and be rich like white men. But how dare I cut off my mother's hair?

It is a bad law and my people cannot obey it. I want my people to stay with me here. All the dead men will come to life again. We must wait here in the house of our fathers and be ready to meet them in the body of our mother.

What the white man often thought was simple laziness or a stubborn unwillingness of the Indian to face the facts of life was, in fact, the very system of belief and values that held Indian society together. Asked to move from their homes and to give up their nomadic hunting life for the sedentary life of the farmer, the Indian responded in the only way he could: by attempting to communicate to the white man the fact that the land, his hunting, his homesite were sacred to him. Altering any aspect of his life threatened the whole of it.

*From Herbert J. Spinden, *The Nez Percé Indians*, p. 261.

Northwest Coast

THE FIRST SHIP SEEN BY THE CLATSOPS*
As Translated from the Chinook of Charles Cultee

THE son of an old woman had died. She wailed for him a whole year and then she stopped. Now one day she went to Seaside. There she used to stop, and she returned. She returned walking along the beach. She nearly reached Clatsop; now she saw something. She thought it was a whale. When she came near it she saw two spruce trees standing upright on it. She thought, "Behold! it is no whale. It is a monster." She reached the thing that lay there. Now she saw that its outer side was all covered with copper. Ropes were tied to these spruce trees and it was full of iron. Then a bear came out of it. He stood on the thing that lay there. He looked just like a bear, but his face was that of a human being. Then she went home. Now she thought of her son, and cried, saying, "Oh, my son is dead and the thing about which we heard in tales is on shore." When she nearly reached the town she continued to cry. The people said, "Oh, a person comes crying. Perhaps somebody struck her." The people made themselves ready. They took their arrows. An old man said, "Listen!" Then the people listened. Now she said all the time, "Oh, my son is dead, and the thing about which we heard in tales is on shore." The people said, "What may it be?" They went running to meet her. They said, "What is it?" "Ah, something lies there and it is thus. There are two bears on it, or maybe they are people." Then the people ran. They reached the thing that lay there. Now the people, or what else they might be, held two copper kettles in their hands. Now the

*From Alfred Powers, *History of Oregon Literature*, pp. 115-116.

271

first one reached there. Another one arrived. Now the persons took their hands to their mouths and gave the people their kettles. They had lids. The men pointed inland and asked for water. Then two people ran inland. They hid themselves behind a log. They returned again and ran to the beach. One man climbed up and entered the thing. He went down into the ship. He looked about in the interior of the ship; it was full of boxes. He found brass buttons in strings half a fathom long. He went out again to call his relatives, but they had already set fire to the ship. He jumped down. These two persons had also gone down. It burnt just like fat. Then the Clatsop gathered the iron, the copper, and the brass. Then all the people learned about it. The two persons were taken to the chief of the Clatsop. Then the chief of the one town said, "I want to keep one of the men with me." The people almost began to fight. Now one of them was taken to one town. Then the chief was satisfied. Now the Quenaiult, the Chehalis, the Cascades, the Cowlitz, and the Klickitat learned about it and they all went to Clatsop. The Quenaiult, the Chehalis, and the Willapa went. The people of all the towns were there. The Cascades, the Cowlitz, and the Klickitat came down the river. All those of the upper part of the river came down to Clatsop. Strips of copper two fingers wide and going around the arm were exchanged for one slave each. A piece of brass two fingers wide was exchanged for one slave. A nail was sold for a good curried deerskin. Several nails were given for long dentalia. The people bought this and the Clatsop became rich. Then iron and brass were seen for the first time. Now they kept these two persons. One was kept by each chief; one was at the Clatsop town at the Cape.

   The emphasis upon material possessions, upon trade, and exchange among the numerous groups of the northwest coast is quite obvious in this narrative. The contrast between such historical accounts and the mythical incorporation of the white man by other Indians is quite marked and suggests the very different kinds of interests that marked the acquisitive and more materialistic groups of the Pacific Northwest from most of their fellow Indians.

CULTEE'S GRANDFATHER VISITS THE GHOSTS*

My grandfather wanted to take a woman from Oak point for his wife. They tried to give him another girl, but he did not like her. He used to make canoes. As soon as he had finished a canoe, he bought a slave with it. He had many slaves. Then an epidemic came. He had a pretty slave girl. She looked just like a chieftainess. Now he heard that the girl whom he wanted to have for his wife had died. The epidemic took the people away. Two days they were sick, then they died. Sometimes they died after three days' sickness. Now his people also were attacked by the epidemic. Several died each day, sometimes three died, sometimes four. Now my grandfather felt sick. After three days he died.

Then he went to the country of the ghosts. He reached that trail. He saw two people carrying a stick. When he came near, he saw that they were posts of a house. These people looked just like posts. Then he came to a person who dragged his intestines on the ground. When he came near, he saw that it was a mat made of rushes. The road was full of tracks of people. Now he came down to a large creek. He looked across and saw a large town. He heard people making canoes. Then a person came up to him. He recognized one of his mother's relatives who had been dead long ago. He said: "Did you come at last? They are waiting for you. The news of your arrival has come already. They will buy for you the girl whom you like. She and her mother have come across." Then that person left him. The grass at that place was three fingers wide and was more than man's height. It was moved by the wind and sounded like bells. He heard it ringing all the time. The grass told the people on the other side what was going to happen. Now he saw that woman and he thought: "I do not like her. She looks just like her mother. Her face is sore all the time." He saw her in that manner. Then another person came to him. He recognized his uncle. They all came up the river. His uncle spoke: "Let us go to catch seals." His uncle took a line. They gave him something that looked just like soap. "Eat that," he said. He ate it, but he did not like it. Then he turned his head toward the land and spit out what was given to him. His uncle, who was looking toward the water, said: "What does he want to eat? He refuses what I give him." Then he thought: "I just came here and they scold me already. I will return." Then the sun shone on his right side. He did not walk. He just turned round and then he fell in a swoon. Now he recov-

*From Franz Boas, *Kathlamet Texts*, pp. 247-251.

ered. He heard people crying. Early in the morning when he had died the people had gone to fetch his aunt from Klatsop. In the evening she arrived and brought two sea-otters which she intended to tie to his body. They had cut their hair and his slaves had been divided. One of his uncles had taken that pretty slave girl. Now his aunt was angry. She wished to have that slave girl. She went home and took the sea-otters along. In the morning his breath had given out. It became night and became day again. The sun was low when he recovered. The people were crying all the time and said: "To-morrow we will bury him." Then that one woman was quiet and looked at him. It looked just as if the mat were moving. She looked at him again and said: "It is an evil omen for me; I see the mat moving." They lifted it. They felt his heart. He was warm and his heart was beating. His feet and his hands were cold. Then they called the conjurers. They warmed his hands at the fire and blew water on his face. He recovered. They gave him water. They poured some into his mouth. It ran down as far as his throat, but ran out of his mouth again. His throat and his chest were dry. Finally he swallowed the water. He drank much and recovered.

Many people died. Sometimes five died in one day, sometimes four, sometimes three. The epidemic killed them.

Then the seers learned what he had seen when he went to the country of the ghosts and saw everything there. Formerly the seers did not know it, but when he had been dead they learned about it.

Interpersonal tensions and concern with the division of property are manifest in this account of a vision brought on by illness. Although the vision is still of importance among these Chinook Indians, its content is more mundane than miraculous and the escape of the narrator from death rests upon his own initiative rather than upon spiritual help.

Duwamish

THERE IS NO DEATH, ONLY A
CHANGE OF WORLDS*

YONDER sky, that has wept tears of compassion on our fathers for centuries untold, and which, to us, looks eternal, may change. Today is fair, tomorrow it may be overcast with clouds. My words are like the stars that never change. What Seattle says, the great chief Washington can rely upon, with as much certainty as our paleface brothers can rely upon the return of the seasons.

The son of the White Chief says that his father sends us greetings of friendship and good will. This is kind, for we know he has little need of our friendship in return, because his people are many. They are like the grass that covers the vast prairies. My people are few, and resemble the scattering trees of a storm-swept plain. . . .

There was a time when our people covered the whole land as the waves of the wind-ruffled sea cover its shell-paved floor. But that time has long since passed away with the greatness of tribes now almost forgotten. I will not mourn over our untimely decay nor reproach my paleface brothers with hastening it.

Your religion was written on tablets of stone by the iron finger of your God, lest you forget it. The red men could never remember it or comprehend it. Our religion is the traditions of our ancestors, the dreams of our old men, given them by the Great Spirit and the visions of our sachems, and is written in the hearts of our people. . . .

Every part of this country is sacred to my people. Every hillside, every valley, every plain and grove has been hallowed by some fond memory or some sad experience of my tribe. Even the rocks which seem to lie dumb as they swelter in the sun . . . thrill with memories of past events connected with the fate of my people. . . .

The braves, fond mothers, glad-hearted maidens and even little children, who lived here . . . still love these solitudes. Their deep fastnesses at eventide grow shadowy with the presence of dusty spirits. When the last red man shall have perished from the earth and his memory among the white men shall have become a myth, these shores shall swarm with the invisible dead of my tribe. . . .

*From Louis Thomas Jones, *Aboriginal American Oratory*, p. 99.

At night, when the streets of your cities and villages shall be silent, and you think them deserted, they will throng with the returning hosts that once filled and still love this beautiful land.

The white man will never be alone. Let him be just and deal kindly with my people, for the dead are not altogether powerless. Dead, did I say? There is no death, only a change of worlds.

CHIEF SEATHE

A prophecy of rebirth forecast upon signing the Treaty of Port Elliot, in 1855. The chief warned the white man, to whom he had surrendered his lands in return for the right to fish, that he was doomed to eternal unrest.

YUROK

ALL IS TROUBLE ALONG THE KLAMATH*

(MRS. OREGON JIM, from the house Erkigér-i or "Hair-ties" in the town of Pékwan, speaking): You want to know why old Louisa and I never notice each other? Well, I'll tell you why. I wouldn't speak to that old woman to save her life. There is a quarrel between her and me, and between her people and my people.

The thing started, so far as I know, with the bastard son of a woman from that big old house in Wáhsek that stands crossways—the one they call Wáhsek-héthlqau. They call it that, of course, because it is *behind* the others. It kind of sets back from the river. This woman lived with several different men; first with a young fellow from the house next door, and then, when she left *him,* with a strolling fellow from Smith River. When she left him for a Húpa, they all began to call her *kimolin,* "dirty." Not one of these men had paid a cent for her, although she came of good people. She lived around in different places. Two of her children died, but a third one grew up at the Presbyterian Mission.

He had even less sense than the Presbyterians have. He came down to Kepél one time, when the people there were making the Fish Dam. It was

*From Elsie Clews Parsons, *American Indian Life*, pp. 289-296.

the last day of the work on the dam. The dam was being finished, that day. That's the time nobody can get mad. Nobody can take offense at anything. This boy heard people calling each other bad names. They were having a dance. The time of that dance is different from all other times. People say the worst things! It sounds funny to hear the people say, for example, to old Kímorets, "Well, old One-Eye! you are the best dancer." They think of the worst things to say! A fellow even said to Mrs. Poker Bob, "How is your grandmother?"; when Mrs. Poker Bob's grandmother was already dead. It makes your blood run cold to hear such things, even though you know it's in fun.

This young fellow I am telling you about, whom they called Fred Williams, and whose Indian name was Sär, came down from the Mission school to see the Fish-Dam Dance at Kepél. He was dressed up. He went around showing off. He wore a straw hat with a ribbon around it. He stood around watching the dance. Between the songs, he heard what people were saying to each other. He heard them saying all sorts of improper things. He thought that was smart talk. He thought he would try it when he got a chance. The next day, he went down by the river and saw Tuley-Creek Jim getting ready his nets. "Get your other hand cut off," he said. "Then you can fish with your feet!" Two or three people who were standing by, heard him. Tuley-Creek Jim is pretty mean. They call him "Coyote." He looked funny. He stood there. He didn't know what to say.

Young Andrew, who was there, whose mother was from the house called "Down-river House" in Qóvtep, was afraid for his life. He was just pushing off his boat. He let go of the rope. The boat drifted off. He was afraid to pull it back. He went up to the house. "Something happened," he told the people there. "I wish I was somewhere else. There is going to be trouble along this Klamath River."

The talk soon went around that Coyote-Jim was claiming some money. It was told us that he was going to make the boy's mother's father pay fifteen dollars. "That's my price," he said. "I won't do anything to the boy, for he isn't worth it. Nobody paid for his mother. Also, I won't charge him much. But his mother's people are well-to-do, and they will have to pay this amount that I name. Otherwise, I will be mad." As a matter of fact, he was afraid to do anything, for he, himself, was afraid of the soldiers at Húpa. He just made big talk. Besides, what he wanted was a headband ornamented with whole woodpecker heads, that the boy's grandfather owned. He thought he could make the old man give it up, on account of what his grandson had said.

The boy went around, hollering to everybody. "I don't have to pay," he said. "I heard everybody saying things like that! How did I know that they only did it during that one day? Besides, look at me! Look at my shirt. Look at my pants." He showed them his straw hat. "Look at my hat! I am just like a white man. I can say anything I please. I don't have to care what I say."

Every day somebody came along the river, telling us the news. There was a big quarrel going on. I was camped at that time, with my daughter, above Metá, picking acorns. All the acorns were bad that year—little, and twisted, and wormy. Even the worms were little and kind of shriveled that year. That place above Metá was the only place where the acorns were good. Lots of people were camped there. Some paid for gathering acorns there. My aunt had married into a house at Metá, the house they call Wóogi, "In-the-middle-House," so I didn't have to pay anything. People used to come up from the river to where we acorn pickers were camped, to talk about the news. They told us the boy's mother's people were trying to make some people at Smith River pay. "He's the son of one of their men," the old grandfather said. "They've got to pay for the words he spoke. I don't have to pay." The thing dragged on. Three weeks later they told us the old man wouldn't pay yet.

Somebody died at the old man's house that fall. The people were getting ready to have a funeral. The graveyard for that house called Héthl-qau, in Wáhsek, is just outside the house door. They went into that kämethl, in that corpse-place, what you whites call a cemetery. They dug a hole and had it ready. They were singing "crying-songs" in that house where the person had died.

Tuley-Creek Jim's brother-in-law was traveling down the river in a canoe. When he got to Wáhsek he heard "crying songs." "Somebody has died up there," they told him. "We better stop! No use trying to go by. We better go ashore till the burial is over." Tuley-Creek Jim's brother-in-law did not want to stop. "They owe some money to my wife's brother," he said. "One of their people said something to Jim. They don't pay up. Why should I go ashore?" So they all paddled down to the landing-place. They started to go past, going down-river. A young fellow at the landing-place grabbed their canoe. "You got to land here," he said. "My aunt's people are having a funeral. It ain't right for anybody to go by in a canoe." The people in the canoe began to get mad. They pushed on the bottom with their paddles. The canoe swung around. Coyote-Jim's brother-in-law stood up. He was pretty mad. They had got his shirt wet. He waved his paddle around. He hollered. He got excited.

One of the men on the bank was Billy Brooks, from the mouth of the river. "Hey! You fellow-living-with-a-woman-you-haven't-paid-for!" he said to Billy Brooks, "make these fellows let go of my canoe."

Billy was surprised. He hadn't been holding the canoe. And anyway, he did not expect to be addressed that way. "Läs-son" is what he had heard addressed to him. That means "half-married, or improperly married, to a woman in the house by the trail." Brooks had had no money to pay for a wife, so he went to live with his woman instead of taking her home to him. That is what we call being half-married. Everybody called Billy that way, behind his back. "Half-married-into-the-house-by-the-trail" was his name.

When Billy got over being surprised at this form of address, he got mad. He pointed at the fellow in the canoe. He swore the worst way a person can swear. What he said was awful. He pointed at him. He was mad clear through. He didn't care what he said. "Your deceased relatives," is what he said to Coyote-Jim's brother-in-law, in the canoe. He said it right out loud. He pointed at the canoe. That's the time he said "Your deceased relatives." "All your deceased relatives," he said to those in the canoe.

Coyote-Jim's brother-in-law sat down in the canoe. Nobody tried to stop the canoe after that. The canoe went down-river. Billy Brooks went up to the house. He waited. After a while the people there buried that person who was dead, and the funeral was over. "I've got to pay money," Billy Brooks said to them then. "I got mad and swore something terrible at Coyote-Jim's brother-in-law. That was on account of you people. If you had paid what you owed to Coyote-Jim, Coyote-Jim's brother-in-law wouldn't have gone past your house while you were crying, and you wouldn't have held his canoe, and he wouldn't have addressed me as he did, and I wouldn't have said what I did. Moreover, Wóhkel Dave was in the canoe, and when I said that which I said, it applied to him, too. I feel terrible mean about what I said. I've got to have trouble with both those men. There were others in the canoe, too, but they are poor people, and don't amount to anything. But Dave is a rich man. Now all this trouble is on your account, and you've got to pay me two dollars and a half."

The old man at Wáhsek was in trouble. "First my mouse says to Coyote-Jim what should not in any case have been said," the old man complained. (We call illegitimate children "mice," because they eat, and stay around, and nobody has paid for them.) "Now on account of what my mouse said, all this other trouble has happened."

Everybody was talking about the quarrel now. That is the time they left off talking about the old man's troubles, and began talking about what Billy Brooks said to the Coyote's brother-in-law in the canoe, and to Wóhkel Dave. It finally came out that the fellow who was steering the canoe, and who called Billy Brooks "Läs-son," was out of the quarrel. His deceased relatives had been referred to, but, on the other hand, his father had only paid twenty-five dollars for his mother, so nobody cared much about him. He talked around but nobody paid any attention, so he decided that he had better keep still about it, and maybe people would forget that he had been insulted.

Wóhkel Dave, however, was a man of importance. His people were married into all the best houses up and down the river. Everybody was wondering what he and Brooks would do. Billy Brooks was kind of a mean man himself. He had a bad reputation. One time he even made a white man pay up for something he did. The white man took a woman from Brooks' people to live with him. Brooks looked him up, and made him pay for her. Everybody was afraid of Brooks. Some people said, "Brooks won't pay. He's too mean. He's not afraid. He'd rather fight it out." Other people said, "That's all right, as far as ordinary people are concerned. Wóhkel Dave, though, is not ordinary. His father paid a big price for his mother. She had one of the most stylish weddings along the river. Dave won't let anybody get the best of him." People used to argue that way. Some said one thing, and some said another. They used to almost quarrel about it.

Suddenly news came down the river that Billy Brooks was going to pay up for what he said. Some one came along and told us that Billy was going to pay. "He offered twenty-five dollars," this fellow said. The next day we heard that Dave wouldn't take it. He wanted forty dollars. They argued back and forth. It was February before they got it settled. Billy had to pay twenty dollars in money, a shot-gun made out of an army musket, bored out, and a string of shell money, not a very good one. The shells were pretty small, but the string was long—reaching from the chest bone to the end of the fingers.

The next thing that happened is what involved me and old Louisa. It came about because Billy didn't have twenty dollars in cash. He had to get hold of the twenty dollars. About that time, certain Indians stole some horses. They were not people from our tribe. They were Chilula from

Bald Hills, or people from over in that direction somewhere. Those people were awful poor. They couldn't pay for a woman. They couldn't pay for anything. They had to marry each other. In the springtime they got pretty wild. They were likely to do things. This time they took some horses from a white man. This white man complained to the agent at Húpa. So some soldiers from Húpa went out to chase these Indians. Billy Brooks was a great hunter. He has been all over everywhere, hunting and trapping. The soldiers needed a guide. They offered Billy twenty-five dollars to serve as a "scout" for the Government, to chase these Indians. So Billy, because he had to have twenty dollars, went as a scout, that time.

The soldiers went to Redwood Creek. Billy Brooks went along. There was a sergeant and six men, they say. Two of the men went to that Indian town six miles above the mouth of Redwood Creek, the name of which is Otlép. That town belongs to the Chilula. These two soldiers went there, looking for the men who stole the horses. There was trouble after a while at that place. The soldiers got into a quarrel with the Indians.

The trouble was about a woman. One of the soldiers wanted her, but the woman would not go with him. She did not feel like it. I don't know exactly what happened, but the soldier insisted, and the woman insisted, and finally her relatives told the soldier that if the woman didn't want to, she didn't have to. There was a fight that time. There was a tussle about the soldier's revolver. Somebody got hit over the head with it. The front sight was sharp. That soldier had filed down the sight on his revolver, to make it fine. That sight dug into a man's face, and cut it open, from his jaw bone up to his eye.

There was big trouble there that time, they say. Everybody got to hollering. That woman had a bad temper. She hit a soldier with a rock. She broke his head open. The man whose face was cut open went for his gun. He couldn't see very well. He didn't get the percussion cap on properly. He tried to shoot the soldier, but the gun wouldn't go off. The cap had dropped off the nipple. The soldier saw the Indian aiming the gun at him, so he fired at the Indian. There was blood in the soldier's eyes, for the woman had cut his head open with a rock. So he missed the Indian who was aiming at him, but he hit old Louisa's nephew, Jim Williams. The bullet went through his thigh. Two years passed before Jim Williams could walk straight after that.

Now that is the trouble between old Louisa and me. Her nephew was hurt, and she blames Billy Brooks, because Billy Brooks was with the soldiers, helping them, the time this happened. Billy would never "pay up" for this. One time it was reported that he was going to pay, but he never did.

Now Billy is a relative of mine by marriage. His sister married my father's brother's oldest boy. That old woman, whose nephew was shot, doesn't like me, because I am a relative of Billy who guided the soldiers.

One time she played me a dirty trick. My nephew was fishing with a gill-net on the river here. The game warden made a complaint and had him arrested, for he had one end of his net fast to the bank. That old woman, that old Louisa, went to Eureka and told the judge there, that one end of the net was fast to the bank. They say she got money for doing that. Somebody said she got two dollars a day. My nephew was put in jail for sixty days. I am not saying anything to that old woman, but I am keeping a watch on her. If anybody talks to her, then I have nothing to do with them.

One time a white man from down below came along this river, asking about baskets. He wanted to know the name of everything. He was kind of crazy, that fellow. They used to call him "Häpó'o," or "Basket-designs." He was always asking, "What does that mean?" or "What is the name of that?" He wanted to know all about baskets. He talked to old Louisa for a day and a half about her baskets. Then he came through the fence to my house. I wouldn't say a word to him, and he went away. My friends won't talk to Louisa, or her friends. It will be that way forever.

It all goes back to that boy Sär. If he had not talked about Tuley-Creek Jim having only one hand, Jim's brother-in-law would not have paddled past a house where there was a person lying dead, and his canoe would not have been seized, and there would have been no quarrel about the canoe, and Billy Brooks would not have sworn at anybody, so he would not have had to pay money, and he would not have hired out as a scout to the Government, and the fellow in Redwood Creek would not have been shot, and old Louisa would not have testified about my nephew. To make people pay is all right. That is what always happens when there is a quarrel. But to put my nephew in jail is not right.

I'll never speak to that old lady again, and neither will any of my people.

as told to T. T. WATERMAN
by MRS. OREGON JIM

The ways in which white culture disrupts and destroys native social organization and values are not always apparent to the casual observer. We are prone to believe that only direct interference by the government affects Indian life. In fact, it is the more subtle disruptions that ultimately are most important. In the narrative account provided here we can quite clearly see how the presence of white "law and order" operates to alienate people from each other, and how the need for money, which demands participation in the white man's world, creates problems for the Indians. The complex family relationships that once made for cooperation now appear to operate to spread dissension, rather than friendship, through the group.

SECTION III

The Present

THE INDIAN'S SOLILOQUY*

To wear hair, or not to wear hair:
That is the question:
Whether 'tis better to be led
Like a sheep to the Shearer's
Or take up a pair of scissors
Of one's own accord
And by the cutting end it?
Long hair: blankets:
A profusion of paint and feathers:
These are truly the outward
Signs of that inward craving
For savage immortality.
Not to be shorn; perchance then
Not to draw ANNUITY.
Ay there's the rub; for in
That drawing of the coin of the realm
What comfort may come
Must give us pause: There's
The respect that makes savagery
Of so long life; for who would
Bear the whips and scorns of work,
The sun's hot rays, winter's
Chilling blasts; the pangs of
Despised hunger, charity's delay,
The insolence of lookers-on
And the spurns that patient
LO of the pale face takes,
When he himself might
Their quietus make
With a sharp shears?   —O. H. L.

*From *The Red Man*, Carlisle Indian Press, November 1914, frontispiece.

287

About the year 1902 an edict went out from the Indian Office at Washington demanding that all long-haired male Indians immediately cut off their hair on pain of having their rations and annuities withheld if they neglected or refused to obey the order.

FRAGMENT*

I rebelled
    I drowned myself in fantasy
To escape your inert living.
And now I gasp for breath
    because I have lingered too long
away from reality.

DONALD REX LANE, Folsom Prison

CAN I SAY**

And it's hard to see the mountains
when you're sitting in the subway
It's hard I said to feel the wind
When you're waiting in some welfare office
but I'm not a case, I'm not a number
I can do quillwork
Mister, I can ride with no
saddle and hey, listen
my brother with his own carved
arrows can stalk a deer.
Why? are you checking boxes
when I am trying to talk   no
I do not have outside income
but there is a tall
cottonwood I know and sometimes
I go to see the leaves and this

*From *Akwesasne Notes*, Vol. 3, No. 8. (1971), p. 48.
**From *Akwesasne Notes*, Vol. 4, No. 3 (1972), p. 48.

morning I heard a meadowlark
     when is the end. . . . to die is not the end
     when is the end. . . . to die is not the end.
he said, I made my ears like a fox stand
to hear and I never even go in
a bank so I got no account
There is an old man I heard
saying, "make moccasins . . ."
no he does not give me money, he
said to the people
"make moccasins for your children, it
is time to go" and I guess we are going
on the plains south where you are always facing
many winters wise. I want someday to bring
when the sun makes white sparks on
the creek like dancing fires, I
want to bring some kinnikinnik to him
he remembers the red willow smoke and a
buckskin bag and why do your eyes
say I tell lies?
I never been insane, I
never been in jail, I do not drink, I am not
an addict. I have no car, I do
not have syphilis or cavities, I did
have TB, I did drop out, and I
did get fired, I did not commit mailfraud, I
did not overthrow the government (lately)
with your pencil flying, mister,
can I say there is a good red road
and a sacred hoop of our people
which was broken but I would like
to help mend so the old man would
be happy. My brother
brought fresh meat to him
but the old man says there is not
much time before he will feed the wolves
I want him to know that the
rivers run free—I do not have
a pen to sign here—the forests grow
tall, the plains—I was just in my mind

thinking mister during this investigation—
of the plains where the dirt is living
and wild horses disappear behind a hill,
I wanted to see the old man at dawn stand
on the living plains with his
horse near, see him raise his
arms to the sun, hear him say
"Thank you father"

                                    . . . again

                                                DOLLY BIRD

STREET KID*

The window opens to a field of sagebrush—
California country northeast of San Francisco.
The sun burns into the hill.
This night is his first taste
of a new ache in the adam's apple,
the hard, dry knot,
a fresh loneliness.
Twilight whirrs with meadowlarks
and insects crawling down the glass
between the bars, and he,
apart from the other boys,
the cool toughs playing ping pong
before lock-up, hears his heart stop
the tear before it leaves the eye.
Injun Joe, the nickname given him
by the brothers, the blacks, the chicanos,
is not afraid of the heart of darkness,
but of his own soul beating like a fist
against the wall.

                                        DUANE McGINNIS

*From *South Dakota Review*, Vol. 9, No. 2 (Vermilion: University of South Dakota Press, 1971), p. 14.

WHITE MAN SAYS TO ME, SAVE*

White Man Says to Me
save,
I save, String. Bricks. Trees.
Horses. Leather. Nobody wants
what I save. So I go into the
desert, rolling my ball of string
which is four feet in diameter.
Two white men come. They look at
the bricks. Trees. Horses.
Leather. String. where'd you
steal them things they ask.
they don't listen. they take
the string from me and they
twist it into rope. Now they
put the rope around my neck.
They hang me from one of the
trees I saved.

FRED RED CLOUD

AN ELEGY TO THE AMERICAN WAY**
(DEDICATED TO: MR. SURE-IS)

*they came by way of transatlantic trauma, shrouded
    in robes of black
and bravely carried their truth between dark covers,
    thrust into golden chastity belts worn around their heads,
pilgrim picnics of burning witch crosses, among other
    degradations, their praise to the New World.*

*in their beginning was the sword & their hearts were
    metallic and tarnished,
brave new world resounding the cannon & a slaughter-house
    mentality*

*From *Akwesasne Notes*, Vol. 4, No. 1 (1972), p. 48.
**From *Akwesasne Notes*, Vol. 4, No. 1 (Later Winter, 1972), p. 48.

of musket balls resembling testimonials of manhood
      lost before being primed,
their voices raised forever lest their neighbors
      neigh more mighty.

for furs and farms a continent was plundered into a
      wasteland of futility, end-of-prizes, Incorpserated,
as Washington crossed the unaware river, his wig
      powerded white in artificial wisdom
while in Detroit a mutual life was benefitted with
      red, white & blue stomping boots
used to thread grapes of wrath in the dustbowl
      pocket of political aspirations.

O, say can you seesaw in mystical middle america
      where the hot dog is a prod & the hamburger god,
& the assets lie down with smiles pinned to their tales
      in the popular mechanics
of computerized rules & regulations formulated in
      goods we trust & the loan is our shepherd
& there, but for the grade of smog, go I.

ever dreaming of wealth on the freeway of mediocrity,
      we see them approach a sterile grave,
a skyscraper tombstone their greatest monument,
      a polluted planet their children's heritage,
go quickly, Mr. & Mrs. American Way, the earth is
      hungry for your passing,
we look over your shoulder to your children, are they,
      we wonder, ready?

coyote 2

THE WORLD OUT THERE CALLED*

The world out there called to my son
And so he went to see if it was a good world
He went to hear its music

*From Myron and Nancy Wood, *Hollering Sun.*

He went because he had to.
A long time passed and then my son returned.
He said the world out there is like
The porcupine that fights with the turtle
Or like fire that has fallen into water.
There is no music either.

TAOS PUEBLO

YOU TELL US TIMES ARE CHANGING*

You tell us times are changing
You say that we do not know
The times in which we live
We say to you that this time is like any other time
If a man's feet are on the ground
And his heart is in the right place
And he does not try to make
The eagle into an airplane

How should I live?
Among my people a small voice?
In your world silent?
Among my people there is no horizon
In your world I have seen the universe contained in glass

What is there for me when I have finished planting?
What is there for me at the end of the row I must hoe?
What is there for me when the harvest is over?
Better corn.
That is all.

TAOS PUEBLO

Because Pueblo dwellers comprise a tight-knit, non-competitive community, literature or other products of community members are not generally attributed to, or signed by, individuals.

*From Myron and Nancy Wood, *Hollering Sun.*.

I HAVE KILLED THE DEER*

I have killed the deer
I have crushed the grasshopper
And the plants he feeds upon
    I have cut through the heart
    Of trees growing old and straight.
I have taken fish from water
And birds from the sky.
In my life I have needed death
So that my life can be.
When I die I must give life
To what has nourished me.
The earth receives my body
And gives it to the plants
And to the caterpillars
To the birds
And to the coyotes
Each in its own time so that
The circle of Life is never broken.

TAOS PUEBLO

THE WAY THE WHITE MAN SAYS HELLO**

We all agreed to gather at his home in the evening. He called on different ones to bring fry bread and chokecherries and jerked meat, "and coffee will be cooked over at my place." So we brought it. And here came the teacher, Three Fingers, and we sat around inside the room. He got charcoal out of the stove for us to write with, and broke up wooden grocery boxes for slates. And he started teaching us the English words he knew.

He lined us up, and told the boy at one end, "Now, you say 'cup'," or whatever the word was, until the boy said it right. Then he moved to the end of the line. After we all said it he wrote the word in charcoal, and we had to write it too. "Every time you see those words," he said,

*From Myron and Nancy Wood, *Hollering Sun*.
**From John Stands-in-Timber, *Cheyenne Memories*, p. 290.

"remember English is different from the Indian language. Make your tongue into a spoon shape. It will sound good, just like white man's talk." So we tried to get our tongues into a spoon shape, and we had trouble with what we were trying to say. Then he went to one side of the house where they had pasted newspapers to the wall. He showed us a picture of two men on horseback facing each other. "They are talking," he said. "They are saying, 'Goddamn'." So we all said that, one at a time. And the next thing was, "You son-of-a-bitch." That was some of the first English we learned. We thought it was the way the white man said "Hello."

JOHN STANDS-IN-TIMBER

FEBRUARY CHILDREN*

we went in uninvited,
spoke too soon of problems,
sat by the stove without asking.
the old man and his wife
shouted at us to leave
because we had no beer,
because we were young and drunk.
my two friends barely stood,
complained of the coldness outside,
that we had no place to stay.
a younger couple who owned
the house staggered in, nodding
the permission. we smiled
at the outcome and proceeded
to drink what was left
of their beer. little kids came
out wrapped in several blankets
and asked their mother for some
food. they were given potato chips
and told to get the hell out.
the old woman passed-out on

*From *South Dakota Review*, Vol. 9, No. 2 (Vermilion: University of South Dakota Press, 1971), p. 34.

the wooden floor. the stove fire
died and no wood was around.
the young man went to the bedroom
and carried out his small son,
talked of his sickness and of
the sister in jail. i looked
at the baby and felt helpless
and sad. i left, and walked for miles
crying, vowing to myself that i
would always love my sons.

RAY YOUNG BEAR

I TRAVELED TO THE WEST*

I traveled to the west
Riding on a coyote's lonely cry.
I saw blackberry shadows turn into death before me.
I stumbled and fell in with the souls that lay
      in this rotting pit.
Everything I touched turned to dust.
I accepted blackness and wondered
      how long a million years would last.
Far off in this blackness I spied a white minute form.
This I fed and nourished with my body,
      giving it my entire self.
Carrying me to the east, I was grateful,
      until finding I could not
Detach myself from it, for this was I, going with myself.

JULIE WILSON

THIEF**

We knew of war
For we were warriors.

*Used by permission of the author, former student at the Institute of American Indian
Arts, Santa Fe, New Mexico. A Bureau of Indian Affairs School.
**From *Akwesasne Notes*, Vol. 3, No. 4 (Late Spring, 1971), p. 48.

The winner takes all.

We knew of lies
For we were diplomats
In a small way.

We knew of politics
For we were democrats;
a man was a man.

You took the land
We tried to understand;
You live on it, not with it.

But my friends
(And you were often good friends
As you understand friendship):

Why did you steal the smiles
From our children?

TOM WHITECLOUD

YOU WHO GROWS TALL LIKE THE CORN*

You
who grows tall like the corn
you are red as the pipestone
eyes of jet
eagle mind
one more indian like you
and i think the nation will stand higher
than it ever did before

you
who spoke to the six grandfathers
who taught again the meaning of the ghost shirt

*From *Akwesasne Notes*, Vol. 4, No. 4 (Summer 1972), p. 48.

indian young
indian old
one more wise man like you
and i think the nation will stand higher
than it ever did before

so last night i prayed
touched the eagle claw around my neck
i wait for your spirit to be born again
guide us Black Elk
    son of Black Elk
one more indian like you
and the nation will stand higher
than it ever did before

LEIGH JOHNSON

WE HOLD IN OUR HAND
FOURTEEN STRINGS OF PURPLE WAMPUM*

We hold in our hand fourteen strings of purple wampum. These we hand, one by one, to you—authors of many American history books; writers of cheap, inaccurate, unauthentic, sensational novels; and other writers of fiction who have poisoned the minds of young Americans concerning our people, the Red Race of America; to the producers of many western cowboy and Indian television programs and moving picture shows; to those Treaty-breakers who delight in dispossessing Indian peoples by constructing dams on Indian lands in violation of sacred treaties; and to those of this, our country, who are prone to build up the glory of their ancestors on the bonds and life-blood of our Old People:

—With this first string of wampum, we take away the fog that surrounds your eyes and obstructs your view, that you may see the truth concerning our people.

—With this second string of wampum we pull away from your imprisoned mind the cobwebs, the net that prevents you from dealing justice to our people!

*Six Nations Pamphlets, Akwesasne Counselor Organization, The People, Hogansburg, N.Y., Vol. I, No. 2 (August 1968).

—With this third piece of wampum, we cleanse your hearts of revenge, selfishness, and injustice that you may create love instead of hate!

—With this fourth string of wampum, we wash the blood of our people from your hands, that you may know the clasp of true friendship and sincerity!

—With this fifth string of wampum, we shrink your heads down to that of normal man, we cleanse your minds of the abnormal conceit and love of self that has caused you to walk blindly among the dark people of the world.

—With this sixth string of wampum, we remove your garments of gold, silver and greed, that you may don the apparel of generosity, hospitality, and humanity!

—With this seventh string of wampum, we remove the dirt that fills your ears so you may hear the story and truth of our people!

—With this eighth string of wampum we straighten your tongues of crookedness, that in the future you may speak the truth concerning the Indian People!

—With this ninth string of wampum, we take away the dark clouds from the face of the sun, that its rays may purify your thoughts that you may look forward and see America, instead of backward toward Europe!

—With this tenth string of wampum, we brush away the rough stones and sticks from your path that you may walk erect as the first American whose name you have defamed and whose country you now occupy!

—With this eleventh string of wampum, we take away from your hands your implements of destruction—guns, bombs, firewater, diseases—and place in them instead the Pipe of Friendship and Peace that you may sow brotherly love rather than bitter hate and injustice!

—With this twelfth string of wampum, we build you a new house with many windows and no mirrors, that you may look out and see the life and purpose of your nearest neighbor, the American Indian!

—With this thirteenth string of wampum, we tear down the wall of steel and stone you have built around the Tree of Peace, that you may shelter beneath its branches!

—With this fourteenth string of wampum, we take from the hen coop the eagle that you have imprisoned that this noble bird may once again fly in the sky over America!

I, Te-ha-ne-to-rens, say this!

OUR WORD FOR THE WHITE MAN IS *WASI' CHU**

Sometimes I lay awake at night . . . and I think of Crazy Horse and of the little stones that walk to the water. . . .

They thought I was going to be a boy so I had to be born among my people at Pine Ridge. My father is Hukpapa and my mother is Oglala. My father had three brothers who were killed at Wounded Knee; they were the grandsons of Big Foot. My other great-grandfather was Chief Gall. . . .

After I was born we went back up to Cheyenne River. I'm enrolled there. My number is 3872. I don't know about that enrollment. The craziest thing happened: my children were all enrolled at Fort Yates and they had a per capita payment. Then they told my children they were never registered. I have some land up there—I don't know how many acres. I get $17 a year for it. There's buffalo grass on it, but alkali water; the water is no good. When my grandmother died, they took her land to pay back her old age assistance she had been paid. They held the lease checks for fourteen years to pay that back. The BIA does that. We're just a bunch of dumb animals to them.

When I was a little girl at Cheyenne River, my grandmother used to part my hair in the middle and color the part yellow and put on a white plume so I wouldn't be struck by lightning. We used to have to go down to the creek every morning. My grandmother talked to the water. Before we washed, she would tell it how beautiful it was and thank it for cleansing her. She used to tell me to listen to the water and then she would sing a song to it. You know the sound water makes? When she sang it sounded just like the water. . . .

We kept ourselves clean; I don't know why they call us dirty Indians. Once I was running away from my daughter's father, and I went through a herd of coyotes and a herd of wild horses, but they didn't bother me, because I had no body odor, nothing but natural. We used to use oil and an herb for scent, and mud to make our skin smooth. . . .

In the thirties we moved back to Pine Ridge. . . . I went to boarding school. You were punished there if you talked Indian. After you got used to it, it wasn't bad.

They called us full bloods "blues" at the boarding school because we were so dark. The mixed bloods were real light. They used to point at us in the shower and the matron punished us more than she punished

*From Earl Shorris, *The Death of the Great Spirit*, pp. 156-158.

the mixed bloods. I was proud to be a full blood, but in my own mind. I didn't express it out loud because it was no use. . . .

I finished the eleventh grade before I ran off and got married. My father wouldn't give me twenty dollars so the next Friday night I eloped and got married on their wedding day. I married Daniel McMasters—he was part Mexican. I didn't want to marry an Indian man because they don't carry their paychecks home; they quit their jobs. Also I promised myself to marry a white man so my children wouldn't be as dark as me. I almost married a Mormon, but I couldn't stand it; I'm too jealous to have sisters.

A Sioux woman don't care nothing for her husband anyway. But my children are my flesh and blood. I live for my children. . . .

I wasn't in love with Daniel McMasters. My mother told me, "When you're in love, it's always like you're at a lake with nice cool water and green trees." It wasn't like that with Daniel McMasters. I regretted it from the day it started. . . . But I stuck it out for four years until my father died because my father didn't believe in divorce. I had two children. After I got divorced I moved to Custer. . . . I worked in civil service in the factory there, cutting mica for airplanes. I met my second husband there. He was working at the planing factory, finishing lumber. He was French and Russian.

We moved to Oakland in '54 and he started drinking. We used to sing and play guitar in the bars. . . . We made money, enough to keep up our bills. . . . We got divorced in '58. He beat me up and broke my jaw so I couldn't eat and I had tuberculosis. The judge put my children in a foster home until I got well.

I got married again in 1960. He passed away in 1965. I had three husbands; when I get to heaven, I won't be lonely. . . .

I don't owe nobody now, but I have my rent, eighteen dollars a week. I'm so worried, I don't know what to do. When you're here you're like in a rat race, wondering what's going to happen. There on the reservation people are happy to see you. Here the people are happy to see you too, but you wonder what they want. Our word for the white man is *wasi'chu*, the one who takes everything, the greedy one. . . .

MARY MCDANIEL

MY FATHER LEARNED TO BE A CHRISTIAN*

My grandfather was a full blood, a chief, but my father went to Haskell and learned to be a Christian. I remember my grandfather riding an old roan with his felt hat turned up in front and wearing his braids. We had a farm; my father worked it. One time my grandfather said to him, "Hitch up a team and get a sack of spuds and a hind quarter of that beef hanging down by the creek and half the coal and some of the wood you cut, and bring them over to that man's house. He's sick and his family's hungry and cold."

There was a big blizzard then and my father didn't want to do it. "Oh shit," he said. But my grandfather told him, "Don't mumble at me. Go do it now."

My father used to get drunk and raise hell with the old man and my grandfather would just sit there and listen and never say anything. Then the next morning he would tell him quietly, like he told me, "You don't eat unless everybody eats, and you don't get warm until all the people are warm. That's our way."

But my father, he went on in his way, being a good Christian until my mother died. Then one day he went up to her grave and cried like an Indian. We do that, we cry and moan asking the one who's gone to take pity on us. We don't cry for them. We cry for ourselves. Then my father came into the cafe and I fixed him a steak, and he said to me, "Roger, did I do right? I don't think I lived a good way and now it's too late to do anything about it."

"You done the best you know how," I told him. "You thought you were doin' good. That's the best you can do."

ROGER STOPS

WHERE HIDDEN FIRES BURN**

across the lake in the darkness
where hidden fires burn
their gambling songs are passed
through the trees

*From Earl Shorris, *The Death of the Great Spirit*, p. 84.
**Used by permission of the author, student, Institute of American Indian Arts, Santa Fe, New Mexico. A Bureau of Indian Affairs School.

they are hidden from the moon's beam
but their drums are not

the lake is full of the evening stars
mirror of the moon is restful
like the quiet shores

the smoke of their hidden fire weakens
like the songs and drums
the moon leaves them
half-sun is opening the day
for the songs and dances
we all see

SUSAN EDWARDS

HANDS THAT KISSED THE EARTH*

Hands that kissed the Earth,
    that know the rain,
Hands that held the clouds,
    that smelled the sun,
        Hands of your breath,
    that sang your song
folded over my eyes
    and landed on my heart.
You soared like the eagle
    and slept in me
with your full awareness
    of my being and your
    full awareness of you.
    I am the deer you hunt.
I am the rain you chase. I am You.

HAROLD LITTLEBUD

*Used by permission of the author, former student, Institute of American Indian Arts, Santa Fe, New Mexico. A Bureau of Indian Affairs School.

POEM*

The sun eloped with you
leaving rainbow illusions.

Muzzled, I stood in Ganado.

Renegade, my heart holds
the gentleness of your hands.

BERTHA FRANCISCO

RELATIONS*

Sky lay Earth
for the third time

Love them

Gentle rains touch
Earth's bosom

She will be pregnant
Love her

Expect a fruitful
summer birth

Love it

BERTHA FRANCISCO

WEST FROM THE RAILHEAD*

Don't we all want to be Oklahoma cowboys
And rough our hands on splintery corrals

*Used by permission of the author, former student, Institute of American Indian Arts, Sante Fe, New Mexico. A Bureau of Indian Affairs School.

And spit tobacco through bunkhouse doors
Singing quiet lonesome cowboy ballads,
Heroes of lonesome cowgirls' square dance dreams?

Singing quiet lonesome cowboy ballads,
Heroes of lonesome cowgirls' square dance dreams?

And don't we want to clean up Loredo,
Polished boot on bar rail, left round
Rotgut in a glass, and right at ease
On pearl-handle at the hip?

But don't we know
How Indiana holds us back,
How New York is so far
From range land hard soil bliss,
And if only the Tucson stage
Left at noon to our wide-eyed gunfighter home.

R. MICHAEL BANTISTA

KIOWA

WE ARE BROTHERS*

Together, side by side, my brothers we
dance the Round Dance, good and free

Cast away your fears and hate
No time left to discriminate
        among ourselves
We are Brothers

Apache, Seminole and Cherokee too

*From *Akwesasne Notes*, Vol. 3, No. 8 (1971), p. 48.

Make room in this Round Dance
      for a Sioux
Says that he's half-breed
has no white kin
Says that he's Indian, let him in
We are Brothers

Together, side by side, my brothers we
dance the Round Dance, good and free
We are Brothers

SEA-FLOWER

OUT OF THE DARKNESS

Out of the darkness
Out of the night
No longer subdued
      Like children afright

Out of the darkness
Into the light
Harsh voices upraised
      In gathering might

Out of the darkness
With memory bright
To avenge past wrongs
      To set their world right

Born in the sunshine
But living in night
How long is the road
      Back into the light?

THE EDITORS

Bibliographies

References

Abbreviations:

AA   American Anthropologist
APAMNH   Anthropological Papers of the American Museum of Natural History
AR of BAE   Annual Report of the Bureau of American Ethnology
BAE   Bureau of American Ethnology
CUCA   Columbia University Contributions to Anthropology
FCM, AS   Field Columbian Museum, Anthropological Series
IUPAL   Indiana University Publications in Anthropology and Linguistics
JAF   Journal of American Folk-Lore
JAMNH   Journal of the American Museum of Natural History
MAAA   Memoirs of the American Anthropological Association
MAFS   Memoirs of the American Folk-Lore Society
PAES   Publications of the American Ethnological Society
SMC   Smithsonian Miscellaneous Collection
TAPS   Transactions of the American Philosophical Society
UCPAAE   University of California Publications in American Archaeology and Ethnology
UWPA   University of Washington Publications in Anthropology
YUPA   Yale University Publications in Anthropology

I. SELECTED GENERAL BIBLIOGRAPHY

Armstrong, Virginia Irving, ed.
 1972 (Orig. 1971) *I Have Spoken: American History Through the Voices of the Indians*. New York: Pocket Books.
Astrov, Margot, ed.
 1962 *American Indian Prose and Poetry: An Anthology* (originally published in 1946 as *The Winged Serpent*). New York: Capricorn Books.
Barrett, Steven Melvil, ed.
 1906 *Geronimo's Story of His Life*. New York: Duffield & Co.
Bierhorst, John, ed.
 1971 *In the Trail of the Wind*. New York: Farrar, Straus & Giroux.
Boas, Franz
 1894 *Chinook Tales*. BAE, Bulletin 20.
 1901 *Kathlamet Texts*. BAE, Bulletin 26.
 1902 *Tsimshian Texts*. BAE, Bulletin 27.
 1913 *Ethnography of Kwakiutl*. In the 35th AR of BAE (1913-14).
 1916 *Tsimshian Mythology*. In the 31st AR of BAE (1909-10).
 1918 *Kutenai Tales*. BAE, Bulletin 59.
 1925 "Stylistic Aspects of Primitive Literature," JAF 38:329-339.
 1928 *Bella Bella Texts*. CUCA, vol. 5.
 1935 *Kwakiutl Tales*. CUCA, vol. 26.
Brant, Charles S., ed.
 1969 *Jim Whitewolf: The Life of a Kiowa Apache Indian*. New York: Dover.
Brown, Joseph Epes, ed.
 1953 *The Sacred Pipe: Black Elk's Account of the Seven Rites of the Oglala Sioux*. Norman: University of Oklahoma Press.
Bunzel, Ruth L.
 1932 *Zuñi Origin Myths*. In the 47th AR of BAE (1929-30).
 1932 *Zuñi Ritual Poetry*. In the 47th AR of BAE (1929-30).
Chafe, Wallace L.
 1961 *Seneca Thanksgiving Rituals*. BAE, Bulletin 183.
Clark, Ella Elizabeth
 1960 *Indian Legends of Canada*. Toronto: McClelland & Stewart.
Clarke, Peter D.

1870   *Origin and Traditional History of the Wyandotts.*

Cronyn, George W.
1962   (Orig. 1918) *American Indian Poetry: An Anthology of Authentic Songs and Chants.* New York: Ballantine Books.

Curtin, Jeremiah, and J. N. B. Hewitt
1918   *Seneca Fiction, Legends, and Myths.* In the 32nd AR of BAE (1910-11).

Curtis, Natalie
1969   (Orig. 1907) *The Indians' Book: Songs and Legends of the American Indians.* New York: Dover.

Cushing, Frank Hamilton
1896   *Outlines of Zuñi Creation Myths.* In the 13th AR of BAE (1891-2).

Day, A. Grove, ed.
1964   (Orig. 1951) *The Sky Clears: Poetry of the American Indians.* Lincoln: University of Nebraska Press.

De Angulo, Jaime
1953   *Indian Tales.* New York: Hill and Wang, Inc.

Densmore, Frances
1910   *Chippewa Music.* BAE, Bulletin 45.
1913   *Chippewa Music—II.* BAE, Bulletin 53.
1917   *Poems from Sioux and Chippewa Songs.* BAE.
1918   *Teton Sioux Music.* BAE, Bulletin 61.
1926   *The American Indians and Their Music.* Reissued 1970 by the Johnson Reprint Corp., New York
1929   *Pawnee Music.* BAE, Bulletin 93.
1929   *Papago Music.* BAE, Bulletin 90.
1941   "Two Songs of the Native American Church," AA 43:81-82.
1943   "A Search for Songs Among the Chitimacha Indians in Louisiana," BAE, Bulletin 133, No. 19, pp. 1-15.
1956   *Seminole Music.* BAE, Bulletin 161.
1957   *Music of Acoma, Isleta, Cochiti and Zuñi Pueblos.* BAE, Bulletin 165.

Dorsey, George A.
1904   *Traditions of the Skidi Pawnee.* Boston: Houghton Mifflin.
1905   *The Cheyenne.* Publication 99, FCM, AS, vol. 9, no. 1.

Dorsey, James Owen
1888   *Osage Traditions.* In the 6th AR of BAE (1884-5).
1891   *Omaha and Ponka Letters.* BAE, Bulletin 11.

Downs, James F.
1966   *The Two Worlds of the Washo: An Indian Tribe of California and Nevada.* New York: Holt, Rinehart & Winston.

Driver, Harold E.
1961   *Indians of North America.* Chicago: University of Chicago Press.

1969 *Indians of North America* (second revised edition). Chicago: University of Chicago Press.

Driver, Harold E., *et al.*
1972 "Statistical Classification of North American Indian Ethnic Units," *Ethnology* 11:311-339.

Driver, H. E., and W. C. Massey
1957 *Comparative Studies of North American Indians.* TAPS, vol. 47.

Driver, H. E., W. C. Massey, *et al.*
1953 *Indian Tribes of North America.* IUPAL, memoir 9.

Dundes, Alan
1965 *The Study of Folklore.* Englewood Cliffs, N.J.: Prentice-Hall.

Dyk, Walter, ed.
1947 *Old Mexican: A Navajo Autobiography.* New York: Viking Fund Publications in Anthropology.
1967 *Son of Old Man Hat: A Navajo Autobiography.* Lincoln: University of Nebraska Press.

Farb, Peter
1968 *Man's Rise to Civilization.* New York: E. P. Dutton.

Fewkes, Jesse Walter
1912 *Casa Grande, Arizona.* In the 28th AR of BAE (1906-7).

Fletcher, Alice C.
1904 *The Hako: A Pawnee Ceremony.* In the 22nd AR of BAE (1900-1).

Fletcher, Alice C., and Francis La Flesche
1911 *The Omaha Tribe.* In the 27th AR of BAE (1905-6).

Forbes, Jack D.
1964 "Voices from Native America," in *The Indian in America's Past.* Englewood Cliffs, N.J.: Prentice-Hall.

Forbes, Jack D., ed.
1967 *Nevada Indians Speak.* Reno: University of Nevada Press.

Ford, C. S.
1968 *Smoke from Their Fires: The Life of a Kwakiutl Chief.* Hamden, Conn.: Archon.

Frachtenberg, Leo J.
1913 *Coos Texts.* CUCA, vol. 1.
1920 *Alsea Texts and Myths.* BAE, Bulletin 67.

Goddard, Pliny Earle
1909 *Putnam Anniversary Volume.* New York: Putnam's.
1911 *Jicarilla Apache Texts.* APAMNH, vol. 8.
1918 *Myths and Tales of the San Carlos Apache.* APAMNH, vol 24, pt. 1.
1933 *Navajo Texts.* APAMNH, vol. 34, pt. 1.

Gooderham, Kent, ed.

1969   *I Am an Indian*. Toronto: J. M. Dent.

Grinnell, George Bird

1962   *Blackfoot Lodge Tales: The Story of a Prairie People*. New York: Scribner's.

Hagan, William T.

1961   *The American Indians*. Chicago: University of Chicago Press.

Hale, Horatio

1883   *The Iroquois Book of Rites*, from *Brinton's Library of Aboriginal American Literature*, no. 2. Philadelphia: D. G. Brinton.

Hamilton, Charles Everett

1950   *Cry of the Thunderbird: The American Indian's Own Story*. New York: Macmillan.

Harrington, J. P., and Helen H. Roberts

1928   *Picuris Children's Stories with Texts and Songs*. In the 43rd AR of BAE (1925-6).

Heizer, Robert F., and M. A. Whipple

1951   *The California Indians*. Berkeley and Los Angeles: University of California Press.

Hirschfelder, Arlene B.

1970   *American Indian Authors: A Representative Bibliography*. New York: Association on American Indian Affairs, Inc.

Hodge, Frederick Webb, ed.

1912   (Orig. 1906) *Handbook of the American Indians North of Mexico* (2 vols.). BAE, Bulletin 30.

Hoffman, Walter James

1896   *The Menomini Indians*. In the 14th AR of BAE (1892-3).

Howard, James H., ed.

1969   *The Warrior Who Killed Custer: The Personal Narrative of Chief Joseph White Bull*. Lincoln: University of Nebraska Press.

Jackson, Donald, ed.

1955   *Black Hawk: An Autobiography*. Urbana: University of Illinois Press.

Jacobs, Melville

1929   *Northwest Sahaptin Texts*. University of Washington Publications in Anthropology, vol. 2, no. 6. Seattle: University of Washington.

1945   *Kalapuya Texts*. University of Washington Publications in Anthropology, vol. 11. Seattle: University of Washington.

1958   *Clackamas Chinook Texts* (2 vols.). Bloomington: Indiana University Research Center in Anthropology, Folklore, and Linguistics.

Johnson, W. Fletcher

1891   *Life of Sitting Bull*.

Jones, Louis Thomas

1965   *Aboriginal American Oratory*. Los Angeles: Southwest Museum.

Josephy, Alvin M., Jr.
  1972   *Red Power: The American Indian's Fight for Freedom.* New York:
          American Heritage Press.
Keesing, Roger M., and Felix M. Keesing
  1971   *New Perspectives in Cultural Anthropology.* New York: Holt, Rinehart
          & Winston. 2d edition.
Kroeber, Alfred L.
  1900   "Cheyenne Tales," JAF 13:161-190.
  1925   *Handbook of the Indians of California.* BAE, Bulletin 78.
  1935   *Walapai Ethnology.* MAAA, no. 42.
  1939   *Cultural and Natural Areas of Native North America.* UCPAAE, vol.
          38.
Kroeber, Theodora
  1961   *Ishi in Two Worlds: A Biography of the Last Wild Indian in North
          America.* Berkeley and Los Angeles: University of California Press.
LeSeuer, Meridel
  1945   *North Star Country.* New York: Book Find Club.
Levine, Stuart, & Nancy O. Lurie
  1968   "The American Indian Today," *Midcontinent American Studies Jour-
          nal*, vol. VI, no. 2. Fall 1965.
Linderman, Frank Bird
  1962   (Orig. 1930) *Plenty-Coups, Chief of the Crows.* Lincoln: University of
          Nebraska Press.
Long, James Larpenter
  1961   *The Assiniboines: From the Accounts of the Old Ones Told to First
          Boy*, edited by Michael Steven Kennedy. Norman: University of
          Oklahoma Press.
Lounsbury, Floyd G.
  1953   *Oneida Verb Morphology.* YUPA, 48.
Lowie, Robert H.
  1909   *The Assiniboine.* APAMNH, vol. 4, pt. 1.
  1918   *Myths and Traditions of the Crow Indians.* APAMNH, vol. 25, pt.
          1.
Lurie, Nancy O.
  1961   *Mountain Wolf Woman, Sister of Crashing Thunder: The Autobiog-
          raphy of a Winnebago Woman.* Ann Arbor: University of Michigan
          Press.
McCreight, M. I.
  1947   *Firewater and Forked Tongues: A Sioux Chief Interprets U.S. History.*
          Pasadena, Calif.: Trail's End Publishing Co.
McLaughlin, James
  1910   *My Friend, the Indian.* Boston: Houghton Mifflin.

McLuhan, T. C., ed.
  1971 *Touch the Earth: A Self-Portrait of Indian Existence.* New York: Outer-
         bridge and Dienstfrey.
MAFS
  1897 "Tsegihi," MAFS, vol. 5, pp. 273-275.
Marriott, A., and C. K. Rachlin
  1968 *American Indian Mythology.* New York: Thomas Crowell Co.
Masson, Marcelle, ed.
  n.d. *A Bag of Bones.* Healdsburg, Calif.: Naturegraph Publishers.
Matthews, Washington
  1894 "Songs of Sequence," JAF 7:185-194.
Michelson, Truman, ed.
  1925 *The Autobiography of a Fox Woman.* In the 40th AR of BAE (1918-9).
  1932 *Narrative of a Southern Cheyenne Woman.* SMC, vol. 87, no. 5.
  1933 "Narrative of an Arapaho Woman," *American Indian Anthropologist*,
         no. 35:595-610.
Mooney, James
  1891 *The Sacred Formulas of the Cherokees.* In the 7th AR of BAE (1885-
         6).
  1896 *The Ghost-Dance Religion and the Sioux Outbreak of 1890.* In the 14th
         AR of BAE (1892-3).
  1898 *Calendar History of the Kiowa Indians.* In the 17th AR of BAE (1895-
         6).
  1900 *Myths of the Cherokees.* In the 19th AR of BAE (1897-8).
  1928 *The Aboriginal Population of America North of Mexico.* SMC, vol.
         80, no. 7.
Morgan, Lewis H.
  1851 *League of the Ho-de-no-sau-nee, or Iroquois.* Rochester: Sage and
         Broa.
Murdock, George P.
  1949 *Ethnographic Bibliography of North America.* Human Relations Area
         Files, Yale University Press. (Expanded edition, 1953. Enlarged edi-
         tion compiled by Timothy J. O'Leary, 1960. Updated version due to
         be published in four volumes during 1974-5.)
Nabokov, Peter
  1967 *Two Leggings: The Making of a Crow Warrior.* New York: Thomas
         Y. Crowell.
Neihardt, John G., ed.
  1961 (Orig. 1932) *Black Elk Speaks: Being the Life Story of a Holy Man
         of the Oglala Sioux.* Simon and Schuster.
O'Bryan, Aileen
  1956 *The Dene: Origin Myths of the Navaho Indians.* BAE, Bulletin 163.

Opler, Morris E.
  1938 *Myths and Folklore of the Jicarilla Apache*. MAFS, vol. 31.
  1938 "Humor and Wisdom of Some American Indian Tribes," *New Mexico
         Anthropologist*, 8:3-10.
  1945 "Mescalero Apache Account of the Origin of Peyote," in *El Palacio*,
         October 1945, pp. 210-212.
Oswalt, Robert L.
  1964 *Kashaya Texts*. University of California Publications in Linguistics,
         vol. 36. Berkeley: University of California Press.
Owen, Roger C., *et al*.
  1967 *The North American Indians: A Sourcebook*. New York and Toronto:
         Macmillan.
Paredos, Americo, and Richard Bauman, eds.
  1972 *Toward New Perspectives in Folklore*. Austin: University of Texas
         Press.
Parsons, Elsie Clews
  1926 *Tewa Tales*. MAFS, vol. 19.
  1962 *Isleta Paintings* (revised, 1970). BAE, Bulletin 181.
  1967 *American Indian Life*. Lincoln, Nebraska, University of Nebraska
         Press.
Pilling, James C.
  1888 *Bibliography of the Iroquoian Languages*. Bureau of Ethnology.
         Washington, D.C.: Government Printing Office.
Powell, John Wesley
  1891 *Indian Linguistic Families of America North of Mexico*. In the 7th AR
         of the BAE (1885-6).
Powers, Alfred
  1935 *History of Oregon Literature*. Portland, Oregon: Metropolitan Press.
Radin, Paul
  1923 *The Winnebago Tribe*. In the 37th AR of BAE (1915-6).
  1957 (Orig. 1927) *Primitive Man as Philosopher*. New York: Dover.
  1963 *Crashing Thunder: The Autobiography of a Winnebago Indian*. New
         York: Dover.
Reichard, Gladys
  1944 *The Compulsive Word*. Seattle: University of Washington Press.
Riggs, Rev. Stephen Return
  1881 "Illustration of the Method of Recording Indian Languages" [a Dakota
         fable by Michel Renville]. Appendix to the 1st AR of BAE.
Rothenberg, Jerome, ed.
  1972 *Shaking the Pumpkin: Traditional Poetry of the Indian North Americas*.
         New York: Doubleday.
Russell, Frank

1908　*The Pima Indians*. In the 26th AR of BAE (1904-5).

Schoolcraft, Henry Rowe
1939　*Algic Researches*. New York: AMS Press, Inc.

Scott, Lalla
1966　*Karnee: A Paiute Narrative*. Reno: University of Nevada Press.

Scoville, Dorothy R.
1970　*Indian Legends of Martha's Vineyard*. Martha's Vineyard: Duke's County Historical Society.

Shipek, Florence C., ed.
1968　*The Autobiography of Delphina Cuero: A Diegueño Indian*. Los Angeles: Dawson's Book Shop.

Shorris, Earl
1971　*The Death of the Great Spirit*. New York: Simon & Schuster.

Simmons, Leo W., ed.
1942　*Sun Chief: The Autobiography of a Hopi Indian*. New Haven: Yale University Press.

Smith, Erminnie A.
1883　*Myths of the Iroquois*. In the 2nd AR of BAE (1880-1).

South Dakota Review
1969　"Poetry, Fiction, Art, Music, Religion by the American Indian," *South Dakota Review*, vol. 7, no. 2.

Speck, Frank G.
1928　*Wawenock Texts from Maine*. In the 43rd AR of BAE (1925-6).
1928　*Native Tribes and Dialects of Connecticut*. In the 43rd AR of BAE (1925-6).
1934　*Catawba Texts*. CUCA, vol. 24.

Spencer, Robert F., J. D. Jennings, *et al*.
1965　*The Native Americans: Prehistory and Ethnology of the North American Indians*. New York: Harper & Row.

Spencer, Robert F., and E. Johnson
1968　*Atlas for Anthropology*. Dubuque, Iowa: Wm. C. Brown Co.

Spinden, Herbert J.
1933　*Songs of the Tewa*. New York: Exposition of Indian Tribal Arts, JAMNH, vol. 15, no. 2.
1908　*The Nez Percé Indians*. Lancaster, Pa. MAAA, vol 2, part 3.

Spier, Leslie
1928　*Havasupai Ethnography*. APAMNH, vol. 29.

Spradley, James P., ed.
1969　*Guests Never Leave Hungry: The Autobiography of James Sewid, A Kwakiutl Indian*. New Haven: Yale University Press.

Stevenson, Mathilde Cox
1894　*The Sia*. In the 11th AR of BAE (1889-90).
1904　*The Zuñi Indians*. In the 23rd AR of BAE (1901-2).

Steward, Julian H., ed.
    1934 *Two Paiute Autobiographies.* UCPAAE, vol. 33, no. 5.
    1943 "Some Western Shoshoni Myths," BAE, Bulletin 136, no. 31, pp. 249-299.
Swanton, John R.
    1905 *Haida Texts and Myths.* BAE, Bulletin 29.
    1909 *Tlingit Myths and Texts.* BAE, Bulletin 39.
    1952 *The Indian Tribes of North America.* BAE, Bulletin 145.
Thatcher, B. B.
    1910 *Indian Life and Battles.* New York & Akron.
Thompson, Stith, ed.
    1972 (Orig. 1929) *Tales of the North American Indians.* Bloomington: Indiana University Press.
Udall, Louise, ed.
    1969 *Me and Mine: The Life Story of Helen Sekaquaptewa.* Tucson: University of Arizona Press.
Underhill, Ruth, ed.
    1936 *Autobiography of a Papago Woman.* MAAA, vol. 46.
    1938 *Singing for Power.* Berkeley: University of California Press.
Vanderwerth, W. C., ed.
    1971 *Indian Oratory.* Norman: University of Oklahoma Press.
Voegelin, C. F., and F. M. Voegelin
    1966 *Map of North American Indian Languages.* Seattle: American Ethnological Society.
Voth, H. R.
    1905 *The Traditions of the Hopi.* Publication 96, FCM, AS, vol. 8.
Washburn, Wilcomb E.
    1964 *The Indian and the White Man.* New York: Doubleday.
Wetherill, Hilda Faunce
    1952 *Navajo Indian Poems: Translation from the Navajo, and other Poems.* New York: Vantage Press.
White, Leslie A.
    1943 "New Material from Acoma," BAE, Bulletin 136, no. 32, pp. 301-360.
Wissler, Clark
    1938 (Orig. 1917) *The American Indian.* New York: Macmillan.
    1966 (Orig. 1940) *Indians of the United States.* Garden City, N.Y.: Doubleday and the American Museum of Natural History.
Wissler, C., and D. C. Duvall
    1908 *Mythology of the Blackfoot Indians.* APAMNH, vol. 2, pt. 1.
Witt, Shirley Hill, and Stan Steiner, eds.
    1972 *The Way: An Anthology of American Indian Literature.* New York: Alfred A. Knopf.

Wood, Myron and Nancy
    1972   *Hollering Sun*. New York: Simon & Schuster, Children's Book Division.

II. SOME WORKS BY AMERICAN INDIANS

American Indian Historical Society
    1970   *Our Inaccurate Textbooks: The American Indian Case*. San Francisco: The Indian Historian Press.
Archiquette, Oscar
    1965   *Oneida Indians of Wisconsin Hymn Book*. Oneida, Wisconsin: Oscar Archiquette.
Bennett, Kay
    1964   *Kaibah: Recollections of a Navajo Girlhood*. Los Angeles: Western Lore Press.
Benson, William
    1932   "The Stone and Kelsey 'Massacre' on the Shores of Clear Lake in 1849, the Indian Viewpoint," *California Historical Society Quarterly* 11:266-273.
Bronson, Ruth Margaret
    1944   *Indians Are People Too*. New York: Friendship Press.
Brown, Dee
    1971   *Bury My Heart at Wounded Knee: An Indian History of the American West*. New York: Holt, Rinehart & Winston.
Buffalo Child Long Lance, Chief
    1928   *Long Lance*. New York: Cosmopolitan Book Corp.
    1933   *Redman Echoes: Comprising the Writings of Chief Buffalo Child Long Lance and Biographical Sketches by His Friends*. Los Angeles: Frank Wiggins Trade School.
Clutesi, George C.
    1969   *Potlatch*. Sidney, British Columbia: Gray's Publishing Ltd.
Cornplanter, Jesse J.
    1963   *Legends of the Longhouse*. Port Washington, N.Y.: Ira J. Friedman.
Costo, Rupert
    1970   *Redman of the Golden West*. San Francisco: The Indian Historian Press.

Deloria, Ella Cara
  1932   *Dakota Texts*. PAES, vol. 14.
  1944   *Speaking of Indians*. New York: Friendship Press.
Deloria, Vine
  1969   *Custer Died for Your Sins: An Indian Manifesto*. New York: Macmillan.
Dockstader, Frederick J.
  1954   *The Kachina and the White Man: The Influences of the White Culture on the Hopi Kachina Cult*. Bloomfield Hills, Michigan: Cranbrook Institute of Science, Bulletin 35.
  1956   *The American Indian in Graduate Studies*. New York: Museum of the American Indian.
  1964   *Indian Art in Middle America*. Greenwich, Conn.: New York Graphic Society.
  1966   *Indian Art in America: The Arts and Crafts of the North American Indian*. Greenwich, Conn.: New York Graphic Society.
Dozier, Edward P.
  1966   *Hano, A Tewa Community in Arizona*. New York: Holt, Rinehart & Winston.
  1970   *Pueblo Indians of the Southwest*. New York: Holt, Rinehart & Winston.

Eagle, Chief
  1968   *Winter Count*. Denver: Golden Bell Press.
Eastman, Charles A.
  1904   *Indian Boyhood*. New York: McClure.
  1904   *Red Hunters and the Animal People*. New York: Harper.
  1911   *Soul of an Indian: An Interpretation*. Boston: Houghton Mifflin.
  1915   *The Indian Today, the Past and Future of the First American*. Garden City, N.Y.: Doubleday.
  1916   *From the Deep Woods to Civilization: Chapters in the Autobiography of an Indian*. Boston: Little, Brown & Co.
Emerson, Gloria
  1972   "Slayers of the Children," *Indian Historian*, Spring, pp. 18-19.
Flying Cloud, Chief
  1967   *The Crimson Carnage of Wounded Knee*. Bottineau, N. Dak.: Edward A. Milligan.
Griffis, Joseph K.
  1915   *Tahan: Out of Savagery into Civilization*. New York: George B. Doran Co.
  1928   *Indian Story Circle Stories*. Burlington, Vt.: Free Press Printing Co.
Henry, Jeannette
  1970   *The American Indian in American History*. Indian Handbook Series #1. San Francisco: The Indian Historian Press.

Hewitt, John Napoleon Brinton
  1904   *Iroquois Cosmology*. In the 21st AR of BAE.
  1937   *Journal of Rudolph Fredrich Kurz*. BAE, Bulletin 115.
Hunter, Lois Marie
  1952   *The Shinnecock Indians*. New York: Buys Brothers.
Joseph, Chief
  1879   "An Indian's View of Indian Affairs," *North American Review*
         269:415-433.
Kilpatrick, Jack F., and Anna G. Kilpatrick
  1964   *Friends of Thunder*. Dallas: Southern Methodist University Press.
  1965   *The Shadow of Sequoyah: Social Documents of the Cherokees, 1862-
         1964*. Norman: University of Oklahoma Press.
  1965   *Walk in Your Soul: Love Incantations of the Oklahoma Cherokees*. Dal-
         las: Southern Methodist University Press.
  1967   *Run Toward the Nightland: Magic of the Oklahoma Cherokees*. Dallas:
         Southern Methodist University Press.
  1968   *New Echota Letters: Contributions of Samuel A. Worcester to the
         Cherokee Phoenix*. Dallas: Southern Methodist University Press.
Laduke, Vincent
  1969   *At Home in the Wilderness*. Sparks, Nevada: Western Printing and Pub-
         lishing Co.
La Flesche, Francis
  1921   *The Osage Tribe*. In the 36th AR of BAE (1914-5).
  1932   *A Dictionary of the Osage Language*. BAE, Bulletin 109.
  1939   *The War Ceremony and Peace Ceremony of the Osage Indians*. BAE,
         Bulletin 101.
  1963   *The Middle Five: Indian Schoolboys of the Omaha Tribe*. Madison:
         University of Wisconsin Press.
Lone Dog, Louise
  1964   *Strange Journey: The Vision Quest of a Psychic Indian Woman*.
         Healdsburg, Calif.: Naturegraph Co.
McNickle, D'Arcy
  1936   *The Surrounded*. New York: Dodd, Mead, & Co.
  1949   *They Came Here First: The Epic of the American Indian*. Philadelphia:
         J. B. Lippincott Co.
  1962   *The Indian Tribes of the United States: Ethnic and Cultural Survival*.
         New York: Oxford University Press.
Mathews, John Joseph
  1934   *Sundown*. New York: Longmans, Green & Co.
  1945   *Talking to the Moon*. Chicago: University of Chicago Press.
  1952   *Life and Death of an Oilman: The Career of E. W. Marland*. Norman:
         University of Oklahoma Press.

1961   *The Osages: Children of the Middle Waters.* Norman: University of
       Oklahoma Press.
1968   (Orig. 1932) *Wah'Kon-Tah: The Osage and the White Man's Road.*
       Norman: University of Oklahoma Press.
Momaday, N. Scott
1969   *House Made of Dawn.* New York: Harper & Row.
1969   *The Way to Rainy Mountain.* Albuquerque: University of New Mexico
       Press.
Monture, Ethel Brant
1960   *Famous Indians: Brant, Crowfoot, and Oronhyatekha.* Toronto: Clarke,
       Irwin, & Co.
Morgan, William
1936   *Human-Wolves Among the Navajo.* YUPA, no. 11.
Nequatewa, Edmund
1967   *Truth of a Hopi: Stories Relating to the Origin, Myths, and Clan His-
       tories of the Hopi.* Museum of Northern Arizona, Bulletin 8. Flagstaff:
       Arizona Northland Press.
Newell, William B.
1965   *Crime and Justice Among the Iroquois.* Montreal: Caughnawaga Histor-
       ical Society.
Ortiz, Alfonso
1965   *Project Head Start in an Indian Community.* Chicago: University of
       Chicago Press.
1969   *The Tewa World: Space, Time, Being, and Becoming in a Pueblo Soci-
       ety.* Chicago: University of Chicago Press.
Oskison, John M.
1929   *A Texas Titan: The Story of Sam Houston.* Garden City, New York:
       Doubleday, Doran & Co.
1935   *Brothers Three.* New York: Macmillan.
1938   *Tecumseh and His Times: The Story of a Great Indian.* New York:
       Putnam's.
Parker, Arthur C.
1919   *The Life of General Ely S. Parker: Last Grand Sachem of the Iroquois
       and General Grant's Military Secretary.* Buffalo Historical Society
       Publications, vol. 23.
1923   *Seneca Myths and Folk Tales.* Buffalo Historical Society Publications,
       vol. 27.
1937   *The Indian How Book.* Garden City, N.Y.: Doubleday, Doran &
       Co.
1952   *Red Jacket: Last of the Senecas.* New York: McGraw-Hill.
1967   (Orig. 1926) *A History of the Seneca Indians.* Empire State Historical
       Publication No. 43. Port Washington, N.Y.: Ira J. Friedman.

1968   *Parker on the Iroquois*. Syracuse, N.Y.: Syracuse University Press.
Phinney, Archie
1934   *Nez Perce Texts*. CUCA, vol. 25.
Ridge, John Rollin
1868   *Poems*. San Francisco: Henry Payot & Co.
1962   *The Life and Adventures of Joaquin Murieta, the Celebrated California Bandit*. Norman: University of Oklahoma Press.
Shaw, Anna Moore
1968   *Pima Indian Legends*. Tucson: University of Arizona Press.
Sitting-Up, Arlene
1971   "Summer Sister," *Indian Historian*, Winter, p. 47.
Standing Bear, Luther
1928   *My Indian Boyhood*. Boston: Houghton Mifflin Co.
1933   *Land of the Spotted Eagle*. Boston: Houghton Mifflin Co.
Stands-in-Timber, John
1967   *Cheyenne Memories: A Folk History*, with Margot Liberty and Robert M. Utley. New Haven: Yale University Press.
Tecumseh
1899   "Father, Listen to Your Children." in *History of the Choktaw, Chickasaw and Natchez Indians*. Greenville, Texas: Headlight Printing House.
Vaudrin, Bill
1969   *Tanaina Tales from Alaska*. Norman: University of Oklahoma Press.
Velarde, Pablita
1960   *Old Father, The Story Teller*. Globe, Arizona: Dale Stuart King.
Villasenor, David
n.d.   *Tapestries in Sand: The Spirit of Indian Sandpainting*. Healdsburg, Calif.: Naturegraph Publishers.
Webb, George
1959   *A Pima Remembers*. Tucson: University of Arizona Press.
White Ghost
1876   *Statement of White Ghost at the Crow Creek Agency, October 21st*. In the Court of Claims: The Sioux Tribe versus the U.S. Vol. 1.
Winnie, Lucille
1968   *Sah-gan-de-oh, the Chief's Daughter*. New York: Vantage Press.
Wright, Muriel H.
1940   *Springplace: Moravian Mission and the Ward Family of the Cherokee Nation*. Guthrie, Oklahoma: Co-operative Publishing Co.
1965   *A Guide to the Indian Tribes of Oklahoma*. Norman: University of Oklahoma Press.
Yellow Robe, Rosebud
1969   *An Album of the American Indian*. New York: Franklin Watts, Inc.

Yellow Wolf
    1962   *The Last Stand of the Nez Percé: Destruction of a People*, with Harvey
            Chalmers II. New York: Twayne Publishers.

III. SOME AMERICAN INDIAN PERIODICALS

Akwesasne Notes. Roosevelt, New York.
Americans Before Columbus. Albuquerque, New Mexico.
The Blue Cloud Quarterly. Marvin, South Dakota.
The Cherokee One Feather. Cherokee, North Carolina.
City Smoke Signals. Sioux City, Iowa.
Early American. Modesto, California.
Fort Apache Scout. Whiteriver, Arizona.
Indian Affairs in California. Sacramento, California.
Indian-Eskimo Association of Canada Bulletin. Toronto, Ontario.
The Indian Historian. San Francisco, California.
Indian Voice. Santa Clara, California.
Institute of American Indian Arts. Santa Fe, New Mexico.
Jicarilla Chieftain. Dulce, New Mexico.
Kanai News. Cardston, Alberta.
Many Smokes: National Indian Magazine. Reno, Nevada.
The Native Nevadan. Reno, Nevada.
The Native People. Edmonton, Alberta.
Native Times. Yellowknife, North West Territory.
The Navajo Times. Window Rock, Arizona.
The NCAI Sentinel [National Congress of American Indians]. Washington, D.C.
Papago Indian News. Sells, Arizona.
Rosebud Sioux Herald (Eyapaha). Rosebud, South Dakota.
Smoke Signals. Parker, Arizona.
Southern Ute Drum. Ignacio, Colorado.
Sun Tracks. Tucson, Arizona.
Talking Leaves. Los Angeles, California.
Tosan. Indianapolis, Indiana.
Tribal Indian News. London, Ontario.
Tundra Times. Fairbanks, Alaska.
The Warpath. San Francisco, California.
The Warrior. Chicago, Illinois.